From Rebels to Rulers

RELIGION IN TRANSFORMING AFRICA

ISSN 2398-8673

Series description
The series is open to submissions that examine local or regional realities on the complexities of religion and spirituality in Africa. Religion in Transforming Africa will showcase cutting-edge research into continent-wide issues on Christianity, Islam and other religions of Africa; Traditional beliefs and witchcraft; Religion, culture & society; History of religion, politics and power; Global networks and new missions; Religion in conflict and peace-building processes; Religion and development; Religious rituals and texts and their role in shaping religious ideologies and theologies. Innovative, and challenging current perspectives, the series provides an indispensable resource on this key area of African Studies for academics, students, international policy-makers and development practitioners.

Please contact the Series Editors with an outline or download the proposal form at www.jamescurrey.com.

Dr Barbara Bompani, Reader in Africa and International Development, University of Edinburgh: b.bompani@ed.ac.uk
Dr Joseph Hellweg, Associate Professor of Religion, Department of Religion, Florida State University: jhellweg@fsu.edu
Professor Ousmane Kane, Prince Alwaleed Bin Talal Professor of Contemporary Islamic Religion & Society, Harvard Divinity School: okane@hds.harvard.edu
Dr Emma Wild-Wood, Senior Lecturer, African Christianity and African Indigenous Religions, University of Edinburgh: emma.wildwood@ed.ac.uk

Previously published titles in the series are listed at the back of this volume.

From Rebels to Rulers

Writing Legitimacy in the Early Sokoto State

Paul Naylor

JAMES CURREY

James Currey
is an imprint of
Boydell & Brewer Ltd
PO Box 9, Woodbridge
Suffolk IP12 3DF (GB)
www.jamescurrey.com
and of
Boydell & Brewer Inc.
668 Mt Hope Avenue
Rochester, NY 14620–2731 (US)
www.boydellandbrewer.com

First published in hardback 2021

British Library Cataloguing in Publication Data
A catalogue record for this book is available from the British Library

ISBN 978-1-84701-270-8 (James Currey hardback)

This publication is printed on acid-free paper

Printed and bound in Great Britain by
TJ Books Ltd, Padstow, Cornwall

FSC www.fsc.org MIX Paper from responsible sources FSC® C013056

For Maria

Contents

Illustrations

Figure

Maps

Table

Acknowledgements

Like the tradition of peripatetic learning common among Muslim scholarly families in the nineteenth-century Sahel, the writing of this book took place across many geographical and institutional settings. To this end, I would first like to thank the UK Arts and Humanities Research Council, the British Library, the UK Economic and Social Research Council, the University of Birmingham, Université Abdou Moumouni, Northwestern University, Tulane University and Loyola University Chicago for their financial and in-kind support during the writing of this book, be that in the form of visiting fellowships, travel grants, residencies, office space and/or food.

The Department of African Studies and Anthropology (DASA) at the University of Birmingham was my home for several years, during which time the idea of this book slowly took shape. The Department's regular series of 'Africa Talks' (every Wednesday evening!) were a constant source of inspiration and enjoyment. I would like to thank Drs Karin Barber, Maxim Bolt, Reginald Cline-Cole, Paulo Fernando de Moraes Farias, Juliet Gilbert, Rebecca Jones, David Kerr, Saima Nasar, Insa Nolte, Benedetta Rossi, Keith Shear, Kate Skinner, Ceri Whatley, and all my DASA friends and colleagues for their intelligence, encouragement and good company. At the British Library, Dr Colin Baker helped me with the initial difficulties of Arabic palaeography, Jody Butterworth and her colleagues introduced me to the Library's Endangered Archives Program, and many other British Library staff generously offered their expert knowledge, as well as table tennis breaks. I am particularly thankful to Marion, Andrew and family for giving me a home away from home. I would like to thank Dr Seyni Moumouni for facilitating my residency at L'institit de recherches en sciences humaines (IRSH) of the Université Abdou Moumouni in Niamey, Niger. My thanks to Dr Moulaye Hassane, director of the Département des Manuscrits Arabes et Ajami Boubou Hama (MARA) and Hadjiya Rahmatou Alkali for facilitating my work with the archives there, and to my companions from the *salle des chercheurs*, among them

Boubacar Moussa, Issaka Yacouba and Salao Alassane. To them and all my fellow colleagues at the IRSH, *merci pour toute l'amitié, et le masa*! Thanks also to the staff at LASDEL for taking care of my accommodation while in Niamey, especially Aghali. Thanks to Dr Rebecca Shereikis for facilitating my visiting fellowship at the Institute for the Study of Islamic Thought in Africa (ISITA) and the Program of African Studies at Northwestern University, Illinois. My thanks also go to Esmeralda Kale, Crystal L. Martin and Gene Kannenberg, Jr. at the Melville J. Herskovits Library of African Studies for facilitating my work with their collection, and to Kelsey Rydland for his help with the maps. At James Currey I thank my two sets of reviewers, my editor Jaqueline Mitchell along with her colleagues Nick Bingham and Emily Champion, who gave prompt and helpful guidance through the publishing process, and Nicholas Jewitt, who provided copy editing services, all of whom made the book infinitely more presentable than it would have been otherwise.

The following scholars, colleagues and friends offered their help, support and ideas, however big or small: Louis Brenner, Ali Diakite, Paulo Fernando de Moraes Farias, Djibo Hamani, Sean Hanretta, Murray Last, Robert Launay, Paul Lovejoy, Ariela Marcus-Sells, Wendell Marsh, Mauro Nobili, Scott Reese, JungRock Seo, Muhammad Shareef, Charles C. Stewart, Amir Syed, Stephanie Zehnle, and many more I undoubtedly will have missed. A special thanks to Dr Benedetta Rossi and Dr Marion Wallace for their support, guidance and warmth, as well as to Joseph Oakley, the first of my history teachers. And last but certainly not least I profoundly thank my wife Maria, to whom this book is dedicated, for her love and encouragement, and for all those discussions about legitimacy!

Abbreviations

AH	*Anno Hegirae* (year of the Islamic Hijri Calendar)
Ar.	Arabic
ALA 2	Hunwick and O'Fahey (1995) *Arabic literature of Africa Volume 2: The Writings of Central Sudanic Africa*
b.	ibn (Ar. 'son of')
BL (EAP)	British Library, Endangered Archives Programme
c.	*circa*
fl.	*floruit*
Dakar (IFAN)	Institut Fondamental d'Afrique Noire Dakar
Ibadan (UC)	University College, Ibadan
Kaduna (NA)	National Archives, Kaduna
Kano (SHCB)	State History and Culture Bureau, Kano
ME	Market edition (see Glossary)
MS	Manuscript
MX	Xerox, Photostat or other copy of an original manuscript
n.d.	no date [of publication]
Niamey (MARA)	Département des Manuscrits Arabes et Ajami Boubou Hama, Niamey
NU/Falke	Northwestern University, Evanston, Illinois, ʿUmar Falke Collection of the Melville J. Herskovits Library of African Studies
NU/Hiskett	Northwestern University, Evanston, Illinois, Mervyn Hiskett Collection of the Melville J. Herskovits Library of African Studies
NU/Hunwick	Northwestern University, Evanston, Illinois, John O. Hunwick Collection of the Melville J. Herskovits Library of African Studies

NU/Paden	Northwestern University, Evanston, Illinois, John Naber Paden Collection of the Melville J. Herskovits Library of African Studies
NU/Wilks	Northwestern University, Evanston, Illinois, The University of Ghana (Ivor Wilks) Collection of the Melville J. Herskovits Library of African Studies
Paris (BnF)	Bibliothèque nationale de France, Paris
Paris (BI)	Bibliothèque de l'institut de France, Paris
r.	reigned
Sokoto (SHB)	Sokoto History Bureau
Timbuktu (BMH)	Bibliothèque Mamma Haidara, Timbuktu/Bamako

Note on Language

All direct quotations translated into English are my own translations, unless otherwise indicated. For quoted translations that are not my own, I have kept to the spelling and orthography of the translator. Words in Hausa, Fulfulde, or other non-European languages follow the standard spelling used in the specialist literature and appear in italics followed by an English translation between square brackets on first occurence, if necessary. Arabic words that commonly occur in English ('imam', 'jihad', 'hadith', etc.) remain in their English approximations. All other Arabic terms not in common use, including the titles of Arabic manuscripts, are transcribed following the *International Journal of Middle East Studies* (IJMES) transcription system and appear in italics followed by an English translation between square brackets on first occurence, if necessary. English translations of the Qur'an are from Pickthall's *The Meaning of the Glorious Koran*.

I will refer to the three protagonists of this study by the versions of their names that have become standard in the literature: Usman dan Fodio, Abdullahi dan Fodio and Muhammad Bello. Dan Fodio is not a 'true' family name but derives from *dan* (Hausa: 'son of') and *Fodio* (Fulfulde: 'learned person' or 'teacher'), a reference to Usman and Abdullahi's father, Muhammad. Although this rendering mixes various linguistic and orthographic conventions, I consider this standardised form easier on the reader than their Arabic transliterations or the less familiar but perhaps more faithful spellings of their names following conventions for Hausa or Fulfulde orthography. When referring to the three men collectively, I will use the term 'Fodiawa'. Again, this is a term that mixes languages and orthographic conventions, being a combination of *Fodio* and the Hausa-*wa* reserved for the plural form of ethnonyms and social groups. Some works of secondary literature use this term, but it is a relatively recent innovation. I prefer Fodiawa to the more frequent 'triumvirate' because the former does not presuppose any notions of shared governance. Fodiawa – to my mind – suggests only that the three men are blood relations and is the most appropriate surrogate for a 'family' or 'surname', for which naming conventions in this time period offer no easy equivalent.

I do not use the term *Sokoto Caliphate* except in reference to the book of this title by Murray Last, or when discussing the concept of a 'Sokoto Caliphate' in other works of secondary literature. I will however use 'Sokoto', 'Sokoto project', 'Sokoto elite' or similar terms, even though Sokoto was not a seat of government in the modern sense. I will refer to the ruler of Sokoto (Usman from c. 1804 to 1817 and Muhammad Bello from 1817 to 1837) by the Arabic term *Amīr al-muʾminīn* [Commander of the Faithful] as this is the term most frequently encountered in the manuscripts. I will refer to the rulers of Gwandu, as well as the heads of the various emirates, sub-emirates and polities under the control of Sokoto and Gwandu as 'Emir'. That said, this book discusses the different terms that denote a Muslim ruler and the significance of these terms in the Sokoto context at some length.

Page references for manuscripts that have been paginated use p. and pp. as for a published work. Page references for unpaginated manuscripts as well as unpaginated market editions use f. and ff. starting from the *basmala*, which may be on the recto (a) or verso (b) of the first folio. Page references for unpaginated manuscripts that have been copied or digitised as separate folio sides use p. and pp. whereas manuscripts that have been digitised or photocopied as full folios use f. and ff.

Glossary

amajegh – imajeghen	(Tamasheq) in Tuareg societies, the aristocratic or warrior class
Amīr al-mu'minīn	(Arabic) Commander of the Faithful, the term given to the political leader of Sokoto
aneslem – ineslemen	(Tamasheq) in Tuareg societies, the Muslim scholarly class, also known as *zwāyā*
Ash'arī	(Arabic) referring to the school of Abū al-Ḥasan al-Ash'arī, who enforced a literalist, anti-rationalist interpretation of the Qur'an, or an adherent thereof
Askiya	(unknown) the title bestowed upon Al-Ḥājj Muhammad, ruler of Songhay, and his descendants after taking power from the family of Sonni Ali
baraka	(Arabic) blessing
batin	(Arabic: *bāṭin*) the hidden aspects of religion, as opposed to *zahir*
bay'a	(Arabic) pledge of allegiance
bid'a	(Arabic) heretical innovation in religious practice
Bilād al-Sūdān	(Arabic) Literally, 'country of the blacks', a geographical term first used by Arab writers to refer to Sub-Saharan Africa[1]
Bori	(Hausa) a spirit possession ritual popular in rural Hausaland

[1] The Fodiawa used both *Bilād al-Sūdān* and *Arḍ* [land of] *al-Sūdān* to refer to the wider area in which they lived, and *Ahl al-Sūdān* or *Sūdānī* to refer to its population. I prefer to use these terms rather than an English approximation. On the rare occasions when the term 'Sudan' appears capitalised and without diacritical marks in unquoted text, it refers to the area of the modern nation state of Sudan.

Caliph	(Arabic: *khalīfa – khulafāʾ*) a deputy or successor of Prophet Muhammad, in the sense of a political figurehead for the Muslim Umma
Dār al-Ḥarb	(Arabic) literally the 'land of war', a place where Muslims are fighting non-believers
Dār al-Islām	(Arabic) the lands of Islam, governed by Muslim rulers, as opposed to *Dār al-Ḥarb* or *Dār al-Kufr*
Dār al-Kufr	(Arabic) literally the 'land of unbelief', a place governed by non-Muslims
emir	(Arabic: *amīr*) in Sokoto, a regional ruler appointed by the *Amīr al-muʾminīn*
fatwa	(Arabic) a legal opinion which may be treated as an authoritive source of law
fiqh	(Arabic) knowledge of Islamic practice, traditions and legal canons, as opposed to *kashf*
fitna	(Arabic) confusion, discord, internecine strife in the Muslim community
Fodiawa	(Fulfulde-Hausa) Usman, Abdullahi and Muhammad Bello, referred to collectively
Fulani	(Fulfulde: *Pulaar*) belonging to the West African people known variously as Fulbe or Peul
hadith	(Arabic: *ḥadīth*) an action or saying of Prophet Muhammad, constituting a source of Islamic law
ḥarbī – ḥarbiyyīn	(Arabic) see *muḥārib*
hijra	(Arabic) emigration, specifically from persecution; originally referring to the emigration of Muhammad and his followers from Mecca, the term was also used by the Fodiawa to refer to their emigration from Gobir
ijāza – ijāzāt	(Arabic) a teaching licence granted at the conclusion of studying a text, containing a list of teachers through whom the work has been transmitted
ijtihad	(Arabic: *ijtihād*) arriving at legal judgement through freely interpreting the sources of law without following the judgements of previous scholars, the opposite of taqlid
ikhtilaf	(Arabic: *ikhtilāf*) absence of consensus among legal scholars over a particular legal question

imajeghen	(Tamasheq) see *amajegh*
imam	(Arabic: *imām*) religious leader of a Muslim community
imāma	(Arabic) Muslim leadership, or else imamate, that is, a country or region ruled over by an Imam
ineslemen	(Tamasheq) see *aneslem*
inkār al-ḥarām	(Arabic) the legal standpoint that one cannot forbid any action over which there is *ikhtilaf*
jamāʿa	(Arabic) community, in this context the reformist community that gathered around Usman dan Fodio
jihad	(Arabic: *jihād*) struggle, and more precisely 'jihad of the sword', with the meaning of Holy War
kāfir – kuffār	(Arabic) one who does not believe in the Islamic faith, an infidel
kalām, ʿilm al-kalām	(Arabic) theology, the study of theology
karāma – karāmāt	(Arabic) spiritual gift, miracles or the working of miracles, as in *karāmāt* literature, texts recalling the miracles of a particular figure
kashf	(Arabic) inspiration and understanding gained through divine revelation in visions and dreams, as opposed to *fiqh*, or book knowledge
kufr	(Arabic) non-belief, infidelity, or an action denoted as such
madhab	(Arabic) an accepted school of Muslim religious and legal practice
Maguzawa	(Hausa) a non-Muslim Hausa people, from Ar. *mājūs* 'Magian', 'Zoroastrian'
Mahdi	(Arabic: *mahdī*; *al-imām al-mahdī*) in Islamic eschatology, a figure whose appearance portends judgement day
mahdiyya	(Arabic) as in, 'claiming the *mahdiyya*', claiming that one is the Mahdi; not to be confused with the Mahdiya, the regime of the Sudanese Mahdi, Muhammad Ahmad
Mai	(Kanuri) term applied to the rulers of the Kanem-Bornu Empire
Maliki	(Arabic: *mālikī*) the madhab of Anas ibn Mālik, predominant in the Sahel region

mallam – *mallamai*	(Hausa) a local practitioner of Islamic knowledge
Market edition	in West Africa, a copy of a manuscript reproduced by local printing presses and commonly found for sale in markets; also called 'market literature' or 'pious print'
muḥārib – *muḥāribūn*	(Arabic) one who refuses to recognise central authority; a rebel, a brigand
mujaddid	(Arabic) a 'renewer' heralded to appear at the start of every Islamic century to reform society and remove corruption
mujtahid	(Arabic) a scholar who engages in *ijtihad*, the opposite of a *muqallid*
mulk	(Arabic) kingship
muqaddam	(Arabic) in Sufism, the regional representative of a Sufi order
muqallid	(Arabic) a scholar who engages in taqlid, the opposite of a *mujtahid*
mustaghraq al-dhimma	(Arabic) a legal term for those who are deemed not to have a legal right to the property they own since they acquired it by theft; a reference to the *muḥāribūn*
mutakallim – *mutakallimūn*	(Arabic) theologian, used pejoratively to refer to the speculative theology of the Muʿtazilites and any scholar whose study of theology has led them to question the beliefs of other Muslims or the validity of Islamic beliefs in general
muwālā – *muwālāt*	(Arabic) variously friendship, good relations, affiliation, alliance
nasab	(Arabic) genealogy, noble heritage
qabīla – *qabāʾil*	(Arabic) the clan groupings that constitute the social architecture of traditional Arab society, although the Fodiawa also used the term to refer to the clans of the Fulani and Tuareg, as well as other West African peoples
Qadiri	(Arabic: *qādirī*) a member of the Qadiriyya Sufi order
the Qadiriyya	(Arabic: qādiriyya) a Sufi order founded in Baghdad by ʿAbd al-Qādir al-Jīlānī, widespread in the Sahel region
Quraysh	(Arabic) the *qabīla* to which Prophet Muhammad belonged

ribat	(*Arabic: rabaṭ – ribāṭ*) fort, garrison
the Rashidun Caliphs	(Arabic: *al-khulafāʾ al-rāshidūn*) a term commonly applied by Muslim historians to the first four 'rightly guided' caliphs after Prophet Muhammad; the historical period of their rule (AD 632–661) is known as the Rashidun Caliphate
Sahel	(Arabic: *sāḥil*) literally 'shore', the southern edge of the Sahara Desert
sarauta	(Hausa) the aristocracy of the Hausa *sarakai* (see next) and members of the royal court, as opposed to the *talakawa* or 'common people'
sarki(n) – sarakai	(Hausa) term applied to the rulers of the Hausa Kingdoms, as in *Sarkin Gobir*, the *sarki* of Gobir
Sharia	(Arabic: *sharīʿa*) Islamic law, derived from the Qur'an, the Sunna and one of the accepted madhabs
sharif	(Arabic: *sharīf – shurafāʾ*) a descendant of Prophet Muhammad; in West Africa, the term was also frequently applied to North Africans of Arab heritage
silsila – salāsil	(Arabic) chain of transmission, notably for a Sufi *wird*
Sunna	(Arabic) the practice of Prophet Muhammad, used as one of the bases for Islamic law
syncretist	(Arabic: *mukhalliṭ*) in this context, a Muslim who allegedly mixes Islamic ritual with the rituals of West African traditional religions
tafsīr	(Arabic) Qur'anic exegesis
takfir	(Arabic: *takfīr*) declaring a Muslim an apostate from Islam because of his or her actions or beliefs; anathematisation
taqlid	(Arabic: *taqlīd*) following only the legal rulings of past scholars, as opposed to *ijtihad*
Taʾrīkh	(Arabic) historical work or chronicle, most often applied to the Timbuktu Chronicles (the *Taʾrīkh al-sūdān* and the so-called *Taʾrīkh al-fattāsh*) as well as the histories of the early Muslim caliphates
tariqa	(Arabic: *ṭarīqa*) a Sufi order

Tawaye	(Hausa: *yan tawaye*) rebel, specifically a participant in the Tawaye Rebellions, in which many (mostly) Hausa communities revolted against Muhammad Bello's rule in the period 1817–1821
Tijani	(Arabic: tijānī) a member of the Tijaniyya Sufi order
the Tijaniyya	(Arabic: tījāniyya) a Sufi order founded in the late eighteenth century by Aḥmad al-Tijānī in present-day Algeria, which quickly spread throughout West Africa
Torobbe	(Fulfulde: *toorodɓe* or *tooroɓɓe*, singular *tooroodo*) a family or clan sub-group of the Fulani, to which the Fodiawa claimed membership; also rendered Torodbe, Turudi, Torodobbe or Toronkawa
Ṭullāb	(Arabic) students, a term used by Usman and Muhammad Bello to refer to various members of the *jamāʿa* or the wider Muslim community who questioned their teachings
ulama	(Arabic: *ʿulamāʾ*) Muslim scholars learned in *fiqh*, who formed a distinct socio-political class in the early history of Islam
Umma	(Arabic) the global Muslim community
walīy – awliyāʾ	(Arabic) one who is close to God, a saint
wazir	(Arabic: *wazīr*) chief minister, in Sokoto a hereditary position granted to Gidado dan Layma and his descendants
wird – awrād	(Arabic) a supplication or litany recited by members of a Sufi tariqa, passed down from the founder of the order and said to bring spiritual benefit; the passing of a *wird* to an initiate marked his or her entry into the order
zahir	(Arabic: *ẓāhir*) the external, or manifest aspects of religion, as opposed to *batin*
zakat	(Arabic: *zakat*) an obligatory religious alms or tax paid by Muslims to support the poor and needy in the community

Introduction

Some time after the year 1854, Al-Ḥājj Saʿīd – a prominent scholar from the region of Masina – completed his history of Sokoto.[1] Sokoto was the largest state to emerge from a series of self-proclaimed jihad movements in the eighteenth- and nineteenth-century Sahel. The leaders of the jihad movements were Muslim scholars and teachers, many of whom identified themselves as Torobbe, a clan of the Fulani, one of the ethnocultural groups of Sub-Saharan Africa.[2] The success of these wars marked an abrupt severance of a politico-religious hegemony that had persisted in the region for many centuries, replacing it with a new form of statecraft explicitly tied to Islamic traditions of governance.

The history of Sokoto had begun some fifty years previously and some 800 miles to the east, in Hausaland. At that time, power lay with the *sarakai*, the hereditary rulers of the *Hausa bakwai* [the seven Hausa kingdoms]. Each *sarki* presided over a large and complex court, which included Muslim scholars. While undoubtedly reliant on various other forms of patronage, the *sarakai* also claimed authority as Muslim rulers. Usman dan Fodio, a scholar and teacher from the Hausa kingdom of Gobir, began to challenge this authority. Assisted by his younger brother, Abdullahi, and later by his son, Muhammad Bello, the Fodiawa (as this

[1] Al-Ḥājj Saʿīd, *Taqāyīd mimmā waṣala ilaynā min aḥwāl umarāʾ al-muslimīn salāṭīn Ḥawsa* [Entries from what came to us regarding the conditions of the Emirs of the Muslims, rulers of the Hausa]. See John O. Hunwick and Rex S. O'Fahey, *Arabic Literature of Africa Volume 2: The Writings of Central Sudanic Africa* (Leiden, 1995), p. 233. The precise identity of Al-Ḥājj Saʿīd and the region he came from are difficult to ascertain.

[2] According to tradition, the Torobbe began migrating eastwards across the Sahel from the region of Futa Toro in the seventeenth century, from which they derive their name. See John Ralph Willis, 'The Torodbe Clerisy: A Social View', *The Journal of African History*, 19:2 (1978), 195–212. However, alternative and more controversial theories exist as to the precise historical identity of Torobbe, which will be discussed in Chapter 1.

book refers to these three individuals collectively) began to militate for a jihad of the sword against the *sarakai*.

The jihad, which began in 1804, destroyed the Hausa kingdoms, precipitated the fall of the ancient Sayfawa dynasty of Bornu, and led to the collapse of the empire of Oyo. The regional flag-bearers of the conflict became emirs of the territories they had captured, although they pledged their loyalty to Usman as *Amīr al-mu'minīn*. In 1811, Muhammad Bello began building the town of Sokoto as a capital city for this evolving state, although it came to rely rather more on established production centres such as Kano (worked by plantation slave labour) for its economic power. Meanwhile, Abdullahi attempted to foster the ideals of the jihad – as well as Fulani hegemony – in his Emirate of Gwandu. After Usman's death in 1817, both he and Bello claimed that they should become *Amīr al-mu'minīn*, while several emirates wavered in their loyalty to this state-building project. Consolidating his control after 1821 through a mixture of military conquest, threats and patronage, Bello extended the administrative reach of the state and ensured that upon his death in 1837, key positions of government, as well as regional emirships, stayed within the extended families of their officeholders. This larger, looser structure of emirates subordinate to a political centre is known today as the Sokoto Caliphate, although this book avoids that term.

Al-Ḥājj Sa'īd drew his history from some twenty years he had spent at the court of Muhammad Bello and his successors at Sokoto, and at Wurno, a nearby garrison town. He had served as Qur'an reader to Sokoto's third ruler, Aliyu, and was a tutor to his sons. He perhaps also offered his ear as a confidante. Because he did not belong to the hereditary elites, Al-Ḥājj Sa'īd probably did not have as much stake in Sokoto's political system as those among whom he moved. An engaging writer with an observer's perspective, he noted that Bello – like other reformist leaders of the period – wrote prolifically in Arabic:

> Questions and disagreements were the reason for the large amount of his compositions. If he was asked something concerning an issue, he would compose a treatise upon it; if it reached him that so-and-so and so-and-so were in disagreement about some issue, then he would compose a treatise upon it.[3]

This observation should alert us to two common features of Muslim reformist movements of the eighteenth- and nineteenth-century Sahel. First, even though they spoke – and wrote – in numerous other tongues,

[3] Al-Ḥājj Sa'īd, *Taqāyīd mimmā waṣala ilaynā min aḥwāl umarā' al-muslimīn salāṭīn Ḥawsa*, Paris (BnF) Arabe 5422, f. 4a.

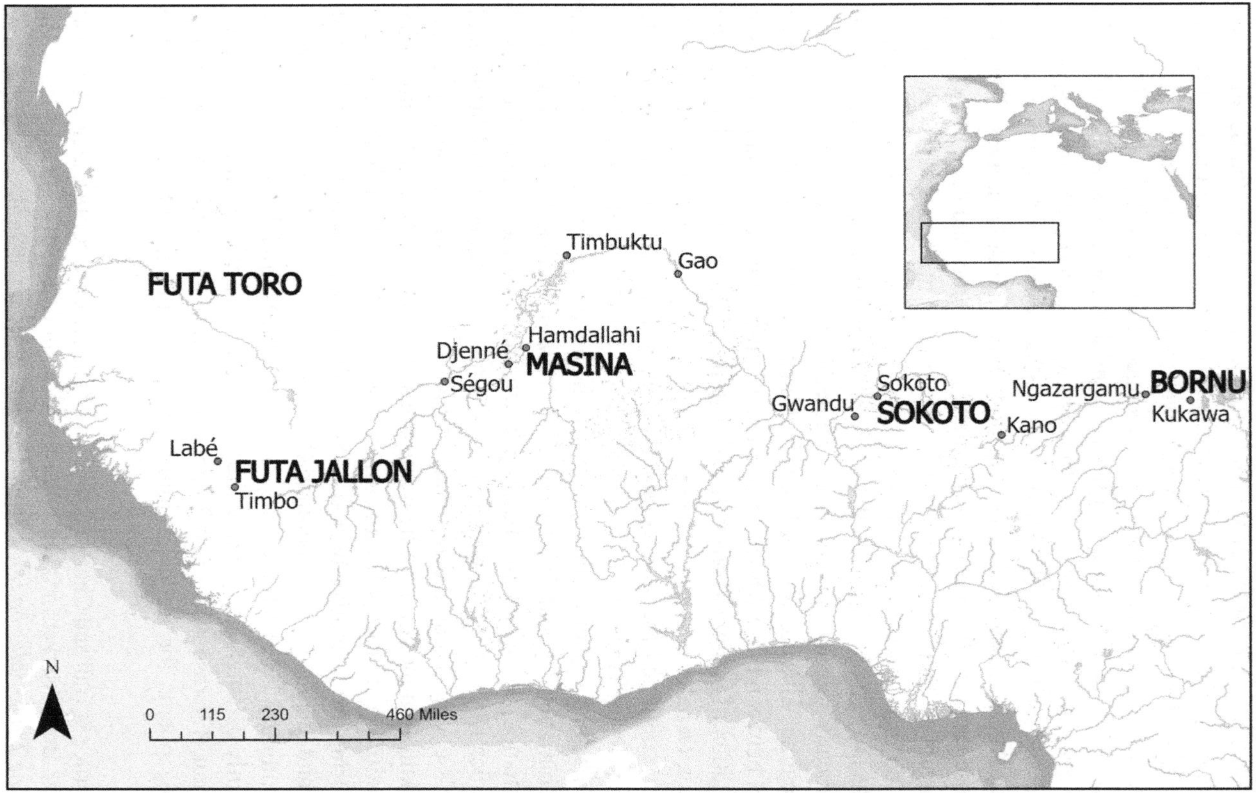

Map 1 Muslim states in the early nineteenth century Sahel. Adapted from Henry B. Lovejoy, African Diaspora Maps Ltd

the leaders of these movements communicated their aims and agendas principally through the medium of the Arabic language. This was because, by the beginning of the nineteenth century, scholarly elites in the Sahel region had developed a shared body of Arabic texts that amounted to a 'core curriculum' of Islamic learning.[4] Arabic was therefore the language in which scholars negotiated, enforced and challenged the ideas within them.[5]

Al-Ḥājj Saʿīd's mention of 'questions and disagreements' as Bello's main motivation for his compositions brings us to the second feature. Despite the impressive victories of the jihad, these leaders and their descendants never ruled entirely unopposed, nor were they ever internally unified. This was because the original impetus of the jihad movements had been the toppling of corrupt systems of governance. However, in a matter of years the rebels who led these movements had become rulers of vast amounts of territory (see Map 1). In order to rule effectively, the erstwhile rebels were compelled to radically reframe the discursive strategies they had used to destroy the old regime. This created a schism, both inside and outside of the reformist camp, between those who accepted a more pragmatic course that would see integration of Islamic ideals with old systems of governance, and those who did not. Debates about how nascent Muslim states should be ruled, and by whom, continued for many years after the conflict and could even lead to new cycles of violence. Al-Ḥājj Saʿīd knew this full well. His patron – for whom he had in fact written his text on the history of Sokoto – was Aḥmad al-Kabīr, son of Umar Tal. In 1862, Tal led a jihad that destroyed Masina, a contemporary of Sokoto, because he claimed that the state had diverged too much from its reformist beginnings. Thus, the frequency of Muhammad Bello's compositions did not suggest that he was some leisurely philosopher-king. On the contrary, he wrote because his authority as a Muslim ruler depended upon distinguishing correct, Islamic actions from their opposites.

During the formative period of Sokoto's history – between the jihad of 1804 and the death of Muhammad Bello in 1837 – the Fodiawa produced an astoundingly vast body of texts. In 1995, John Hunwick gave the number of firmly established Arabic writings as 100 prose works and 3 poems for Uthman, 87 prose works and 26 poems for Abdullahi, and 108 prose works and 67 poems for Bello.[6] While Usman, Abdullahi and Bello were the

[4] Bruce S. Hall and Charles C. Stewart, 'The Historic "Core Curriculum" and the Book Market in Islamic West Africa', in G. Krätli and G. Lydon (eds), *The Trans-Saharan Book Trade* (Leiden, 2011), pp. 109–74.

[5] Ahmad M. Kani, *Ḍiyāʾ al-siyāsāt wa-fatāwī-l-nawāzil mimmā huwa fī furūʿ al-dīn min al-masāʾil* (Cairo, 1988), pp. 73–4.

[6] See Hunwick and O'Fahey, *ALA 2*. During my own relatively short period

most prolific writers in the early Sokoto state, their family members and contemporaries from the new elite were likewise engaged in intensive literary activity during this period.[7] In addition, their compositions in the West African languages of Hausa and Fulfulde await comprehensive cataloguing and study.[8] As such, this is perhaps the most documented period in West African history before the twentieth century.

The heirs to the Fodiawa's legacy – descendants of the Fodiawa themselves, and of the wazirs, emirs and other titled positions they established – became the custodians of this written record. They used the texts of their forefathers to create a stable narrative of the jihad and its aftermath that justified their own hereditary rule. Officially, this rule ended in 1903, when Britain annexed Sokoto's territories to form the protectorate of Northern Nigeria which later became the northern portion of colonial Nigeria. However, during the colonial period, Sokoto's elites continued to hold metaphorical and actual power as the 'native authority' under the British system of indirect rule.

With decolonisation and a growing northern Nigerian nationalism, northern elites guided historians – both Nigerian and non-Nigerian – as they worked to move Sokoto's written record from private hands to a series of regional archives and synthesise the writings that the Fodiawa left behind them into a convincing and engaging narrative of revolution and conquest, followed by a robust tradition of statecraft that had continued up to the present day. In modern Nigeria, the Sultan of Sokoto, regional emirs and a wealth of titled officials remain important players in local and national politics, as do traditional leaders in many other regions of the nation state.[9]

---

of research I have come across additional material not included in *ALA 2*, which is listed in the appendices.

[7] For a full list of other Sokoto scholars and their works, see *ALA 2*, pp. 150–255.

[8] See Hunwick and O'Fahey (*ALA 2*) for a preliminary list of titles and extant academic research on this topic. See also the British Library's Endangered Archives Programme no. 387: Safeguarding Fulfulde ajami manuscripts of Nigerian Jihad poetry by Usman dan Fodio (1754–1817) and contemporaries, accessible online at https://eap.bl.uk/project/EAP387 [accessed 29 March 2020].

[9] Abubakar Aliyu Gwandu, Aminu S. Mikailu and S. W. Junaidu, *The Sokoto Caliphate: A Legacy of Scholarship and Good Governance – Proceedings of the Conference of ʿUlamāʾ Organised to Commemorate the 200 Years of the Establishment of the Sokoto Caliphate* (Sokoto, 2005).

So intensive was the study of these writings in the post-colonial period that we can properly speak of a whole genre of 'Sokoto studies' in Nigeria itself and across the neighbouring countries of Niger, Burkina Faso, Togo, Benin, Chad and Cameroon, which all formed a part of Sokoto's territories, as well as in Britain and the Western world. In northern Nigeria, this work took place in the context – or, in some cases, as part and parcel of – a nationalist project to elevate northern elites to prominent roles in the government of independent Nigeria through demonstrating the region's impressive pre-colonial history. The very concept of a 'Sokoto Caliphate' arose during this period, with the publication in 1967 of Murray Last's book of that title. Others disputed this triumphalist narrative by, for example, emphasising Sokoto's reliance on slave labour, or the violence of the jihad. They questioned how important the Fodiawa's writings really were as a tool for the historian, pointing out the narrow scope of their audience and the fact that many seemed to contain mostly arcane theological points. They looked to 'alternative' sources such as oral histories, resuscitated colonial records and early European travel accounts of the region, or employed an emancipatory 'against the grain' reading of Arabic sources to complicate established paradigms.

Going back to Al-Ḥājj Saʿīd's questions and disgreements, the narrative that these writings are simply an historical record of the ascendancy of the Sokoto Caliphate appears to contrast sharply with the circumstances of their composition. An alternative reading sees the writings of the Fodiawa and their contemporaries as a sustained and, in the Fodiawa's case, successful attempt to legitimise political power. What is more, the vision of a 'Sokoto Caliphate' has misled historians into considering the Fodiawa as a collective 'triumvirate', reconceptualising their profound differences as unique contributions to a shared idea. On the contrary, the fact that Usman, Abdullahi and Muhammad Bello produced so much writing is testament to the depth of their disagreements regarding the correct form of Muslim government, among many other subjects. Read in their own context, Arabic texts of the nineteenth-century Sahel are the vehicles for what Roman Loimeier characterises as the 'discourses of legitimation and delegitimation' that dominated political life in the nineteenth-century Sahel.[10] They are an indelible record of the evolving politico-intellectual projects of their authors, and their descendants. As such, their use in constructing a stable, 'official' history of Sokoto has been flawed, while the role they

[10] Roman Loimeier, *Muslim Societies in Africa: A Historical Anthropology* (Bloomington, 2013), p. 114.

played in shaping the early political developments in that state is far *more* important than oral historians and their ilk have presupposed.

This book does not use the writings of the Fodiawa to add to the 'official' historiography of early Sokoto, or to question it fundamentally. Neither does it seek to engage in a Benjaminist 'against the grain' reading that would subvert their meaning and create space for under-represented actors in Sokoto society.[11] What I am proposing is that, with Laura Ann Stoler, we read these documents *along* the grain.[12] This is to say, we read them in *the way that they were meant to be read* at the time of their creation. Stoler's essay – and subsequent book – focuses on the colonial archive. For Stoler, sustained engagement with this archive as a subject, rather than a source of knowledge production, reveals 'disparate notions of what made up [colonial] authority'. The archive is not an all-powerful record of things that were, but a 'system of expectation' for things that should be, 'identifying how nations, empires, and racialized regimes were fashioned – not in ways that display confident knowledge and know-how, but in disquieted and expectant modes'.[13] Bearing the above interpretation of the role of Arabic texts in the nineteenth-century Sahel in mind, one could argue that the archives of the Fodiawa's writings as they appear today are no different from the colonial archives that Stoler describes.

Is this book then about the texts themselves, or the historical context in which they were created? In a sense, it is about both and neither. Moving beyond the narrow confines of 'Sokoto studies', this book suggests that there is perhaps a whole other sub-discipline of African studies lying here, somewhere between history and political science, that applies a context-critical methodology not only to primary sources from the African past, but to the historiography developed around them. Paulo Moraes Farias said as much when he tasked historians to look beyond Arabic sources as 'raw evidence' of the African past, and rather as windows into the 'social relations and political-ideological issues at the time of their writing'.[14]

[11] Walter Benjamin, *Illuminations*, trans. Zohn (New York, 2007), p. 257. The phrase comes from *Thesis VII* of his original 1942 essay, *Theses on the Philosophy of History.*

[12] Laura Ann Stoler, 'Colonial Archives and the Arts of Governance', *Archival Science*, 2 (2002), 87–109.

[13] *Ibid.*, pp. 91; 109.

[14] Paulo F. de Moraes Farias, 'Intellectual Innovation and Reinvention of the Sahel: The Seventeenth-Century Timbuktu Chronicles', in S. Jeppie and S. B. Diagne (eds), *The Meanings of Timbuktu* (Cape Town, 2008), pp. 95–107, at p. 96.

Between 1804 and 1837, the Fodiawa rose from a local band of rebels to the rulers of a vast territorial empire. A close and chronological analysis of these documents reveals the various discursive strategies through which they legitimised their actions, and how these strategies changed over time. Such a context-specific reading offers remarkable insights into the way in which legitimacy was constructed and sustained in the nineteenth-century Sahel, and indeed in the wider Islamic world. It also presents a vivid picture of Muslim intellectual life in Sokoto – at that time the region's largest Muslim state – during a critical formative period of its history.

The rest of this introductory chapter familiarises the reader with the Fodiawa's writings, exploring the form of these documents as we encounter them today and places them in their historical context. It explains how the book's structure is predicated upon dividing these writings into distinct groupings that are not only chronological but also based on the changing function of writing and the Arabic text in the Fodiawa's world. Following this, it summarises the long history of engagement with the Fodiawa's writings and its shortcomings, outlining a new methodology for thinking with these texts drawing upon related scholarly work and qualifying the nature of the book's contribution to the literature. It discusses evolving approaches to legitimacy and to Islam in West Africa, establishing the theoretical framework and terminology used in the book, and emphasising the causal relationship between the production of texts, structures of (de) legitimation, and patterns of state formation and collapse in Muslim West Africa of the nineteenth century.

The Arabic Writings of the Fodiawa in their Context

The Fodiawa's writings as we encounter them today are preserved in handwritten texts in the Arabic language, or in African languages rendered in Arabic script. Historians have hitherto treated this physical form as a challenging lock, which, through linguistic and paleographical specialisation, can be opened to extract meaning. But to focus solely on the content of these documents at the expense of the form belies the fact that both the act of writing itself and the copying and safeguarding of written texts were inseparable from their function as legitimising devices. It follows that these aspects should feature in any study centred around the analysis of primary source material. Simply describing the physical form of these documents and the process of their archivisation may also allow specialists in manuscript studies to see them with new eyes, while perhaps demystifying the field for non-specialists and alerting them to some important questions they may not otherwise have asked about these texts.

At the time the Fodiawa were writing, paper was a luxury foreign commodity. The paper that they used was probably manufactured in France or Italy. It reached Hausaland across the Sahara from North Africa on camelback. It may also have come upriver and overland from ports on the West African coast.[15] Either way, it should be stressed that the import of paper – and indeed the periods of free time that the scholar required to write – was inextricably tied to the institution of slavery and the trade in enslaved Africans specifically.[16] It is also impossible to ignore the highly gendered aspect of writing. Texts were, for the most part, copied by and for men.[17] Writing was best undertaken in the cooler nights and early mornings of the dry season. It therefore required a source of light – another luxury. The manufacture of pens and ink took place locally and, in some cases, preparing these items was part and parcel of the scholar's work. Storage of texts was also a major concern. Finished manuscripts as well as reams of blank writing paper were tied between leather boards to protect them from heat, humidity, insects and rodents. Some items were also held in embossed leather carrying cases. This was yet another luxury. In short, the physical and material requirements of writing underpin the fact that it was an elite but also supremely purposeful pursuit. However, the discursive power of texts belies the fragile nature of their physical form.

[15] For more on the West African paper trade see Jonathan M. Bloom, 'Paper in Sudanic Africa', in S. Jeppie and S. B. Diagne (eds), *The Meanings of Timbuktu* (Cape Town, 2008), pp. 45–58; Terence Walz, 'The Paper Trade of Egypt and the Sudan in the Eighteenth and Nineteenth Centuries and its Re-export to the Bilād as-Sūdān', in G. Krätli and G. Lydon (eds), *The Trans-Saharan Book Trade: Manuscript Culture, Arabic Literacy and Intellectual History in Muslim Africa* (Leiden & Boston, 2011), pp. 73–108.

[16] For example, Ayuba Sulayman Diallo, a notable from Bundu, was attempting to sell several captives so that he could buy writing paper for his father when he himself was taken captive and shipped to the Americas in 1731. See Thomas Bluett, *Some Memoirs of the Life of Job, the Son of Solomon, High Priest of Boonda in Africa* (London, 1734), p. 16 and analysis in Paul Naylor and Marion Wallace, 'Author of His Own Fate? The Eighteenth-Century Writings of Ayuba Sulayman Diallo', *The Journal of African History,* 60:3 (2019), 343–77.

[17] There will have been exceptions. In the family libraries of Timbuktu, recently digitised and available online, one can find a handful of copyists with female names, although most of these texts were copied at a much later date to the period we are discussing here. See www.vhmml.org/readingRoom.

At the time that the Fodiawa wrote, paper did not have a long life. Any 'manuscript' of a Fodiawa text today will generally be a late nineteenth- or early twentieth-century copy. In the mid-twentieth century, printing presses in northern Nigeria began to mass-produce freshly written manuscript copies of many Fodiawa texts. Such 'market literature'[18] or 'pious print'[19] often included parallel Hausa translations rendered in Arabic (*ajami*) or typed Latin (*boko)* script. However, the majority of Fodiawa texts available to researchers today reside in public or private archive collections, whether in their original paper form, on microfilm or increasingly as a digital copy accessed through online platforms.[20] The question of how the increasing digitisation and transnationalisation of Sokoto's archives will affect the way scholars of the future will portray this same historical period is beyond the scope of this book, but should indeed be a subject of reflection.

While the Fodiawa wrote on a wide range of topics, the textual layout and presentation across manuscript copies of these works is remarkably formulaic. This formalism is the result of a rich tradition of copying and recopying Arabic texts in the West African region. First the copyist pens an introduction, consisting of the *basmala*,[21] the name of the author and some information about him or her. Here are two examples:

[18] See Nikolai Dobronravine, 'Design Elements and Illuminations in Nigerian "Market Literature" in Arabic and 'Ajamī', *Islamic Africa,* 8:1–2 (2017), 43–69.

[19] See Ami Ayalon, *The Arabic Print Revolution: Cultural Production and Mass Readership* (Cambridge, Mass., 2016).

[20] The collection of Fodiawa manuscripts held by the Bibliothèque nationale de France is available via its online platform www.gallica.bnf.fr. Most are from the library of Al-Ḥājj 'Umar, which the French colonial authorities seized after the conquest of Ségou in 1890. Fodiawa manuscripts held at branches of the Nigerian national archive collections in Kano (State History and Culture Bureau), Kaduna (National Archives) and several other collections are now available through the British Library's Endangered Archives Programme at www.eap.bl.uk. Perhaps the most ambitious digitisation project of West African manuscripts is being undertaken by the Hill Museum and Manuscript Library (HMML), who are currently overseeing the digitisation of dozens of family libraries from Timbuktu which will be uploaded to their online platform www.vhmml.org.

[21] I.e. *bismillāh al-raḥmān al-raḥīm* [In the name of God, the Most Righteous, the Most Merciful].

> In the name of God, the Most Gracious the Most Merciful. May God bless our master Muhammad, his family and Companions. The humble servant in need of his Lord's mercy, ʿUthmān ibn Muḥammad ibn ʿUthmān ibn Ṣāliḥ ibn Muḥammad, known as Ibn Fūdī – may God protect him with His grace, Amen – says:[22]

> In the name of God, the Most Gracious the Most Merciful. May God bless our master Muhammad, his family and Companions. The one humble to his Lord, doomed from the wickedness of his making (he is) ʿUthmān ibn Muhammad ibn ʿUthmān, Fulani in origin, Maliki in legal school, Ashʿarī in belief, says:[23]

This is followed by the doxology of the original author. In many examples, this is simply a short, pious statement of intent. In others, it is a general statement reflecting the content of the work and its virtues. Here, as an example, is the start of Abdullahi's *Ḍiyāʾ al-siyāsāt* [Guidance on policies], a compilation of Islamic law:

> In the name of God, the Most Gracious the Most Merciful. May God bless our master Muhammad, his family and Companions. Praise be to God, sole possessor of judgement, whose decree is absolute. He enacts the laws for His servants and through their implementation averts them from iniquity and corruption. He gives them sufficient and correct policies to prevent them from ignorance and heretical innovation. Blessings and praise upon our messenger Muhammad – may God bless him – who made clear what is permissible and what is forbidden, and upon his family, Companions and followers.[24]

Below is an example of another work by Abdullahi. This one concerns the rules of buying and selling:

> In the name of God, the Most Gracious the Most Merciful. May God bless our master Muhammad, his family and Companions. Praise be to God, who allowed us to sell and thereby receive money that was not our own, so that we might be content and so that living on the earth might be made easier. He sent to us the Messenger of Islam – Muhammad, may God bless him, his Companions and those who follow him – to distinguish the permissible from the forbidden.[25]

22 Usman dan Fodio, *Ajwiba muḥarrara ʿan asʾila muqarrara fī wathīqat al-Shaykh Al-Ḥājj al-maʿrūf bi-laqabihi Shīṣumaṣ ibn Aḥmad,* Kaduna (NA), digitised as BL (EAP) 535 1/4/2/18, f. lb.

23 Usman dan Fodio, *Miʿrāj al-ʿawām* (Zaria, n.d.), p. 2.

24 Abdullahi dan Fodio, *Ḍiyāʾ al-siyāsāt*, Ibadan (UC), f. la.

25 Abdullahi dan Fodio, *Kifāyat al-ʿawām fī-l-buyūʿ*, NU/Falke 117, f. la.

The author indicates the end of the doxology by the Arabic words *amma ba'd*, meaning something akin to 'and now…' or, 'to move on'. Copyists often bolden this phrase or write it out in red ink to help the reader locate the start of the text proper. The doxology is followed by the author's introduction. The introduction may include the title of their work, its structure (such as the number of chapters it has), the principal sources from which they drew, and the reason they composed it. Alternatively, it may simply consist of the words: 'I say, trusting in God', followed by the main body of the text. Here are two examples from works by Muhammad Bello:

> When I came across the preface of our Shaykh and teacher, blessed in vowelled and vowelless consonants, named *The Repository of Texts Concerning those Shaykhs from whom I Took Knowledge*, as well as the versified treatise of my brother, al-Muṣṭafā ibn Muḥammad ibn Muḥammad, mentioning what he took [of texts], my soul yearned to add to them. Even though I had already made note of them in my book, *Easy Expenditure Regarding the History of the Lands of Takrur,* nevertheless my soul set out to allude to them and the individuals mentioned by making a commentary to the preface of our Shaykh, as well as noting some of the things he mentioned that are untrue. By my objection, I do not wish to attack him nor overlook him, but only to bring benefit to the quest for knowledge.[26]

> This book is [named] *Revealing the Cover and the Veil Concerning Friendship with the Infidels, that is to say, Aiding them*, according to what is said on this topic by the specialists in Qur'anic exegesis and Islamic jurisprudence.[27]

After this introduction, the author begins the main body of the text. This can range between unstructured works of a few folios in length to more than a hundred folios divided into *abwab* [chapters] and *fuṣūl* [sections]. Following the author's conclusion, the copyist sometimes adds a note to announce that the copy is complete and asks for blessing from God for their labour. These statements are anonymous in the majority of texts I have consulted, and the copyist therefore impossible to identify.[28] Some copies in archive collections do include cover sheets that give this information,

[26] Bello, *Ḥāshiya 'alā muqaddimat Īdā' al-nusūkh*, Paris (BnF) MS Arabe 543, f. 298b.

[27] Bello, *Kashf al-ghiṭā' wa-l-sitr fī muwālāt al-kuffār (bi-ma'nā al-naṣr)*, Kaduna (NA), f. la.

[28] See Murray Last, 'The Book in the Sokoto Caliphate', in S. Jeppie and S. B.

although this tends to be the case only for more recent and prolific copyists such as Muhammadu Junaidu, Waziri of Sokoto from 1948 until his death in 1997 and thus custodian of the Sultan's private manuscript collection.

The body of Fodiawa texts surviving today is commonly presupposed to represent a historical moment of unity, when in fact it preserves profound questions and disagreements. These texts speak to one another because of their similar conventions and presentation on the page, but at times literally speak to one another by name. Each had a precise function within their 'meta-function' as vehicles of (de)legitimation: (de)legitimation of what, and for whom, in which precise circumstance? This relationality creates context. But these texts do not speak to each other in an echo chamber. Conversely, a close reading of these texts within their contexts reveals how profoundly and directly they affected historical events.

This methodology also addresses a question which, amazingly, has been generally overlooked: whom were the Fodiawa writing for? The Fodiawa's correspondence with regional figures of course records the intended recipient. Aside from this, a number of Fodiawa texts had clearly stated audiences. For example, Muhammad Bello wrote his treatise on government, *al-Ghayth al-shuʾbūb* [Abundant rain], to guide the Emir of Bauchi, Yaʿqūb. Usman wrote *Taḥdhīr al-ikhwān* [Warning to the brothers] in response to a Tuareg group asking his advice about a local Mahdi claimant. Abdullahi wrote *Ḍiyāʾ al-ḥukkām* [Guidance for the judges] at the insistance of the people of Kano, who sought his legal guidance. In other cases, these texts are part of a dialogue between the Fodiawa themselves. Abdullahi's *Ḍiyāʾ al-sulṭān* [Guidance for the ruler] is a reaction to Usman's works, *Miṣbāḥ li-ahl hadhā-l-zamān* [A lamp for the people of this time] and *Sirāj al-ikhwān* [Light of the brothers] to which Usman wrote *Najm al-ikhwān* [Star of the brothers] as a counter-response. Bello's works, *al-Inṣāf fī dhikr mā fī masāʾil al-khilāfa min wifāq wa-khilāf* [Fair judgement of conflicting views on questions concerning the caliphate] and *Ḥāshiya ʿalā muqaddimat Īdāʿ al-nusūkh* [A commentary to the preface of the Repository of texts] are direct responses to Abdullahi's *Sabīl al-salāma fi-l-imāma* [The way of safety concerning the imamate] and *Īdāʿ al-nusūkh* [Repository of texts] respectively.

Extrapolating these contexts allows us to create a fairly precise chronology for these writings, corroborated against those rare instances in which Usman, Abdullahi and Muhammad Bello gave a date for their

---

Diagne (eds), *The Meanings of Timbuktu* (Cape Town, 2008), pp. 135–63, at p. 154.

compositions.[29] These relatively distinct chronological periods of activity are the basis for the division of this book's chapters.[30] However, these distinctions are not only temporal. This book will demonstrate how the developing political and intellectual projects of the Fodiawa led to changes in the *function* of writing and written texts as they rose from rebels to rulers.

A History of the Historiography[31]

We have already discussed how, in Sokoto, descendants of the Fodiawa preserved and re-copied the written texts of their forefathers over several generations. Their function essentially remained one of legitimation for the jihad and, following the jihad's conclusion, the hereditary rule of the Sokoto elite, although this was manifested in the preservation, copying and quoting of extant texts, and not necessarily the composing of new ones.[32] Copies of the Fodiawa's writings also circulated throughout Muslim scholarly circles in North and West Africa, where

[29] Usman, Abdullahi and Muhammad Bello sometimes added the date on which they had finished their composition, expressing the Hijri year using the abjad system that assigns numerical values to each letter of the Arabic alphabet. But of the one hundred or so texts analysed in preparation for this book, less than a dozen bear a date of composition.

[30] See Appendix. For the first three terms and date ranges I rely on Muhammad A. Al-Hajj, 'A Tentative Chronology for the Writings of Shehu 'Uthmān dan Fodio', delivered at Bayero University College Department of History Postgraduate Seminar, 18th January 1977, Kano, Nigeria and Ahmad M. Kani, 'Some Reflections on the Writings of Shaykh 'Uthman b. Fudi', *Kano Studies,* 2:1 (1980), 1–9.

[31] For this analysis of Sokoto historiography I am indebted to Professor Charles C. Stewart, who allowed me to consult a draft of his unpublished study, provisionally entitled *A Condensed Summary of Historians and History Writing in Nigeria: Sokoto's Past through 180 Years*, which he completed in 1979.

[32] Of course, descendants of the Fodiawa continued to produce compositions of their own (*ALA 2* dedicates almost one hundred pages to these writers) but on the whole these compositions were derivative works based on the Fodiawa and their writings, whether hagiographies, elaborations on certain of their texts and their benefits, descriptions of their character or defences of their reputation. This literature and the reasons for the decline in the production of Arabic texts in Sokoto after the rule of Muhammad Bello is discussed in the concluding chapter.

they served similar functions.[33] The Fodiawa's writings, as well as other manuscript material collected in West Africa, also began to circulate in the Western world, where a different, decontextualised function for these texts began to emerge in tandem with a growing European interest in the African continent.[34]

In the case of the Fodiawa's writings, this decontexualisation started when, in 1824, British explorer Hugh Clapperton passed through Sokoto, meeting Muhammad Bello at his court. This was the first interaction between a ruler of Sokoto and the representative of a European power. Clapperton came back to Britain bearing two Arabic texts. One of these was Bello's *Infāq al-maysūr fī Taʾrīkh bilād al-Takrūr* [Easy expenditure regarding the history of the lands of Takrur], a voluminous work that includes a detailed history of the jihad between 1804 and 1812.

In the published account of Clapperton's travels, only the first five chapters of the *Infāq* were translated into English. These outline the geography, topography and natural resources of various regions of the Sahel.[35] In this era of European exploration, Bello's account informed Europeans about parts of the world they barely knew existed. As Clapperton's translator noted, the rest of the work concerned, 'only the details of the actions and battles that took place when Bello's father conquered these countries'.[36] Such a level of detail must have seemed irrelevant to current European

[33] See Hall and Stewart, *"Core Curriculum"* and Hunwick and O'Fahey, *ALA 2* who mention extant copies in archive collections in Ghana, Mali, Mauritania and Morocco, among other places. It is difficult to know how recently these copies were acquired, although we do know that Fodiawa texts were certainly being read and quoted from during the nineteenth century. For example, Umar Tal defended his decision to attack Hamdallahi citing one of Usman's texts.

[34] Although the decontextualisation of West African texts that resulted from European intervention in the region and Western scholarship in general is a topic that remains largely unexplored, several works carefully trace the decontextualisation of borders and spatial concepts in West Africa during the colonial period. See Camille Lefebvre, *Frontières de sable, frontières de papier. Histoire de territoires et de frontières, du jihad de Sokoto à la colonisation française du Niger (XIXe–XXe siècles)* (Paris, 2015); Vincent Hiribarren, *A History of Borno: Trans-Saharan African Empire to Failing Nigerian State* (London, 2017).

[35] Dixon Denham and Hugh Clapperton, *Narrative of Travels and Discoveries in Northern and Central Africa: In the Years 1822, 1823, and 1824* (Cambridge, 1826), pp. 158–67 (in appendices).

[36] *Ibid.*, p. 167.

preoccupations, such as the search for the source of the Nile. More than a century passed after Clapperton's visit before Bello's history was published in full, albeit under quite different political circumstances.

On 15 March 1903, following Britain's growing colonial ambitions in Sokoto territories, British troops defeated the armies of Sokoto, killing *Amīr al-mu'minīn* Muhammadu Attahiru I and declaring the British Protectorate of Northern Nigeria. Installing a new ruler more amenable to British demands, one of Britain's first actions was to request the wazirs of Sokoto and Gwandu to write histories of their emirates from the jihad of 1804 to the present.[37] In emphasising the importance of the jihad and its legacy, the northern elites ensured for themselves a prominent role in the Native Administration that served as intermediary for British rule.[38]

In 1922 Edward J. Arnett, British Resident of Kano, published *The Rise of the Sokoto Fulani*, a translation and paraphrase of Bello's *Infāq al-maysūr*.[39] In his preface, Arnett noted the disparity between the disinterest that Clapperton's translator had shown in this work a century previously to the importance it now assumed in advancing British indirect rule in Northern Nigeria. As he put it, 'it may assist those who are directing the destinies of the Hausa States to have access to a record of that movement written by one of the principal actors in it'.[40]

[37] Muḥammad al-Bukhārī, *Ta'nīs al-ikhwān bi-dhikr al-khulafā' al-'uzamā' fī-l-Sūdān*, written in 1905; Aḥmad b. Sa'd, *Lubāb mā fī Tazyīn al-waraqāt wa-Infāq al-maysūr*, written in 1908. For further details see Hunwick and O'Fahey, *ALA 2*, pp. 191–3; 240–1.

[38] Frederick Lugard, Governor of Nigeria 1914–1919, supposedly modelled the system of native courts in Northern Nigeria on Abdullahi dan Fodio's legal works *Ḍiyā' al-ḥukkām* and *Ḍiyā' al-siyāsāt*. See Michael G. Smith, 'Hausa Inheritance and Succession', in J. Duncan and M. Derrett (eds), *Studies in the Laws of Succession in Nigeria* (Oxford, 1965), pp. 230–83, at pp. 264–5. Herbert Palmer, an assistant Resident of Northern Nigeria, used Muhammad Bello's account of the origin of the Fulani in the *Infāq* to argue that the Sokoto elite were descended from a naturally dominant, non-African people. See Herbert R. Palmer, *The Carthaginian Voyage to West Africa in 500 B.C. Together with Sultan Mohammed Bello's Account of the Origin of the Fulbe* (Bathurst, 1931).

[39] Edward John Arnett, *The Rise of the Sokoto Fulani: Being a Paraphrase and in Some Parts a Translation of the Infaku'l Maisuri of Sultan Mohammed Bello* (Kano, 1922). Arnett had in fact requested Mallam Haruna, brother of the Wazir of Sokoto, to give an oral rendering of Bello's Arabic manuscript in Hausa, which Arnett then translated into English. Such collaboration typifies the relations between colonial administrators and the Sokoto elite.

[40] *Ibid.*, p. II.

As British rule of Nigeria reached its end, the region's pre-colonial history – notably, the 1804 jihad and its legacy – assumed a growing political relevance among Nigeria's newly founded political parties, divided along geographical, ethnic and religious lines. Of the two major political parties of northern Nigeria, both the Sokoto elite and the British gave their support to the Northern People's Congress (NPC), rather than the more egalitarian Northern Elements Progressive Union (NEPU). This was in order to preserve the prominent role of the northern elites, whom the British presumed would be essential for a smooth transfer to independence. The leader of the NPC at that time was Sir Ahmadu Bello, Muhammad Bello's great-grandson.

Nigeria's first independent elections in 1959 brought the NPC to power. The deputy leader of the NPC, Abubakar Tafawa Balewa, became Prime Minister, with Bello serving as Premier of Northern Nigeria. During the colonial period, these two men had developed close ties to historians of Sokoto.[41] After independence, Ahmadu Bello used his premiership to fund a number of regional 'Northern History Research Schemes'. Under the schemes, Fodiawa texts were systematically located, documented and transferred from private hands to the archives of northern Nigeria's many new universities and colleges, where a new generation of historians would add to Sokoto's historiography.[42]

These individuals were no longer British colonial administrators with a leisurely interest in history, but (mostly British) academics based at the history departments of Nigerian universities, and in particular the University of Ibadan.[43] They were informed by the written texts now accessible due

[41] Balewa and Ahmadu Bello were taught at Katsina College by Sidney Hogben, author of *The Muhammadan Emirates of Nigeria*, the best-known account of Sokoto's history written during the colonial era. In November 1964, Balewa wrote the foreword to the second edition of Hogben's work. Sir Ahmadu Bello wrote the foreword to Hogben's *Islamic States of Northern Nigeria* in December 1965, less than a month before his assassination.

[42] Some regional facilities, key figures and dates of foundation are as follows: Centre of Arabic Documentation, Ibadan (John Hunwick, 1965); Arewa House, Kaduna (Abdullahi Smith, 1970); Northern History Research Scheme, Zaria (Murray Last, 1966). William (Bill) Kensdale assisted with cataloguing the Arabic manuscript collection of University College, Ibadan (1958), while Adrian Bivar helped to establish the Arabic manuscript collection at the Department of Antiquities, Jos (founded in 1952).

[43] The Department of History at the University of Ibadan was under the direction of Abdullahi Smith. Smith supervised the dissertations of both Murray Last (*The Sokoto Caliphate*) and Roland Adelẹyẹ (*Power and Diplomacy in*

to Bello's Northern History Research Schemes, but also through close conversation and collaboration with members of the Sokoto elite such as Waziri Junaidu, custodian of Sokoto's archives and also the grandson of Wazir Muḥammad al-Bukhārī, who had first acted as official historian to British colonists some sixty years previously.[44] This continuity is a typical feature of early post-colonial scholarship which – as Sean Hanretta aptly puts it – tended to 'downplay the imprint of colonial transformation of the political economy and ignored the way nationalist projects and their elite leaders had come to be saturated in colonial ideologies'.[45]

In the same way, Ahmadu Bello's aim for the Northern History Research Schemes (as Ousmane Kane has it, 'to promote the unity of Muslims in Northern Nigeria on the basis of their common heritage of the jihad of the nineteenth century') closely mirrored Britain's policy of indirect rule in the region.[46] By emphasising the order, unity and continuing legacy of a 'Sokoto Caliphate', a term largely absent from the writings of the Fodiawa but, again, of interest to the British colonial project in Nigeria, Bello hoped to preserve the prominent role of northern Nigeria and its British-sponsored elites after independence.

In 1966, some two years after Murray Last completed his dissertation that would become *The Sokoto Caliphate*, Premier Bello and Prime Minister Balewa were both assassinated in a bloody coup, and the country drifted into civil war. In these tumultuous years, Nigerian scholarship on the writings of

---

Northern Nigeria), the most commonly referenced and best-known general histories of Sokoto. Theirs was part of a wider effort by historians such as Jacob Ajayi, often collectively referred to as the Ibadan School, to create a 'usable' past for Nigeria. See Paul E. Lovejoy, 'The Ibadan School of Historiography and Its Critics', in T. Falola and J. F. Ade Ajayi (eds), *African Historiography* (London, 1993), pp. 195–202. Stephanie Zehnle, *A Geography of Jihad: Sokoto Jihadism and the Islamic Frontier in West Africa* (Berlin, 2020), pp. 29–44, discusses this period in detail. See also Ousmane Kane, 'Arabic Sources and the Search for a New Historiography in Ibadan in the 1960s', *Africa,* 86:2 (2016), 344–6.

44 For example, whereas Johnston was firmly in the colonial historian camp and Murray Last of the Ibadan School, both relied on Waziri Junaidu as a final authority. See Hugh A. S. Johnston, *The Fulani Empire of Sokoto* (London, 1967), p. xi; Murray Last, *The Sokoto Caliphate* (New York, 1967), p. lii.

45 Sean Hanretta, *Islam and Social Change in French West Africa: History of an Emancipatory Community* (Cambridge, 2009), pp. 4–5.

46 Ousmane Kane, *Beyond Timbuktu: An Intellectual History of Muslim West Africa* (Cambridge, Mass., 2016), pp. 34–5. For more on Sir Ahmadu Bello, see Sir Ahmadu Bello, *My Life: Autobiography* (Cambridge, 1962).

the Fodiawa became thoroughly entrenched in present political concerns.[47] Given the formal introduction of Sharia Law to northern Nigeria from 1999 and the rise of the jihadi-salafi group, Boko Haram, from 2002, this trend has not abated. In fact, scholars in the fields of global Islamic fundamentalism and security studies are becoming interested in the history of Sokoto because of the frequent references to the 'Sokoto Caliphate' in Boko Haram propaganda.[48] Following the group's 2015 declaration of allegiance to the Islamic State group, it is inevitable that studies in this field will continue to be framed in relation to ever-wider global events.

Over two hundred years of engagement with the Fodiawa's writings has allowed scholars to recreate Sokoto's early history in a level of detail unusual for pre-modern Africa. Yet, tracing the development of this historiography reveals a serious problem. Whether we are talking about the Sokoto elite, British colonial administrators, or historians of newly independent Nigeria, there has been little attempt to understand the Fodiawa's writings within their own context, or to think seriously about the function of the written word at that time. Rather, the aim has been to selectively mine those details that fitted the political exigency of a unified and eminently 'usable' past for northern Nigeria. But as we shall see, these texts do not project unity at all. Rather, they reveal questions and disagreements between the Fodiawa themselves, as well as regional powers, and demonstrate an ongoing need to legitimate the jihad of 1804 and subsequent developments well after the fact.

The non-critical approach to the Arabic writings of the Sokoto Fodiawa taken thus far is typical of the treatment of other bodies of Arabic writings from the West African past. Such approaches favoured synthesis over analysis, flattening the contours of the contextual landscape within which these diverse writings were being produced, and leaving questions about genre, audience and motivation largely unanswered. The attitude seems to have been that Arabic primary source material from Africa existed so that historians could create events-based histories of the pre-modern African past and, that work done, had no further use.[49]

[47] For an excellent analysis of post-independence Nigerian scholarship on the Sokoto Caliphate see Zehnle, *A Geography of Jihad*, pp. 29–44.

[48] See Abdulbasit Kassim, 'Defining and Understanding the Religious Philosophy of Jihādī-Salafism and the Ideology of Boko Haram', *Politics, Religion & Ideology*, 16:2–3 (2015), 173–200.

[49] Hadrien Collet, 'Le sultanat du Mali (XIVe-XVe siècle): Historiographies d'un État soudanien, de l'Islam médiéval à aujourd'hui' (Unpublished PhD dissertation, Université Paris 1, 2017).

The recent excitement over 'Arabic Sources for African History' disguises the fact that, by the 1980s, the topic had become relatively passé among many historians of Africa.

Paulo Farias's provocative demonstration that the Timbuktu Chronicles – and the historiography developed from them – actually contradicts the archaeological evidence has prompted a number of scholars to critically re-examine primary sources hitherto taken for granted in West African historiography.[50] Although not always stated explicitly, these studies also reveal the key role of written texts in discourses of (de)legitimation. Recent work by Paul Lovejoy has shown that the Kano Chronicle (which records the rulers of Kano going back to the tenth century) was likely compiled in the 1880s by Dan Rimi Barka, a high official of the Kano Emirs. [51] Benedetta Rossi has investigated the Chronicles of Agadez, suggesting that the version presented to the French colonial authorities was altered to further the territorial claims of certain Tuareg groups.[52] Mauro Nobili and Mohamad Shahid Mathee demonstrate that the so-called *Taʾrīkh al-fattāsh* is in fact an apocryphal nineteenth-century creation to further the legitimacy claims of Ahmad Lobbo, written by one of his followers.[53] Nobili went on to examine the wider role of Arabic texts in the legitimation of Masina, the Muslim state founded by Lobbo and centred in the town of Hamdallahi.[54] Meanwhile, Ariela Marcus-Sells argues that the autobiographical writings of the Kunta of Azawad should be considered first and foremost as legitimating devices for their spiritual and commercial hegemony in the wider region.[55] Other recent scholarly work has used both established and newly

[50] Paulo F. de Moraes Farias, *Arabic Medieval Inscriptions from the Republic of Mali: Epigraphy, Chronicles and Songhay-Tuareg History* (Oxford, 2004).

[51] Paul E. Lovejoy, 'The Kano Chronicle Revisited', delivered at Landscapes, Sources, and Intellectual Projects in African History: Symposium in Honour of Paulo Fernando de Moraes Farias, University of Birmingham, 12–14 November 2015.

[52] Benedetta Rossi, 'The Agadez Chronicles and Y Tarichi: A Reinterpretation', *History in Africa*, 43 (2016), 95–140.

[53] Mauro Nobili and Mohamed S. Mathee, 'Towards a New Study of the So-Called Tārīkh Al-Fattāsh', *History in Africa*, 42 (2015), 37–73. See also Mauro Nobili, Ali Diakite and Zachary Wright's forthcoming critical edition and parallel translation of *Taʾrīkh al-fattāsh* and *Taʾrīkh ibn al-Mukhtār*.

[54] Mauro Nobili, *Sultan, Caliph, and the Renewer of the Faith: Ahmad Lobbo, the Tārīkh Al-Fattāsh and the Making of an Islamic State in West Africa* (Cambridge, 2020).

[55] Ariela Marcus-Sells, 'Realm of the Unseen: Devotional Practice and Sufi

discovered Arabic primary source material to explore concepts of justice, diplomacy, history and authority in pre-colonial West Africa.[56]

My focus on discursive strategies of legitimation in Sokoto specifically owes much to Murray Last's exploration of the topic in a number of articles.[57] It also draws inspiration from other studies which use the Fodiawa's writings to explore topics as diverse as music,[58] ransoming,[59] geography,[60] and urban planning.[61] Developing an understanding of the Fodiawa as distinct voices whose varying dispositions, ambitions and opinions shaped the discursive strategies they used was aided by close biographical studies such as as M. T. Minna's work on

---

Authority in the Kunta Community' (Unpublished PhD dissertation, Stanford, 2015).

[56] Among them Collet, *Le sultanat du Mali*; Rémi Dewière, *Du lac Tchad à la Mecque: Le sultanat du Borno et son monde (XVIᵉ–XVIIᵉ siècle)* (Paris, 2017); 'Les lettres du pouvoir au Sahel islamique. Marques, adaptations et continuités administratives Au Borno (1823–1918)', *Cahiers d'études africaines,* 236 (2020), 1047–90; Amir Syed, 'Al-Ḥājj ʿUmar Tāl and the Realm of the Written: Mastery, Mobility and Islamic Authority in 19th Century West Africa' (Unpublished PhD dissertation, University of Michigan, 2017).

[57] Murray Last, '"Injustice" and Legitimacy in the Early Sokoto Caliphate', in J. F. Ade Ajayi and J. D. Y. Peel (eds), *People and Empires in African History: Essays in Memory of Michael Crowder* (New York & London, 1992), pp. 45–57; 'From Dissent to Dissidence: The Genesis & Development of Reformist Islamic Groups in Northern Nigeria', in A. R. Mustapha (ed.), *Sects & Social Disorder: Muslim Identities & Conflict in Northern Nigeria* (Woodbridge, 2014), pp. 18–53.

[58] Veit Erlmann, 'Music and the Islamic Reform in the Early Sokoto Empire: Sources, Ideology, Effects', *Abhandlungen für die Kunde des Morgenlandes,* 48:1 (1986), 1–56.

[59] Jennifer Lofkrantz, 'Protecting Freeborn Muslims: The Sokoto Caliphate's Attempts to Prevent Illegal Enslavement and its Acceptance of the Strategy of Ransoming', *Slavery & Abolition,* 32:1 (2011), 109–27; 'Intellectual Discourse in the Sokoto Caliphate: The Triumvirate's Opinions on the Issue of Ransoming, ca. 1810', *The International Journal of African Historical Studies,* 45:3 (2012), 385–401.

[60] Zehnle, *A Geography of Jihad.*

[61] Mark D. DeLancey, 'Moving East, Facing West: Islam as an Intercultural Mediator in Urban Planning in the Sokoto Empire', in T. Falola and S. J. Salm (eds), *African Urban Spaces in Historical Perspective* (Rochester, 2005), pp. 3–22; Besim S. Hakim and Zubair Ahmed, 'Rules for the Built Environment in 19th Century Northern Nigeria', *Journal of Architectural and Planning Research,* 23:1 (2006), 1–26.

Muhammad Bello,[62] Sidi Mohamed Mahibou's study of Abdullahi,[63] Seyni Moumouni's work on Usman,[64] as well as Beverly Mack and Jean Boyd's biography of Usman's daughter, Nana Asmau.[65] Slavery in Sokoto has also been an important area of scholarly research. While institutionalised slavery in the Sokoto state probably did not begin until after Bello had firmly established his rule in 1821, studies on this topic by Paul Lovejoy, Sean Stillwell and Muhammad Bashir Salau – among others – inform my later chapters.[66]

Approaching Legitimacy

This book contends that in the nineteenth-century Sahel, Arabic texts were primarily vehicles for political legitimation among a Muslim intellectual elite. While the use of these texts to create an objective account of this particular historical period is limited by their inherent biases, these very biases can inform our understanding of legitimacy and the process by which legitimacy was created, maintained and destroyed in the Muslim societies of this region. But we must first take pause to consider what exactly we mean by legitimacy, and the scope of this book's intervention. This section will first discuss the definition of legitimacy more generally, before exploring studies of legitimacy in West African Muslim movements of the nineteenth century and comparing these studies with conceptualisations of legitimacy in extant literature on Sokoto. It will then introduce the theoretical framework of the book, and the new terms and concepts I will be using to talk about legitimacy and processes of legitimation.

[62] Mahmud T. M. Minna, 'Sultan Muhammad Bello and His Intellectual Contribution to the Sokoto Caliphate' (Unpublished PhD dissertation, SOAS, 1982).

[63] Sidi Mohamed Mahibou, *Abdullahi dan Fodio et la théorie du gouvernement islamique* (Paris, 2010).

[64] Seyni Moumouni, *Vie et œuvre du Cheikh Uthmân Dan Fodio (1754–1817): De l'islam au soufisme* (Paris, 2008).

[65] Beverly B. Mack and Jean Boyd, *One Woman's Jihad: Nana Asma'u, Scholar and Scribe* (Indianapolis, 2000).

[66] Paul E. Lovejoy, *Slavery, Commerce and Production in the Sokoto Caliphate of West Africa* (Lawrenceville, 2005); Sean Stilwell, *Paradoxes of Power: The Kano 'Mamluks' and Male Royal Slavery in the Sokoto Caliphate, 1804–1903* (London, 2004); Mohammed Bashir Salau, *Plantation Slavery in the Sokoto Caliphate: A Historical and Comparative Study* (Rochester, 2018).

In his groundbreaking work on governance in Hausaland, social anthropologist M. G. Smith attempted to distinguish authority and legitimacy, speaking of *authority* as the power to make decisions based upon a commonly agreed system of rules, and *legitimacy* as the harmony of this system of rules with a given society's moral principles.[67] In sum, the former derives from formalised institutions and structures, whereas the latter does not necessarily require such structures. For example, the *authority* of a court of law pertains to the extent of that court's jurisdiction in a given matter. Its broader *legitimacy* relates to its fundamental right to exist as an organ of justice. Thus, while it seems possible to have authority without legitimacy or legitimacy without authority, this condition cannot last for long. But arguably the difference comes down to usage and linguistic convention. Authority is spoken of as 'possessed' or 'wielded' from within while legitimacy is earned, granted or conferred from without. Weber's commonly accepted definition of authority as 'legitimately exercised power' (with power being the probability of carrying out one's will) demonstrates the fundamental connection between the two terms.[68] This book takes care to use *authority* and *legitimacy* with this distinction in mind, acknowledging that it can oftentimes be unclear.

Legitimacy is thus a complex and multi-faceted concept. While it may be straightforward for societies and individuals to 'know' when leaders, power structures and thought systems become legitimate or illegitimate, the process of (de)legitimation and its components demand greater scrutiny. But to be clear, I am not using the texts of the Fodiawa to talk about legitimacy *in the abstract*. That is to say, these texts do not reveal innate human behaviours or contribute to interpretive sociological theory. Rather, legitimacy here is endogenous to the act of writing, sanctioning a particular social class to hold political power. Contained within the world of these texts, we cannot then extrapolate arguments about legitimacy beyond this precise social context. This allows us to step back from a broad, Weberian discussion of authority and legitimacy – which some Africanists have pursued – and instead follow the discursive processes

[67] See Michael G. Smith, *Government in Zazzau, 1800–1950* (London, 1964), pp. 18–21.

[68] Bryan S. Turner, *Weber and Islam: A Critical Study* (London & Boston, 1974), p. 23; Max Weber, *The Theory of Social and Economic Organization*, trans. Parsons and Henderson (New York, 1947), p. 152.

by which legitimacy was created, maintained and destroyed within the 'meta' world of Arabic texts.[69]

There are a few studies of Muslim movements in Africa that explore legitimacy in some detail. In his study of Muslim holy men in the Nilotic Sudan, Neil McHugh found that successful claims to *walīy* status depended upon divine election, Islamic learning and a good ancestry. Essentially, holy men had to demonstrate that they had been personally chosen by God, that they had, through systematic and rigorous study, gained an acceptable degree of Islamic learning, and that they came from a line of holy men, or at least could claim an ancestor who had also been a *walīy*.[70] Similarly, David Robinson, an authoritative source on the jihad movement of Umar Tal, concluded that Tal's legitimacy derived from 'religious affiliation, ethnic identity and class position'.[71] Meanwhile, Bruce Hall has analysed extensively the connection between race and the legitimacy to rule in West Africa, making clear that race is only one of several 'constructors of authority' in the Sahel region.[72] Muslim actors thus seemed to construct their identities from distinct but interlinked components that acted collectively as sources of legitimation.

Scholarship on Sokoto makes no comparable attempt to explore how the Fodiawa's movement gained its legitimacy. While scholars have identified various reasons why the jihad of 1804 was successful, they have tended to argue for one factor over the others, rather than approaching legitimation itself as a multi-faceted phenomenon. This, I would argue, is another consequence of the various phases of historiographical work on Sokoto and the different aims and ideologies of each.

[69] Ernest Gellner uses his interpretation of baraka among Sufi leaders in the Atlas Mountains to both engage with and to challenge Weber's three types of authority; John Hanson uses Weber's model of the 'suffocation' of charisma to interpret the various internal conflicts, contradictions and – in the case of the Futunke in Karta – failures of West African jihad movements. See Ernest Gellner, *Saints of the Atlas* (London, 1969); John H. Hanson, *Migration, Jihad, and Muslim Authority in West Africa: The Futanke Colonies in Karta* (Bloomington, 1996).

[70] Neil McHugh, *Holymen of the Blue Nile: The Making of an Arab-Islamic Community in the Nilotic Sudan, 1500–1800* (Evanston, 1994), p. 18.

[71] David Robinson, *The Holy War of Umar Tal* (Oxford, 1985), p. 3.

[72] Bruce S. Hall, *A History of Race in Muslim West Africa, 1600–1960* (New York, 2011), p. 67.

The first British colonial administrators in northern Nigeria tended to frame the jihad as an ethnic takeover disguised as a religious movement.[73] This theory is inseparable from the colonial policy at that time, which was to idealise the Fulani as a natural ruling race through which to project British power. Later advocates for a northern Nigerian nationalism – tied as it was to the historical prestige of a 'Sokoto Caliphate' – tended to emphasise the Fodiawa's religious authority as orthodox reformers speaking to a receptive audience of pious Muslims.[74] After Nigerian independence (and influenced by political Islamist thought) the Islamic Legitimist school in Nigeria placed the movement of the Fodiawa within a global movement of revolutionary change driven by reformist ideology.[75] Meanwhile, economic historians argued that the movement gained its legitimacy through the articulation of socio-economic issues in religious terms and, after the jihad was won, by their monopoly over means of production and patronage networks.[76]

[73] John A. Burdon, 'The Fulani Emirates of Northern Nigeria', *The Geographical Journal,* 24:6 (1904), 636–51, at pp. 640–1; Arnett, *Infaku'l Maisuri*, p. 12. That said, some administrator-historians also recognised the religious leadership of Usman dan Fodio as a source of baraka, as well as the link between knowledge of Islamic texts and authority to rule. See for example Sidney J. Hogben, *The Muhammadan Emirates of Nigeria* (Oxford, 1930).

[74] H. F. C. (Abdullahi) Smith, 'A Neglected Theme of West African History: The Islamic Revolutions of the 19th Century', *Journal of the Historical Society of Nigeria*, 2:2 (1961), 169–85; John Ralph Willis, 'Jihād fī Sabīl Allāh – Its Doctrinal Basis in Islam and Some Aspects of its Evolution in Nineteenth-Century West Africa', *The Journal of African History,* 8:3 (1967), 395–415. A noticeable exception is Mervyn Hiskett, who emphasised Usman's adherence to the Qadiriyya and alleged link to the Mahdi as decisive factors in the legitimacy of the jihadist movement. See Mervyn Hiskett, *The Sword of Truth: The Life and Times of the Shehu Usuman Dan Fodio* (Oxford, 1973); 'The Nineteenth-Century Jihads in West Africa', in J. E. Flint (ed.), *The Cambridge History of Africa* (8 vols, Cambridge, 1977), vol. 5, pp. 131–51; *The Development of Islam in West Africa* (New York, 1984).

[75] See Ibraheem Sulaiman, *The Islamic State and the Challenge of History: Ideals, Policies, and Operation of the Sokoto Caliphate* (London, 1987), pp. 1–2; *A Revolution in History: The Jihad of Usman Dan Fodio* (London, 1986). For more on the context of the Islamic Legitimist movement, see Lovejoy, *The Ibadan School of Historiography.*

[76] Joseph P. Smaldone, *Warfare in the Sokoto Caliphate: Historical and Sociological Perspectives* (Cambridge, 1977), p. 20; Lovejoy, *Slavery, Commerce*

Further, discussions about the legitimacy of the Fodiawa's movement (and Sokoto more generally) tended to focus predominantly on the jihad itself. No attempt has been made thus far to track how concepts of legitimacy – and as such, discourses of legitimation – may have changed after this time, along with the evolving political exigencies of Sokoto's foundational period. While scholars have noted that the Fodiawa's legitimation came from the 'integrating force of Islamic ideology', there has been little attempt to explore what this ideology was or entertain the possibility that ideologies can be subject to historical change.[77]

But such oversights are also due to underlying assumptions about Islam, and specifically Islam in Africa, that were typical until fairly recently in African studies. Robert Launey and others have summarised this 'Islamisation' theory, whereby a foreign ideology – Islam – is first quarantined within African societies, then mixes with endemic religious practices, and finally returns to its orthodox roots through the efforts of Muslim reformers. Such a way of thinking does not credit Muslim actors with any agency or discursive flexibility in their religious practices. Instead, it conceives only of a 'reified, primordial, and a-historical entity called "Islam"', which African societies either follow correctly, only nominally, or not at all.[78] More recent scholarly work has recentred African Muslims in the process of forming ideas about what is Islamic, which Mauro Nobili terms a 'discursive approach'.[79]

---

and Production; 'Plantations in the Economy of the Sokoto Caliphate', *The Journal of African History,* 19:3 (1978), 341–68.

[77] See Roland A. Adelẹyẹ, *Power and Diplomacy in Northern Nigeria 1804–1906: The Sokoto Caliphate and Its Enemies* (London, 1971), p. 21. See also 'Hausaland and Borno, 1600–1800', in J. F. Ade Ajayi and M. Crowder (eds), *History of West Africa* (2 vols, Harlow, 1971), vol. 1, pp. 577–623, at p. 622. See also *Power and Diplomacy*, pp. 5–12; 21–2; 38–44.

[78] See Mauro Nobili, 'Reinterpreting the Role of Muslims in the West African Middle Ages', *The Journal of African History*, 61:3 (2020) 327–40, quoting Robert Launey, *Beyond the Stream: Islam and Society in a West African Town* (Berkeley, 1992), p. 17. Interestingly, Mauro Nobili points out that adherents of the Islamisation theory, such as Nehemia Levtzion, took these rigid ideas about Islam from the texts of nineteenth centry jihad leaders themselves.

[79] *Ibid.* This approach is grounded in the work of Talal Asad, 'The Idea of an Anthropology of Islam', *Qui Parle,* 17:2, 1–30, who conceived of Islam as a 'discursive tradition', an idea adapted by Shahab Ahmed, *What Is Islam? The Importance of Being Islamic* (Princeton, 2016).

Taking this approach further, it is possible to conceive of West Africa of the nineteenth century as its own discursive space. By putting forward such a term I do not suggest that discourse in this period was limited, closed or isolated. Rather that there existed at this time and in this geographical region a robust and well-defined *'Maliki-Ashʿarī'* discursive tradition through which new ideas were expressed and discussed, as well as a 'core curriculum' of Islamic texts judged worthy of informing such discussions[80] – and that *this* particular, discursive 'Islam', as Roman Loimeier had it, 'became both the most important foundation of political legitimacy and a major ideological source'.[81]

However, what remains unanswered are the processes through which Muslim scholars such as the Fodiawa, working *within* the 'meta' level of legitimacy bestowed through belonging to a West African discursive space, shifted discourses of legitimacy to suit their evolving political needs. Jean-Louis Triaud suggests that analysing moments of conflict between Muslim leaders in West Africa – in his case, between Amadu Amadu of Masina and Umar Tal – might expose *les outils juridiques* [the juridical tools] that gave Muslim actors the flexibility they required to maintain authority even as their need for pragmatic solutions ran up against the established understanding of correct 'Islamic' actions.[82]

Triaud points to two distinct 'modes' – and, extrapolated, two different 'Islams' – that could be employed within this West African discursive space. I call the first of these modes a 'discourse of dissent'.[83] When examined closely, the 'Islam' of this mode is exactly the 'Islam' which historians of Africa imbibed from the early writings of the Fodiawa

[80] See Loimeier, *Muslim Societies in Africa*; Rudolph T. Ware III, *The Walking Qur'an: Islamic Education, Embodied Knowledge, and History in West Africa* (Chapel Hill, 2014); Rüdiger Seesemann, 'Embodied Knowledge and the Walking Qur'an: Lessons for the Study of Islam and Africa', *Journal of Africana Religions,* 3:2 (2015), 201–9.

[81] Loimeier, *Muslim Societies in Africa*, p. 114.

[82] Jean-Louis Triaud, 'Le renversement du souverain injuste: Un débat sur les fondements de la légitimité islamique en Afrique noire au XIXᵉ siècle', *Annales. Histoire, Sciences Sociales,* 40:3 (1985), 509–19, at p. 510.

[83] Triaud (*ibid.*, p. 516) suggested the term *madhdhab maghīlite,* after the dogmatic preacher (and Qadiri Sufi) ʿAbd al-Karīm al-Maghīlī, discussed below. Murray Last has also discussed the concept of 'dissent' in several articles (Last, '"Injustice" and Legitimacy'; 'The Pattern of Dissent: Boko Haram in Nigeria 2009', *Annual Review of Islam in Africa,* 10 (2009), 7–11; 'From Dissent to Dissidence').

and their contemporaries and, taking it out of its historical context and function, turned into the Islamisation theory. In essence, Muslim actors engaged with classical Islamic texts to make rigid distinctions between what (and who) was and was not Muslim, thus delegitimising the ostensibly Muslim forms of government in the region by pointing out their inevitable deviances from, for example, Muhammad's rule of Medina, while seriously threatening the local Muslim rulers themselves by suggesting that they tolerated *bid'a* [heretical innovation] and as such were not Muslims at all.

By linking deviations from religious practices with wider societal issues, and (through *takfir*) implicitly condoning violence against the political elite, such discourse aimed to rapidly overturn the extant political order. Although they had not generally been politically powerful before the conflict, Muslim reformers garnered the necessary authority to rule with the promise to reinstate the law of 'Islam'.[84] This programme was, by design, destructive rather than constructive, in that its aim was to delegitimise existing structures by invoking abstract ideals. It was inevitable that Muslim actors integrated some precedents from former power structures for the sake of quickly consolidating their rule. But any pragmatism threatened to alienate their followers, who could after all invoke the same discursive tools to unseat them. To avoid fresh cycles of violence and eventually, anarchy, a second discursive process was necessary.

Essentially, Muslim rulers attempted to moderate Islamic discourse so that it conformed to their new-found political power, replacing an emancipatory yet orthodox 'Islam' with a cautious, pragmatic and ambiguous discourse that served to justify 'might makes right' and enforce the status quo, stressing the importance of unity in the Muslim community under their new leaders.[85] This second discursive mode, which I call a 'discourse of moderation', frequently referenced legal texts from the Abbasid period, a time in which the *ulama* sought compromise with local rulers and found creative ways to excuse the evaporation of a centralised caliphal power. Thus, durable state-building in the Sahel depended upon a smooth transition between these two discursive modes, as Muslim leaders moved beyond jihadism while maintaining the veneer of Islamic

[84] See Gellner, *Saints of the Atlas*, p. 10, who explains how rural religious figures could unseat existing and largely urban religious elites by appealing to the ultimate sources of Muslim authority: the Qur'an, the hadith and the books of law.

[85] A phenomenon which Triaud, *Renversement*, amply demonstrates in his analysis of Amadu Amadu of Masina's arguments against Umar Tal.

orthodoxy. Over time, the authority of the Muslim ruler himself precluded the need to engage in discursive work at all, and 'Islam' became simply what the ruler said it was.

This book makes several contributions. Having demonstrated that Islamic movements derive legitimacy from distinct but interlinked sources, this book undertakes theoretical work to explore these sources, constructing a new typology of legitimacy as it was understood within nineteenth-century Sahelian discursive space. Likewise, accepting Islam as a discursive tradition, this book demonstrates that tradition in action, charting the Fodiawa's shift between discourses of dissent and moderation from the jihad of Usman through the rise of Muhammad Bello and the Sokoto state. But, while discursive flexibility was the key to creating a stable and cohesive Muslim state in Sokoto, and indeed in other Muslim societies, it also left many questions and disagreements. I argue that the explosion of Arabic texts in the nineteenth-century Sahel represents the collective response of Muslim intellectuals to a changing discursive space. Analysis of these Arabic texts is thus our principal window into a pivotal moment of West African history.

That being said, I must also point out several limits to this book's contribution. Arabic texts are useful concepts for thinking through how legitimacy was conceived within the Muslim, literate, predominantly male and Arabic-speaking intellectual elite to which the Fodiawa claimed membership. However, I accept that there were undoubtedly sources of legitimation for the jihad and for the construction of a Sokoto state that neither derived from Islamic discourse, nor from the discursive tools offered through Arabic texts. As such, the book can offer only a limited insight as to what legitimacy meant for non-elite and non-Muslim actors during this same time period. Further, while Arabic was the Fodiawa's preferred medium for discourses around legitimacy such as I have described, the Fodiawa also left behind them numerous compositions in the languages of Hausa and Fulfulde. In this sense, the Fodiawa had several author identities, only one of which I am capturing in this study.

For a book so highly reliant on texts, we must also make several assumptions and ignore certain unknowns. We must assume that these texts were indeed written by their stated authors, and that the form they are in now is roughly the same as when first composed. For a book so dependent on accurate chronology, we must also assume that manuscripts with a date bear the correct one. We do not know whether the texts that survive today are an accurate representation of the Fodiawa's historical oeuvre. Whether accidental or deliberate, a certain degree of selectivity will have played a part in those works frequently copied, and thus preserved today. It is possible that during the jihad years the Fodiawa destroyed a certain amount of material that ran contrary to the narrative they wished to portray. But the more likely scenario is that texts which no longer had a political relevance simply stopped being copied. This perhaps explains the almost total lack of documentation from Gwandu Emirate. Governed by Abdullahi, it seemingly failed to remain cohesive after his death, and was apportioned between France, Germany and Britain at the turn of the twentieth century. Such was also the case for Masina. After the sack of Hamdallahi in 1862 and the fall of the Lobbo dynasty, the state's foundational texts all but disappeared.[86]

Whereas I have attempted to the best of my abilities to ascertain questions of motivation and audience when not clearly stated, these can be at best well-reasoned hypotheses. Constant figures in the daily lives of the Fodiawa who may have influenced their thinking and motivations (brothers, sisters, wives, servants, concubines) are never mentioned, while we can assume numerous events of vital importance to our understanding of this historical period will never have been written down. But this is not a problem exclusively associated with the writings of a group of religious leaders from the nineteenth-century Sahel. The question of how much we can really understand of a society's values, or of a person's life, hopes, and dreams through the written record they leave behind is a constant and largely unknowable one for the historian.

[86] The *Tārīkh al-Fattāsh*, a text legitimising Ahmad Lobbo's rule of Masina, is one of the only documents to survive from Hamdallahi, with only eight extant copies. See Mauro Nobili and Mohamed Diagayeté, 'The Manuscripts That Never Were: In Search of the *Tārīkh Al-Fattāsh* in Côte d'Ivoire and Ghana', *History in Africa*, 44 (2017), 309–321.

CHAPTER 1

Sources of Legitimacy in the Nineteenth-Century Sahel

Since at least the sixteenth century, it has been possible to talk of an intellectual elite of Muslim scholars in the Sahelian milieu. These scholars were not 'elite' in the sense that their position brought them political influence, universally acclaimed high status or significant personal wealth. On the contrary, many subsisted on very few resources, had little interaction with West African political systems, and were often relegated to a low status within them. Rather, I call them an 'elite' in the sense that a long-established tradition of peripatetic scholarship and migratory practices, as well as family, clan and tariqa affiliation, created a shared body of values, pursuits and conceptions of the world that I have termed a Sahelian discursive tradition, and which was believed was superior to other knowledge systems. Members of this elite, such as the Fodiawa, appealed to the understanding of legitimacy that existed within this tradition as it stood in the early nineteenth century, through the medium of Arabic texts.

It follows that if we are to make the writings of the Fodiawa recognisable in their intellectual context, as discussed in subsequent chapters, we must first understand the markers of authority and the structures for receiving, managing and transferring it as they existed within this discursive tradition. This chapter offers a novel way to think through legitimacy's composite nature in the Sahel, introducing the terms *fiqh*, *kashf* and *nasab*, and explaining how they worked together to create a durable authority that could be invoked by Muslim actors.

Fiqh

Among the names of God in the Muslim tradition is *al-ʿalīm* [the supreme knower]. Knowledge, in a scholarly milieu such as that of the Sahel, essentially meant *fiqh*. Although often translated as 'Islamic jurisprudence', *fiqh* is rather more expansive than that. In essence, the science of *fiqh* is man's attempt to interpret God's wishes for how humankind should behave and order itself, as revealed in the Qur'an and distilled from the hadith, and to implement this Divine Will to further the goal of a just, harmonious and vibrant Muslim society. But the task of interpretation is challenged by the inferior intellect of man. God's word is infallible, but an erroneous interpretation of it is possible, and holds catastrophic consequences for the Umma and the fate of Muslim souls.[1]

Early *fiqh* scholars constructed a stable and authoritative interpretation of the Divine Will through Qur'anic exegesis and the compilation and curation of hadith that became known as the Sharia. In Sunni Islam, further elaboration of the Sharia produced four universally recognised madhabs [legal schools]. After the creation of the madhabs, *ijtihad* – or the free interpretation of Qur'anic law using *manṭiq* [logic] rather than close reference to any one of these traditions – became highly controversial. However, the fundamental limits of *fiqh* remained. Since the text being interpreted is the direct word of God (or, in the case of the hadith the actions of His perfect creation, Muhammad), scholars could hardly question the basis of a free interpretation of these texts. As the maxim goes, 'every *mujtahid* is correct'.[2] This introduced considerable flexibility to legal judgements or what was otherwise considered an authoritative *fiqh* tradition, to say nothing of contemporary notions of a 'rigid' Sharia Law.

By the nineteenth century, Sahelian scholars had formed consensus on a remarkably standardised body of writings that they equated with *fiqh*. This 'core curriculum' resulted from the labours of generations of

[1] In a rebuke to a man who supposedly interpreted the Qur'an without sufficient training, Usman warned that his actions could result in 'plague, hunger, lack of rain, poverty, maladies, house fires, an outbreak of discord and bloodshed, enmity and hatred between the Muslims for no reason'. Usman, *Wathīqa ilā al-rajul yadʿī annahu ʿālim yufassir al-Qurʾān bi-ghair itqān qawānīn al-tafsīr* (Sokoto, n.d.), p. 3.

[2] Usman set down what we can assume was a commonly accepted hierarchy of *mujtahids*. He started with scholars who freely abrogated Qur'anic verses (*mujtahidūn al-tarjīḥ*), moving to those who used the legal reasoning of existing judgements to make new ones (*mujtahidūn al-tafrīʿ*), to those who made new legal judgements without reference to any preceding ones (*mujtahidūn al-taʾsīl*). See Usman, *Taḥdhīr al-ikhwān min iddiʿāʾ al-mahdiyya al-mawʿūda ākhir al-zamān* in Muhammad A. Al-Hajj, 'The Mahdist Tradition in Northern Nigeria' (Unpublished PhD dissertation, Ahmadu Bello University 1973), pp. 224–72.

discerning legal minds. Charting a path from the legal compendiums of Malik ibn Anas (711–795) through established commentaries made in the early period of Islam, to commenteries and abridgements of these works produced in the Sahelian milieu, can provide us with one dimension of this local tradition, dating back to at least the fifteenth century.[3] Many authors in the Sahelian core curriculum were alive at this time, and several were (or tradition claimed them to be) physically present in the Sahel region. But the development of the Sahelian *fiqh* tradition also went hand in hand with a gradual interpretation and rewriting of the historical past that came to equate knowledge of the *fiqh* tradition with legitimacy to rule.

Two critical figures in this regard are Jalāl al-dīn al-Suyūṭī (1445–1505) and ʿAbd al-Karīm al-Maghīlī (1425–1505). Egyptian polymath al-Suyūṭī authored works on *tafsīr* and Islamic history, as well as several on Arabic grammar and rhetoric, that feature heavily in the Sahelian core curriculum.[4] Not incidentally, he is the most frequently cited author in the Fodiawa's bibliographical works. This prominence can be traced to the fact that al-Suyūṭī actively disseminated his texts among the West African scholars who passed through Cairo on their way to pilgrimage, and directly corresponded with West African rulers such as Ibrahim of Katsina, for whom he wrote a treatise on Muslim governance.[5]

Al-Maghīlī was born in Tlemcen, north-western Algeria, but fled across the Sahara after inciting a failed rebellion against the Waṭṭasid dynasty of Morocco. He passed through Hausaland, writing a kingship manual for

[3] See Lamin Sanneh, 'The Origins of Clericalism in West African Islam', *The Journal of African History,* 17:1 (1976), 49–72; Finn Fuglestad, 'A Reconsideration of Hausa History before the Jihad', *The Journal of African History*, 19:3 (1978), 319–39; Paul E. Lovejoy, 'The Role of the Wangara in the Economic Transformation of the Central Sudan in the Fifteenth and Sixteenth Centuries', *The Journal of African History*, 19:2, 173–93; Murray Last, 'The Early Kingdoms of the Nigerian Savanna', in J. F. Ade Ajayi and M. Crowder (eds), *History of West Africa*, 2nd edn (2 vols, New York, 1985), vol. 1, pp. 167–224.

[4] See his *Tafsīr al-Jalālayn* (along with Jalāl al-Dīn al-Maḥallī) and *Taʾrīkh al-khulafāʾ*.

[5] See Elizabeth M. Sartain, 'Jalal ad-Din as-Suyuti's Relations with the People of Takrur', *Journal of Semitic Studies,* 16:2 (1971), 193–8. Usman dan Fodio quotes this letter in *Tanbīh al-ikhwān ʿalā aḥwāl Arḍ al-sūdān* in Herbert R. Palmer, 'An Early Fulani Conception of Islam (Continued)', *Journal of the Royal African Society,* 14:53 (1914), 53–9, at pp. 55–9. Abdullahi also refers to this letter in *Ḍiyāʾ al-muqtadīn.*

Muhammadu Rumfa of Kano (r. 1463–1499)[6] as well as a second short treatise in 1491 or 1492, an event possibly recorded in the Kano Chronicle.[7] More significant for the wider Sahelian *fiqh* tradition is the treatise that he prepared in 1498 for *Askiya* Al-Ḥājj Muhammad of Songhay.[8] *Askiya* Muhammad (originally Muhammad ibn Abī Bakr al-Ṭūrī), an army commander, seized power upon the death of his predecessor, Sonni Ali. He supposedly wrote to al-Maghīlī, claiming that during his rule Sonni Ali had made offerings to idols, persecuted the *ulama* and enslaved free Muslims. In his reply, al-Maghīlī declared *takfir* upon Sonni Ali and said that *Askiya* Muhammad had been correct to take power. As Songhay's territories expanded under the *Askiya* dynasty, al-Maghīlī's legitimation of that family's power earned him a prominent place in the Sahelian tradition.[9] Such at least is clear from a well-known scholar of the late Songhay Empire, Ahmad Baba (1556–1627), whose bibliographical work *Nayl al-ibtihāj* [Attainment of joy] dedicates a substantial portion to the biography of al-Maghīlī and his extant writings.[10]

The kingship guides written by al-Maghīlī and al-Suyūṭī, themselves based on Abbasid standards such as al-Māwardī's *al-Aḥkām al-sulṭāniyya*, introduced certain expectations for a Muslim ruler. For example, the *Amīr*

[6] *Tāj al-dīn fī-mā yajib ʿalā al-mulūk* [The crown of religion in what is obligatory for kings]. See Abd al-Aziz A. Batran, 'A Contribution to the Biography of Shaikh Muḥammad ibn ʿAbd-Al-Karīm ibn Muḥammad ('Umar-A'mar) Al-Maghīlī Al-Tilimsānī', *Journal of African History*, 14:3 (1973), 381–94; Humphrey Fisher, 'The Eastern Maghrib and the Central Sudan', in R. Oliver (ed.), *The Cambridge History of Africa* (8 vols, Cambridge, 1977), vol. 3, pp. 232–330.

[7] Fisher, *The Eastern Maghrib and the Central Sudan*, p. 296.

[8] *Ajwiba li-asʾilat al-amīr Askiya Al-Ḥājj Muḥammad* [Answers to the questions of Amir Askiya Al-Ḥājj Muhammad]. See John O. Hunwick, *Timbuktu and the Songhay Empire: Al-Saʿdī's Taʾrīkh al-Sūdān down to 1613, and Other Contemporary Documents* (Leiden, 1999), p. 102.

[9] John Hunwick's 'Al-Maghīlī's Replies to the Questions of Askia Al-Hajj Muhammad, Edited and Translated with an Introduction on the History of Islam in the Niger Bend to 1500' (Unpublished PhD dissertation, University of London, 1974), p. 389n provides a succinct summary of their relationship of mutual benefit: 'It was important for Al-Maghīlī to establish that Sunni ʿAlī and his aides were unbelievers, since it legitimised Askia Muḥammad's seizure of power from [Sonni Ali, as well as] his son and successor Sunni Abū Bakr Dāʿū. On this, in turn, hinged the propriety of Al-Maghīlī's association with the Askia'.

[10] Baba's father, as well as his son, also wrote commentaries on al-Maghīlī's works. Historians date the effective end of the Songhay Empire to the Moroccan conquest of 1591.

al-mu'minīn should rule justly and according to Islamic law; he should appoint judges and other state officials, as well as representatives to govern the provinces; he should maintain and promote the Islamic faith by the construction of mosques and other public works; and he should lead a yearly expedition against the unbelievers to defend his territories and extend the frontiers of Islam.[11] However, in practice the machinery of government and the terminologies of political office were defined by the Sahelian political context. Local terms of authority such as *Mai* in Bornu, *Sarki* in Hausaland and *Elimān* in Bundu and the Futas complemented *Amīr al-mu'minīn.*[12]

Having explained the foundations of the Sahelian knowledge tradition, it is important to demonstrate clearly the link between *fiqh* (understood in this tradition as consisting of commentaries, abridgements and versifications of Maliki legal works) and legitimacy. Internalising the Sahelian core curriculum of some one hundred works through rigorous study constituted the foundations of 'knowing' and, as such, the authority to make judgements based on this knowledge. It is no surprise that the majority of Arabic texts written during this period consist of extended quotations from this core curriculum of authors, the Fodiawa's writings being no exception. In this tradition, to be called a *muqallid* (that is, a scholar whose compositions simply compile the views of other scholars) was an honour, not a slur, especially since the inverse – *mujtahid* – carried multiple risky connotations. This was not because imitation was prized over originality. On the contrary, quotations functioned to legitimate one's own thoughts and ideas by melding them to established legal minds. Of course, thoughts and ideas were, in turn, influenced by training in the core curriculum. Yet, as we shall see, the writings of the Sahelian elite were replete with personal and political projects hiding behind quoted text.

A further point to consider is that *fiqh* knowledge and the legitimacy that came with it did not simply exist in the texts themselves. Like other learning traditions, it was not *what* one learned that mattered, so much as *who* one

[11] See Usman, *Bayān wujūb al-hijra* in Fathi H. El-Masri, *Bayān wujūb al-hijra 'alā al-'ibād* (Khartoum, 1978); Abdullahi, *Ḍiyā' al-umarā'* in Hamidu Alkali, *Diya Al-'Umara: A Guide for Rulers Concerning Their Demands and Obligations* (Sokoto, 2004), Chapter 1; Bello, *al-Ghayth al-wabl* in Omar Bello, 'The Political Thought of Muhammad Bello (1781–1837) as Revealed in his Arabic Writings, more especially al-Ghayth al-Wabl fī Sīrat al-Imām al-'Adl' (Unpublished PhD dissertation, University of London, 1983).

[12] See Paul E. Lovejoy, *Jihād in West Africa During the Age of Revolutions* (Athens, Ohio, 2016), pp. 37–8, who provides a useful chart comparing the political titles of Muslim leaders during the West African jihad period.

learned it with. Teachers did not only pass on their understanding of the work, but also a licence to teach it – the *ijāza* – that connected the student to the author of the original text through a list of former teachers. Some *ijāzāt* were more prestigious than others, and teachers often specialised in teaching a single work. For example, Abdullahi dan Fodio remarks that one of his teachers was 'famous as the sun in our country' for his teaching of Khalīl ibn Iṣhāq's *Mukhtaṣar*, a versified primer on Maliki law.[13] It was expected that scholars produce bibliographies of the texts that they had studied, a vital part of which was the teacher they had studied each text with. Scholars learned most of the basic texts of the core curriculum within their own families.[14] However, the *ijāza* system fuelled peripatetic learning. Promising students travelled great distances to seek out knowledge, again using family connections. Thus, aside from the intellectual skills necessary to engage with the texts themselves, access to *fiqh* knowledge was further restricted by pedagogical processes that ensured it stayed within a narrow elite.

Kashf

In nineteenth-century West Africa, as in other parts of the Islamic world, Muslims believed that God had hidden secrets within each of His creations. Islamic thought represents this division by speaking of the *zahir* [manifest] and *batin* [hidden] worlds.[15] A certain awareness of the *batin* could be achieved through exercises of the mind and heart. However, unlike *fiqh*, knowledge of the *batin* world did not depend wholly upon human reason and logic. It also required faith.[16] God, as a wilful being, decided when

[13] Abdullahi, *Īdā' al-nusūkh man akhadhtu 'anhu min al-shuyūkh* in Mervyn Hiskett, 'Material Relating to the State of Learning among the Fulani before their Jihād', *Bulletin of the School of Oriental and African Studies,* 19:03 (1957), 550–78, at p. 567.

[14] Abdullahi and Bello studied around half of the texts they learned during their early education at the feet of direct family members. See Abdullahi, *Īdā' al-nusūkh* in *ibid.* and Bello, *Ḥāshiya 'alā muqaddimat Īdā' al-nusūkh.* The section of the text detailing Bello's learning does not appear in Delafosse's part-translation into French (Maurice Delafosse, 'Traditions Musulmanes relatives à l'origine des peuls', *Revue du monde musulman,* 19 (1912), 242–67.

[15] See Louis Brenner, *Réflexions sur le Savoir Islamique en Afrique de l'ouest* (Talence, 1985).

[16] A notion expressed most clearly in Ibn Khaldūn's *Muqaddima.* See Franz Rosenthal (ed.), *The Muqaddimah: An Introduction to History* (3 vols, New York, 1958), vol. 1, pp. 184–246.

to grant such knowledge to humankind and when to withhold it. *Batin* knowledge was not the structured 'knowing' achieved through study, but a mystical and spontaneous 'unveiling' known as *kashf*.[17]

Consensus around *kashf* arose from a complicated series of debates about the nature of God in the mid-Abbasid period between two theological schools. The Muʿtazalites argued that God was a supremely logical being, and thus had put in place consistent rules to manage His world which humans could access through rational enquiry. The Ashʿarīs argued that this reasoning effectively placed limits on God's actions and was thus heretical, a view that became dominant throughout the Muslim world.[18] *ʿIlm al-batin* – the science of understanding the hidden – thus became a key component of Islamic knowledge systems.[19] In the Sahel, as Charles Stewart has it, 'mysticism was accepted among leading Saharan scholars as a logical complement to any advanced studies in jurisprudence', while the aforementioned core curriculum was intended to cultivate both 'effective judicial administration and mystical insight'.[20] Like *fiqh*, *kashf* knowledge also had structures of production and control that offered legitimation in several distinct spheres of the nineteenth-century Sahelian discursive world: from Mahdist thought to Sufism, to the study of *ʿilm al-ghayb*, each of which I will discuss.

As demonstrated above, the Sahelian concept of *fiqh* arose from centuries of legal scholarship and pedagogical training. However, Ashʿarī thought regards time as a retrogressive force, anticipating that man's ability to interpret the Divine Will irreversibly declines the further in time from the perfect Islamic governance of the Rashidun age.[21] Early Muslim

[17] For another discussion of *kashf* see Rüdiger Seesemann, *The Divine Flood: Ibrahim Niasse and the Roots of a Twentieth-Century Sufi Revival* (Oxford, 2011), p. 19.

[18] This classical repudiation of the Muʿtazalites can be found in the theological works of all three Fodiawa.

[19] This development can be traced to the writings of the eleventh-century theologian al-Ghazālī who presented the *zahir* and the *batin* as equally important components of Islam. Al-Ghazālī sought to prevent a schism between dogmatic legal scholars and mystical orders who dispensed with the outward meaning of the Qur'an all together in pursuit of spiritual truth.

[20] Charles C. Stewart, 'Southern Saharan Scholarship and the Bilad Al-Sudan', *The Journal of African History,* 17:1 (1976), 73–93, at pp. 87; 89.

[21] For more on Ashʿarī theology in relation to West African statecraft see Mohamed S. Mathee, 'A Seventeenth-Century Songhay Chronicler Learning (and Teaching) to be Muslim through Historiography: The Case of the Tarikh al-Sudan', delivered at Cadbury Conference 2016: Bodies of Text: Learning to Be Muslim in West Africa, Birmingham, UK, 30 June – 1 July 2016.

scholars gradually reinterpreted the caliphal title of *al-Mahdī* [guider; redeemer] to refer to an expected figure whose appearance would return the Umma to an age of perfect Muslim governance, pre-ordaining the end of the world.[22] This interpretation probably drew on a hadith stating that the true caliphate would emerge again after a period of tyranny.[23]

Later scholars elaborated upon the Mahdi's characteristics further, stating that he would be a *mujtahid muṭlaq*, meaning that he could interpret Divine Will directly from the Qur'an with no reference to any previous legal interpretations. This had profound implications for *fiqh* knowledge, based as it was upon the work of generations of scholars. In the Muslim world, Mahdist movements had long been the established means of directing popular discontent towards the professed holders of authority and bringing about radical societal change. But Mahdism was of course a double-edged sword. While temporarily effective in garnering massive popular support, barring the actual appearance of the Mahdi such movements had no long-term adhesive qualities. As more radical groups splintered from the original movement, they became highly destructive.

In another hadith, which al-Maghīlī had relayed in his answers to *Askiya* Muhammad, Prophet Muhammad announced that a *mujaddid* [renewer] was fated to appear at the start of every Islamic century to reform society and remove the corruption built up over the previous years.[24] The identities of the *mujaddids* were a topic of debate. Al-Suyūṭī hoped that he would be the *mujaddid* of the ninth century, while the Kunta – taking the view that there could be several renewers, each of them specialised in different fields – named *Askiya* Muhammad and al-Maghīlī, along with al-Suyūṭī

[22] See Wilfred Madelung, 'Al-Mahdī', in P. Bearman, Th. Bianquis, C. Bosworth, E. van Donzel and W. Heinrichs (eds), *Encyclopaedia of Islam* (Leiden, 2012).

[23] *Musnad Aḥmad ibn Ḥanbal*, Hadith no. 18406: 'Prophethood will remain with you for as long as God wills, and God will put an end to it whenever He wills. Then Caliphate in the way of Prophethood, and it will remain with you for as long as God wills, and God will put an end to it whenever He wills. Then rapacious kingship, and it will remain with you for as long as God wills, and God will put an end to it whenever He wills. Then tyrannical kingship, and it will remain with you for as long as God wills, and God will put an end to it whenever He wills. Then Caliphate in the way of Prophethood [My emphasis]'. The Fodiawa quoted this hadith in their works.

[24] Hunwick, *Al-Maghīlī's Replies*, p. 290, which he correctly identifies as a hadith rather than – as Batran, *A Contribution* has it – being of al-Maghīlī's own invention. See *Sunan Abū Dāwūd*, Hadith no. 4291: 'At the head of every hundred years God sends to this Umma one who renews its religion'.

and Muḥammad ibn Yūsuf al-Sanūsī (famous for his didactic 'creeds') as the *mujaddids* of the tenth century.[25] As opposed to the destructive tendencies of Mahdism, speculation about the *mujaddid* figure on the part of the scholarly elite served instead to facilitate the ordering of West African discursive space, reinforcing the prominent place that this tradition gave to certain historical figures.

However, Mahdist expectations and speculation over the identity of the *mujaddids* converged around the hadith that twelve caliphs would rule after Muhammad.[26] Jalāl al-Dīn al-Suyūṭi's interpretation, that the first ten *mujaddids* were historical caliphs, that the twelfth caliph would be the awaited Mahdi and that the eleventh was yet to come, was well known in the Sahel, as was his relation of earlier prophecies that the Mahdi would appear in the year AH 1200 or 1204 (AD 1785–1786 or 1789–1790).[27] Some Sahelian scholars therefore equated the *mujaddid* heralded to appear at the start of the twelfth Islamic century (equating to AD 1785–6) with the twelfth and final caliph, in turn conflated with the Mahdi.

It is therefore very probable that the late eighteenth to early nineteenth century was a time of widespread millenarianism in the Sahel, corresponding to the time that Usman dan Fodio first began his preaching tours of the Hausa countryside. *Kashf* knowledge in this context, that is, both the ability to know the identity of the mahdi-caliph, the date of his appearance, and a demonstrated connection to him, carried a latent legitimising force. Further, Mahdism appealed directly to the popular and non-literate imagination in a way that *fiqh* tradition could not. As such, written sources from the period – and historical scholarship – may vastly underestimate the extent to which beliefs around the Mahdi contributed to legitimacy in the nineteenth-century Sahel.

Sufism [Ar. *taṣawwuf*] also offered the possibility of *kashf* – more commonly known within the tradition as *maʿrifa* – through the belief that certain people could draw closer to God, obtain divine knowledge and pass baraka to others. This individual – the *walīy* – or his followers, established a tariqa that provided a set of ritualised practices to achieve *kashf*. This could involve *dhikr* [sessions of recitation and intercession], *wird*, communal and solitary retreats, visitations to the

25 Hunwick, *Al-Maghīlī's Replies*, pp. 380–1.

26 'This religion will remain until twelve Caliphs have been with you'. The hadith, in various iterations, is recorded as sound in *Saḥīḥ al-Bukhārī*, *Ṣaḥīḥ Muslim* and *Musnad Aḥmad ibn Ḥanbal*.

27 Jalāl al-dīn al-Suyūṭī, *al-ʿArf al-wardī fī akhbār al-Mahdī*; *al-Kashf ʿan mujāwazat hadhihi al-Umma al-alf*.

tomb of the *walīy*, as well as *silsilas* that, similar to the function of the *ijāza*, passed on the spiritual genealogy of the order to novices.[28] A *silsila* related the chain of *muqaddams* [local leaders of a tariqa] from the *walīy* himself to the *muqaddam* who initiated the holder of the *silsila*, and therefore differed from region to region. The tariqa structure allowed for the spreading of *kashf* to others, but also ensured that it was 'routinised' within the leadership of a tariqa, resulting in regional, political and commercial orderings.[29]

In the early nineteenth-century Sahel, the control and supply of *kashf* was not connected exclusively with any one tariqa. The Khalwatiyya and Sanusiyya were active in the region, as well as the Tijaniyya later in the century. However, it was the Qadiriyya that took precedence. Sahelian discursive tradition credits al-Maghīlī with the introduction of the Qadiriyya south of the Sahara, meaning that *fiqh,* Sufi practice and movements of religious reform were – or could be – explicitly linked.[30] The Qadiriyya in the Sahel revolved around the Kunta, a family of Sanhaja scholars from the Azawad region. This was because al-Maghīlī had allegedly passed the *wird* of the Qadiriyya to the ancestor of the Kunta, Sīdī ʿUmar al-Shaykh, in the sixteenth century, when both men were living in Touat.[31] This ensured that spiritual knowledge – like *fiqh* – remained within a select elite, and that the Kunta family were the supreme holders of *kashf* in the region.

Demonstrating membership of this 'Qadiriyya Mukhtariyya' was an important legitimising device. However, the nature of *kashf* also allowed for 'jumps' in this spiritual chain of *muqaddams*. Adherents of a tariqa

[28] See R. G. Jenkins, 'The Evolution of Religious Brotherhoods in North and Northwest Africa', in J. R. Willis (ed.), *Studies in West African Islamic History* (London, 1979), pp. 40–77, at p. 58.

[29] See Gellner, *Saints of the Atlas*, p. 12; Knut S. Vikør, 'Sufi Brotherhoods in Africa', in N. Levtzion and R. L. Pouwels (eds), *The History of Islam in Africa* (Athens, Ohio, 2000), pp. 441–76.

[30] Brenner, *Réflexions*, p. 12.

[31] Al-Mukhtār ibn Aḥmad al-Kuntī, *al-Ṭarāʾif wa'l-talāʾid*. Al-Mukhtār (1729–1811) headed the Kunta family during this period. See Marcus-Sells, *Realm of the Unseen*, p. 62; Abd al-Aziz A. Batran, 'The Kunta, Sīdī Al-Mukhtār Al-Kuntī, and the Office of Shaykh Al-Ṭarīq Al-Qādiriyya', in J. R. Willis (ed.), *Studies in West African Islamic History* (London, 1979), pp. 113–46, at p. 120. A separate tradition from Kano is reported in Priscilla E. Starratt, 'Oral History in Muslim Africa: Al-Maghili Legends in Kano' (Unpublished PhD dissertation, University of Michigan, 1993), pp. 91–2, who states that al-Maghīlī passed the *wird* to one Malam Bawa while the former was staying with *Sarkin Kano* Muhammadu Rumfa.

cultivated a spiritual state in which visions and dreams of the order's founder, as well as Prophet Muhammad himself, were anticipated and even expected. However, miraculous happenings could threaten local spiritual-political hierarchies if they presented a more direct path to *kashf* than through the existing *silsila* held by the *muqaddam*. Seekers who had experienced visions and were able to amass a following could and did found their own orders, subverting elite groups. However, various other factors dictated whether such visions were accepted as *kashf* or rejected as spurious.

Kashf knowledge can also be found in a branch of Islamic sciences known as *ʿilm al-ghayb* [knowledge of the hidden]. A significant proportion of archived Arabic manuscript material from West Africa fits into this genre.[32] Although the genre itself is described in vague terms both by practitioners and in scholarly literature, the most commonly encountered text in this genre – the *fāʾida* – is extremely formulaic.[33] *Fāʾidas* consist of instructions for the preparation of Qur'anic text to achieve a specific personal benefit. The instructions may call for the verses to be copied down on a writing slate, and the ink washed off and consumed or applied to parts of the body.[34] Other recipes call for the verse to be written out on paper or an object and then buried, or worn on certain parts of the body for protection. Instructions also demand the performance of certain physical actions such as the genuflections of prayer, oral repetition of prayer formulas, the preparation of tree barks and other pharmacological substances, or the slaughtering of animals of a certain colour. Thus, like other forms of

32 The British Library's Endangered Archives Project no. 488: Major project to digitise and preserve the manuscripts of Djenné, Mali, found that 'more than 50% [...] dealt with "esoteric" subjects'. See https://eap.bl.uk/project/EAP488 [accessed 11 August 2020]. Charles Stewart, 'What's in the Manuscripts of Timbuktu? A Survey of the Contents of 31 Private Libraries', *History in Africa*, 48 (forthcoming), estimates that *fāʾidas* and associated texts could make up to at least one quarter of the manuscripts in Timbuktu's SAVAMA collections. Nehemia Levtzion found that 'over ninety per cent' of the Royal Danish Library's collection of Arabic manuscripts from Kumasi, Ghana, 'may be described as magical formulas, or prescriptions for preparing amulets'. See Nehemia Levtzion, 'Early Nineteenth Century Arabic Manuscripts from Kumasi', *Transactions of the Historical Society of Ghana,* 8 (1965), 99–119, at p. 100.

33 So-called since each text starts with the Arabic word فائدة [of benefit; a useful thing].

34 Last, 'The Book in the Sokoto Caliphate', p. 151, refers to this substance as *rubutu.*

Muslim knowledge, the *fā'ida* also depends on the Qur'an, albeit decontextualised through 'linguistic, graphic and numerical processes'.[35]

Al-Mukhtār ibn Aḥmad al-Kuntī described such practices as 'breakings-of-the norm' – evidence of God's unknowable nature. Whereas others decried it as *bidʿa*, the sheer volume of surviving manuscript material suggests that the use of *ʿilm al-ghayb* was extremely widespread.[36] Like Mahdism, *ʿilm al-ghayb* had a strong popular appeal, and even more so given the universal belief in the supernatural among both Muslim and non-Muslim populations in the Sahel. Connection to supernatural forces, whether the ability to create esoteric devices, converse with spirits or otherwise affect the normal order, could therefore be a powerful legitimising element in the Sahel that cut across religious and cultural divides.

Nasab

As we recall from the preceding chapter, scholars have recognised that one aspect of legitimacy in the nineteenth-century Sahel concerned affiliation with an ethnocultural group, or to a particular genealogy or historical personage that conferred status. However, we are confounded here by the modern concepts of these terms. The nineteenth-century Sahel was certainly a multi-ethnic, multi-cultural society. But within the Sahelian Muslim elites of the nineteenth century, identity was in many cases synonymous with and indistinguishable from political, economic or religious networks. In turn, genealogy, like the other areas of knowledge we have explored, was inseparable from religious identity, and from the political and intellectual projects of the scholar.

The concept of *nasab*, which I translate as 'noble origin', emerged from the tribal society of the pre-Islamic period. Genealogical records passed down through the generations maintained the collective memory of the *qabīla.* After Muhammad had united the Arabian Peninsula under Islam, affiliation with the Quraysh (the *qabīla* of Muhammad) became one of the

[35] Constant Hamès, 'Problématiques de la magie-sorcellerie en islam et perspectives africaines', *Cahiers d'études africaines,* 189–190 (2008), 81–99, at p. 89.

[36] Marcus-Sells, *Realm of the Unseen,* pp. 9–10. This uncertain attitude is mirrored in Abdullahi (*Ḍiyāʾ al-siyāsāt*), who suggests that *fā'idas* were acceptable only if written in Arabic and only if the buyer understood the content. For a wider discussion of *ʿilm al-ghayb* in West Africa, see Hamès, *Problématiques.*

conditions for caliphal office.[37] Versions of the hadith of the twelve caliphs state that all twelve will come from the Quraysh, and most scholars agreed that the Mahdi must be of Qurayshi descent. Descendants of Prophet Muhammad – known as *sayyids* or sharifs – traced their genealogies from the children of Muhammad's daughter, Fatima, and Ali and commanded universal respect in the Muslim world.

Biographies of Muhammad and the early Muslim histories mention a huge number of individuals by name. This can be explained in part by the social prestige and – under the policy of the Rashidun Caliphs – financial rewards that came from tracing family involvement in the early Muslim community. This tradition of genealogical recordkeeping spread to the lands of the early Muslim conquests, where an Arabic *nisba* – indicating *qabīla* affiliation, place of origin or ancestry – quickly became a marker of social and political status.[38]

Arabic origin as a status marker in the Sahel again goes back to political developments of the fifteenth and sixteenth centuries. In this period, there was an increased migration of *ineslemen* groups from the north across the Sahara. The influence of North Africans such as al-Maghīlī upon West African rulers increased the cultural and social dominance of Arab and Berber groups. To justify their new-found prominence, these groups reimagined their pasts to connect themselves to known individuals who had first brought Islam across the Sahara from North Africa such as ʿUqba ibn Nāfiʿ, an army general under Caliph Umar who led the Muslim conquest of the Maghreb.[39] Over time, as Bruce Hall explains, claims to Arab heritage became a benchmark for social stratification.[40]

[37] See Hugh Kennedy, *The Prophet and the Age of the Caliphate* (New York & London, 1986), p. 50.

[38] Albrecht Noth, *The Early Arabic Historical Tradition: A Source-Critical Study* (Princeton, 1994), pp. 109–72. The *nisba* or 'attribution' occurs at the end of an Arabic name and is usually adjectivised and preceded by the Arabic definite article '*al-*'.

[39] For more on the ʿUqba myth, see Mauro Nobili (2012) 'Back to Saharan Myths: Preliminary Notes on 'Uqba al-Mustajab', *Annual Review of Islam in Africa*, 11 (2012), 79–84; Paul Naylor, 'Abdullahi Dan Fodio and Muhammad Bello's Debate over the Torobbe-Fulani: Case Study for a New Methodology for Arabic Primary Source Material from West Africa', *Islamic Africa,* 9:1 (2018), 34–54.

[40] Hall, *History of Race*, pp. 33; 40–1. See also Harry T. Norris, *The Arab Conquest of the Western Sahara: Studies of the Historical Events, Religious Beliefs and Social Customs which Made the Remotest Sahara a Part of the Arab World* (London, 1986); Abdel Wedoud Ould Cheikh, 'Nomadisme,

In the Sahel, like in other parts of the Muslim world, sharifian descent carried immense social prestige. Association and endorsements from such figures undoubtedly lent legitimacy to political movements. Abdullahi describes Nūḥ ibn al-Ṭāhir, the emissary of the Kunta who initiated Usman into the Qadiriyya Mukhtariyya, as a sharif.[41] Shortly after the start of the jihad the Fodiawa report receiving blessings from sharifs arriving from the north.[42] On the other hand, sharifs often made demands on the legitimised party such as lodging and financial help.[43] Sharifian tradition also limited the scope of Muslim authority that could be acquired in the Sahel. Both the Saadian and Alaouite dynasties of Morocco claimed sharifian descent and as a result addressed themselves as caliphs.[44] But until the nineteenth century, Muslim rulers south of the Sahara did not do the same. This was because, following *fiqh* tradition, caliphs must come from the Quraysh.[45]

---

islam et pouvoir politique dans la société maure précoloniale (XIème siècle–XIXème siècle): essai sur quelques aspects du tribalisme' (Unpublished PhD dissertation, Université Paris V, René Descartes, 1985).

[41] Abdullahi, *Tazyīn al-waraqāt bi-jamʿ baʿḍ mā lī min al-abyāt* in Mervyn Hiskett, *Tazyīn al-Waraqāt* (Ibadan, 1963), p. 104.

[42] For Sharif ʿAbd Allāh Ḥanuna Gīwa see Abdullahi, *Kashf al-liʾm la-nā wa-li-man tabiʿnā fī amr al-sharīf ʿAbd Allāh Ḥanuna Gīwa*; Bello, *Miftāḥ al-baṣāʾir*. Hunwick (*ALA 2*, pp. 111; 145) notes that Waziri Junaidu dismissed these documents as forgeries. For Sharif Qamr al-Dīn, see Bello *[Majmūʿ baʿḍ al-rasāʾil]*, NU/Hunwick 162, pp. 37–9.

[43] Bello *[Majmūʿ baʿḍ al-rasāʾil]*, instructed that Qamr al-Dīn be accommodated in Sokoto and given cowries and a guide for his onward journey. See also Richard Lander, *Records of Captain Clapperton's Last Expedition to Africa with the Subsequent Adventures of the Author* (2 vols, Cambridge, 1830), vol. 1, p. 276, who mentions the 'swarms of sheriffs, or emirs, the real or fictitious descendants of Mohammed and Ali' demanding money from the courts of Sokoto and Gwandu. Clapperton (Denham and Clapperton, *Narrative of Travels and Discoveries*, p. 91) had earlier remarked: 'both Bello and his father have, it seems, been much cheated by the Arabs [in all] their dealings, twenty sometimes coming at a time on a begging excursion, with the story of being poor shreefs; and, if not presented with thirty or forty slaves, besides food and camels, they were sure to bully the Felatahs, telling them they were not Mussulmans, and would never see paradise, on account of the number of the faithful they had put to death in the conquest of Soudan'.

[44] Hunwick, *Timbuktu and the Songhay Empire*, p. 297. In two extracts of a letter from Mūlāy Aḥmad al-Mansūr (r. 1578–1603), al-Manṣūr talks of the 'complete obedience that God has imposed towards this Prophetic caliphate'.

[45] Contrary to Last's assertions (Last, *Sokoto Caliphate*, p. 46 n.) the term 'Sokoto Caliphate' was not used by the Fodiawa before the 1820s and neither

Sahelian Muslim elites not only refashioned their genealogies to conceivably involve them in the story of Islam. They also recontextualised the wider societies in which they lived using the lexicon of Islamic historical tradition. As Murray Last describes it, 'history – in this case, the history of the ancient Middle East – provided the blueprint for the relationships between groups defined in religious terms'.[46] Among Sahelian Muslim elites, merit was accorded to theories about the physical world by its harmony not with local, observable criteria but with wider Muslim discursive tradition, a phenomenon Paulo Farias refers to as 'cognitive dissonance'.[47] This also applied to theories of race. Scholars such as the Fodiawa described the region in which they lived as *Bilād al-Sūdān*. In so doing, they drew upon a tradition of geographical knowledge of the Sahel that pivoted around the question of where captive labour could be legally acquired, and with it – in the words of Bruce Hall – a 'complex set of ideas bound up with blackness'.[48]

---

was the term *khalīfa* [Caliph] the standard term by which Usman or Bello were referred to or referred to themselves. Bello refers to Usman as Caliph on a single occasion in *Infāq al-maysūr*, Chapter 5, as well as once in his debates with Ahmad Lobbo, discussed in Chapter 3 of this book. There are only two other instances of the term before the 1820s other than in reference to the Rightly Guided. The first is by Abdullahi in *Ḍiyā' ūlī-l-amr* (1810), where he says (Paris (BnF) Arabe 5364, f. 2b) 'The Imam should ... be a *khalīfa* of the Messenger of God for the Muslims, and their emir'. Here he is clearly using the term in its original meaning of 'deputy': for this see Patricia Crone and Martin Hinds, *God's Caliph: Religious Authority in the First Centuries of Islam* (Cambridge, 1986). The second is in the title of Bello's work of 1817, *al-Inṣāf fī dhikr mā-fī masā'il al-khilāfa min wifāq wa-khilāf*, or '*Fair Judgement of conflicting views on questions concerning the Caliphate*'. Here, the term *khilāfa* is arguably used only as a play on words with *khilāf* (difference). The term does not occur again at any point in the text.

[46] Murray Last, 'History as Religion: De-constructing the Magians "Maguzawa" of Nigerian Hausaland', in J.-P. Chrétien (ed.), *L'invention religieuse en Afrique: Histoire et religion en Afrique noire* (Paris, 1993), pp. 267–96, at p. 268. As Last explains, *Maguzawa* derives from *mājūs*, a Qur'anic term meaning Zoroastrians, perhaps for the pragmatic reason that Zoroastrians were 'people of the book' and thus trade with them was permitted.

[47] Paulo F. de Moraes Farias, 'Local Landscapes and Constructions of World Space: Medieval Inscriptions, Cognitive Dissonance, and the Course of the Niger', *Afriques: Débats, méthodes et terrains d'histoire*, 2 (2010), 1–21.

[48] Hall, *History of Race*, p. 104; John O. Hunwick and Fatima Harrak, *Mi'rāj al-Su'ūd: Ahmad Baba's Replies on Slavery* (Rabat, 2000).

But at the same time, genealogies, origin stories and readings of historical events were remarkably fluid. Nowhere is this clearer than in the case of the *Torobbe*, a term by which many leaders of the nineteenth-century reform movements – the Fodiawa included – referred to themselves. Variously rendered TorobBe, Torodbe, Turudi, Torodobbe or Toronkawa, and in Arabic *al-Turūdī*, the simplest meaning of Torobbe (singular Torodo) suggests 'those from [Futa] Toro', from which the Fodiawa maintained their ancestors had migrated.[49] However, scholars talk of a distinct Torobbe 'clerisy', caste or *métier* that coalesced in Senegal in the 1650s following the movement of Nāṣir al-Dīn, a scholar from Mauritania who led a failed uprising against the European slave trade. According to John Ralph Willis, a distinct group calling itself Torobbe 'evolved out of that mass of rootless peoples who perceived in Islam a source of cultural identity' as the adherents of Nāṣir al-Dīn's movement migrated eastwards across the Sahel.[50] Meanwhile, Moustapha Kane and David Robinson state that the Torobbe earned their name from their reputation for begging, from the Fulfulde verb *toraade* [to beg for alms].[51] On the other hand, traditions from Futa Toro say that the Torobbe were originally manumitted slaves, or a Bambara group who became clients of the Fulani before slowly adapting their language and customs.[52] Other theories of origin reference a 'Toro' idol that certain Fulani worshipped, or a reference to Mount Sinai – in Arabic, *Jabal Ṭūr* – from which the Torobbe supposedly migrated.[53] In short, scholars have long searched in vain for the 'correct' origin theory of the Torobbe and other West African groups. However, it is more likely the case that different origin stories emerged at different times depending on their required function.

[49] Willis, 'Torodbe Clerisy', at p. 195; Abdullahi, *Aṣl al-fulātiyyīn*; *Īdā' al-nusūkh*.
[50] *Ibid.*, p. 201.
[51] Moustapha Kane and David Robinson, *The Islamic Regime of Fuuta Tooro: An Anthology of Oral Tradition* (East Lansing, 1984), p. 5. Alternatively, Willis, 'Torodbe Clerisy', p. 200 suggests that the meaning is '"to implore Allah", or "to ask Allah for a favour"'.
[52] For manumitted slaves see Michael A. Gomez, *Pragmatism in the Age of Jihad: The Precolonial State of Bundu* (Cambridge, 1992), p. 36, quoting Rançon, *Le Bondou: Etude de geographie et d'histoire soudaniennes de 1681 a nos jours (Bordeaux, 1894)*; Willis, 'Torodbe Clerisy', p. 196, quoting Gaden, *Proverbs et maximes peuls et Toucouleurs (Paris, 1931)*. For Bambara origins, see Muhammad Bello, *Ḥāshiya 'alā muqaddimat Īdā' al-nusūkh,* f. 299a, quoting al-Ḥasan al-Bilbālī.
[53] For the 'Toro' idol see Willis, 'Torodbe Clerisy', p. 198n, quoting Mūsā Kamara. For Mount Sinai, see Abdullahi, *Aṣl al-fulātiyyīn*.

Similarly, problems presented by classical Islamic genealogical traditions could be navigated by simply rewriting or reinterpreting the past. In some accounts of the *Askiya* dynasty, Al-Ḥājj Muhammad was made a representative (*khalīfa*) of the *Bilād al-Sūdān* by the Abbasid Caliph in Cairo.[54] A prophecy in the apocryphal *Ta'rīkh al-fattāsh*, written by Ahmad Lobbo's supporter, Nūḥ ibn al-Ṭāhir, stated that Lobbo was the rightful successor of the *Askiya* and thus could also claim a caliphate in the *Bilād al-Sūdān*.[55] Thus, Sahelian Muslim elites constantly reshaped their origin stories, and with it their relation to the Arab world, to suit the changing exigencies of what made best sense in the present.[56]

Conclusion

The leaders of the jihad period drew upon a common discursive tradition of legitimacy making that had been present in the Sahel region for several centuries. Elite actors identified a prominent historical role for themselves in the Islamisation of the *Bilād al-Sūdān* using a select group of stock characters, such as the 'Uqba figure. They demonstrated thorough knowledge of a select body of Maliki legal texts, learned through a standardised pedagogical chain, and adhered to the Qadiriyya Mukhtariyya, a specific branch of the Qadiriyya connected to the Kunta family. Spiritual, pedagogical and ancestral genealogies affirmed and reinforced one another, as key personalities such as al-Maghīlī formed the lynchpin of both pedagogical and Qadiri pedigree.

But such a narrowly defined path to legitimacy did not restrict those who walked it to a similarly narrow set of actions. Rather, as the history of the Sahel region tells us, discursive tradition was a tool kit through which

[54] Muḥammad al-Ifrānī (1669–1745), account of the Saadian conquest of Songhay in Hunwick, *Timbuktu and the Songhay Empire*, p. 310, quoting Imam al-Takrūri, *Naṣiḥat Ahl al-Sudan*.

[55] See Nobili and Mathee, 'Towards a New Study of the So-Called *Tārīkh Al-Fattāsh*'.

[56] For example, Starratt, *Al-Maghili Legends in Kano*, p. 58, suggests that the Kano elite justified their position by discovering Islamic origins for the social practices and traditional institutions over which they presided. In turn, reformist scholars could delegitimise these elites by presenting evidence that these same practices had pagan origins. For an equivalent phenomenon in East Africa, see the discussion of *dini* (orthodox religion) and *mila* (local tradition) in Roman Loimeier and R. Seesemann (eds), *The Global Worlds of the Swahili: Interfaces of Islam, Identity and Space in 19th- and 20th-Century East Africa* (Berlin, 2006), pp. 7–13.

Muslim actors could legitimise a wide range of actions. The remainder of this book details how the Fodiawa used this tool kit over a period of roughly thirty years during which they rose from rebels to rulers. Drawing on the Sahelian discursive tradition gave the Fodiawa the flexibility to maintain their legitimacy in the face of radical policy changes, but also allowed for others to challenge and question it.

CHAPTER 2

Discourses of Dissent and Moderation

This chapter is both a narrative and an explanation of how the Fodiawa moved from discourses of dissent to discourses of moderation in their writings during the period c.1790 to 1814. During both phases they used familiar legitimising strategies from the Sahelian discursive tradition. Recognising this discursive shift allows us to explain both the meteoric success of the 1804 jihad and the emergence of a stable and legitimate Sokoto state. The chapter begins in the 1790s, the period of Usman dan Fodio's earliest surviving works. It then introduces the more militant writings Usman produced in the years directly preceding the jihad of 1804. The remainder of the chapter explains how after their victory the Fodiawa radically amended their judgements on a number of issues to facilitate their rule of Hausaland. The concluding part of this chapter demonstrates that the shift from dissent to moderation was also observed by Muslim scholars at the time, including Usman's brother, Abdullahi, and had serious repercussions for the legitimacy of Usman and Muhammad Bello.

Laying Claims to Legitimacy: Usman's Writings in the 1790s

Throughout the 1780s and 1790s, Usman dan Fodio travelled the Hausa countryside accompanied by his younger brother, Abdullahi.[1] Usman's voluminous work, *Iḥyāʾ al-Sunna wa-ikhmād al-bidʿa* [Revival of the Sunna and the destruction of innovation], composed in 1793, may represent a summary of what he preached on these tours, as well as a teaching guide for others.[2] During this time, the young Abdullahi became an accomplished Arabist, translating Usman's Fulfulde poetry into Arabic

[1] See Fathi H. El-Masri, 'The Life of Shehu Usuman Dan Fodio before the Jihād', *Journal of the Historical Society of Nigeria*, 2:4 (1963), 435–48. Last, *Sokoto Caliphate*, p. 6, states that Usman was about 20 years old when he began these tours, making Abdullahi around eight.

[2] See Ismail A. Balogun, 'A Critical Edition of the Iḥyāʾ al-Sunna wa-Ikhmād

and composing his own *qaṣāʾid* [epic poems]. From Muhammad Bello's highly detailed account of his father's lectures, it is clear that Usman's main purpose was to teach rural Muslim communities the basics of Islamic practice, while also exposing the *bidʿa* that these communities may have unknowingly incorporated into their religious life.[3] Separately, Usman was also writing a set of works that would establish the grounds for *takfir* which pre-empted, in various ways, the jihad against the Hausa *sarakai*, of which *takfir* was a vital component.[4]

As Last and Al-Hajj explain, Usman's exploration of *takfir* reflected concern among 'a number of scholars, largely Fulani and Tuareg, who were not involved in the Gobir administration', over who or what was and was not Muslim.[5] As such, opinion on these topical matters would have been an effective way to establish scholarly credentials. Although the precise identities of these scholars are unclear, one of them was certainly Jibril ibn ʿUmar, Usman and Abdullahi's teacher in Agadez. Jibril may have been the first to introduce Usman to al-Maghīlī's *Ajwiba*, which undoubtedly influenced Usman's ideas about *takfir* in a significant way. His works on this subject bear no date but overlap with much of the contents of *Iḥyāʾ al-Sunna*.[6] Thus, Usman seemed to have developed his judgements on *takfir* several years before the jihad.

---

al-Bidʿa of ʿUthmān b. Fūdī, popularly known as Usumanu Ḍan Fodio' (Unpublished PhD dissertation, University of London, 1967).

[3] Bello, *Infāq al-maysūr* in Bahīja Shādhilī (ed.), *Infāq al-maysūr fī taʾrīkh bilād al-Takrūr* (Rabat, 1996), Chapters 13–19. Muhammad Bello, born in 1781, likely did not travel with his father and uncle, and did not begin producing his own compositions until the turn of the century. His observations must therefore date to a later period, or else were not firsthand.

[4] These are *Naṣāʾiḥ al-umma al-Muḥammadiyya li-bayān al-firāq al-shayṭāniyya allatī ẓaharat fī bilādinā al-sūdāniyya* 'Pieces of advice to the Umma of Muhammad, making them aware of the satanic parties who have appeared in our Bilād al-sūdān' and *Ifhām al-munkirīn ʿalayya fī-mā āmur al-nās bihi wa-fī-mā anhāhum ʿanhu fī dīn Allāh* 'Informing those who disavow me regarding what people are ordered to do and prevented from doing in God's religion'.

[5] See Murray Last and Muhammad A. Al-Hajj, 'Attempts at Defining a Muslim in 19th Century Hausaland and Bornu', *Journal of the Historical Society of Nigeria,* 3:2 (1965), 231–40, at p. 232.

[6] Mervyn Hiskett, 'An Islamic Tradition of Reform in the Western Sudan from the Sixteenth to the Eighteenth Century', *Bulletin of the School of Oriental and African Studies,* 25:1 (1962), 577–96, at p. 578.

Both texts are premised on the idea that Hausaland was prey to several 'satanic parties' whose conditions for defining belief in Islam and their use of *takfir* were erroneous and damaging the religious fabric holding communities together. The first 'satanic group' were 'those who deny that there are those born unbelievers in our *Bilād al-Sūdān'*, or otherwise did not declare *takfir* upon 'those mixing Islam with the words and actions of the pagans'.[7] Usman argued that this position was itself a justification for *takfir*:

> the consensus of the Muslims holds that those who venerate rocks and trees with sacrifices, even if they claim to practice Islam, are infidels [...] and there is also a consensus that those who do not anathematise them are anathematised[8]

The second group were scholars who, conversely, declared *takfir* on good Muslims on account of differences in positions on minor points of *fiqh*, or their level of religious knowledge. Usman describes these people as *mutakallimūn* [theologians] or more commonly as *Ṭullāb* [students], a term which he had also used in *Iḥyā' al-Sunna*. As Usman explained, the *Ṭullāb* were:

> the ones who do not believe the faithful and do not judge that anyone has faith except after learning their beliefs ... which they have found in their books in theology, namely that whoever believes this thing and that is an unbeliever, and whoever is ignorant of such and such a thing is an unbeliever[9]

Usman also declares *takfir* upon this group, following the logic that calling good Muslims infidels was in effect calling Islam unbelief.[10]

[7] Usman, *Naṣā'iḥ al-umma al-Muḥammadiyya li-bayān al-firāq al-shayṭāniyya allatī ẓaharat fī bilādinā al-sūdāniyya*, Niamey (MARA) 264, Chapter 1. The Arabic term for 'born unbeliever' is *kāfir aṣlī.*

[8] Usman, *Ifhām al-munkirīn 'alayya fī-mā āmur al-nās bihi wa-fī-mā anhāhum 'anhu fī dīn Allāh*, Niamey (MARA) 229, page 9 (labelled as 3–11). Reminiscent of Qur'an 5:44 'Whoso judgeth not by that which Allah hath revealed: such are disbelievers' quoted by al-Maghīlī (Hunwick, *Al-Maghīlī's Replies*, p. 284).

[9] Usman, *Naṣā'iḥ al-umma*, Chapter 2.

[10] According to Muhammad Bello (Shādhilī, *Infāq al-maysūr*, Chapter 11) Usman wrote over fifty works against the *mutakallimūn*, the majority of them before the jihad. They include *Mi'rāj al-'awām ilā samā' 'ilm al-kalām*

The third group were scholars anathematising Muslims who had sinned.[11] Usman identifies this group with his former teacher, Jibril ibn ʿUmar, and questioned how Jibril could claim consensus 'on [a subject] which no scholars of the Sunna have accepted'.[12] He maintained the standard position that *shirk* [polytheism] is the only sin that demands *takfir*, but only when it has been committed knowingly.[13] Significantly, he did not anathematise this group as he did the previous ones, perhaps because of his close personal connection with Jibril.[14]

The fourth and final 'satanic party' were 'those ones who follow the blameworthy practices of their fathers', that is to say, innovations in ritual washing, the performance of prayers, the recitation of the Qur'an,[15] laws relating to inheritance or other aspects of Islamic ritual and legal norms.[16]

(1784–5); *Kifāyat al-muhtadīn; Ḥiṣn al-afhām* and *Mirʾāt al-ṭullāb* (all presumed written 1774–1804).

[11] The Arabic term is *maʿāṣī,* literally 'disobediences' with the meaning of major sins such as neglecting prayers, not paying zakat, gambling, drinking alcohol, etc. Usman identifies these groups with the *khawārij* [kharijites]. The original kharijites were a faction of the supporters of ʿAlī ibn Abī Ṭālib who turned against him after he sought arbitration with Muʿāwiya at the Battle of Siffin, and who later fled from the Hijaz. There is evidence that the Ibadis, whose origins can be traced back to the kharajite movement, played an important role in the early history of Islam in Africa. See Elizabeth Savage, 'Berbers and Blacks: Ibāḍī Slave Traffic in Eighth-Century North Africa', *The Journal of African History,* 33:3 (1992), 351–68. Hiskett, *An Islamic Tradition of Reform*, p. 596 convincingly argues that by Usman's time, kharajite probably meant simply 'schismatic' or 'innovator'.

[12] Usman, *Naṣāʾiḥ al-umma,* Chapter 3.

[13] Usman *Ifhām al-munkirīn,* page 8 (3–12) citing Qur'an 4:48: 'Lo! Allah forgiveth not that a partner should be ascribed unto Him. He forgiveth (all) save that to whom He will'. Usman added that anyone committing polytheism unknowingly was a *fāsiq* (immoral person), and that *takfir* cannot be declared for *fisq* alone. See for comparison al-Maghīlī, *Ajwiba* in Hunwick, *Al-Maghīlī's Replies*, p. 303–4.

[14] Usman also composed a second text explaining in more detail the difference between their respective positions on *takfir* and excusing Jibril for his inconsistencies and errors. The text is entitled *Shifāʾ al-ghalīl fī-mā ashkala min kalām shaykh shuyūkhinā Jibrīl* [Quenching the thirst concerning what is dubious from the words of the Shaykh of our Shaykhs Jibrīl].

[15] See *Ifhām al-munkirīn*, where Usman refers to a *tajwīd* [Qur'anic recitation] school using certain elisions to ease pronunciation.

[16] Usman also makes extensive lists of these practices in works such as *Kitāb al-farq* and *Nūr al-albāb.*

Usman ruled that, like committing major sins, these innovations did not constitute *kufr* if done without the knowledge that they are wrong. Bello later specified that this group consisted of ignorant jurists who passed fatwas based on 'bizarre and unusual' authorities and taken from books 'of the most loathsome nature', as well as those who pretended to have hidden knowledge and claimed to be Sufis.[17]

Usman's writings on *takfir* give us a window into the religious landscape of Muslim Hausaland before the jihad, or at least the conception that Usman had of that landscape. Aside from Jibril ibn 'Umar, Usman did not mention the precise identities of these groups. However, we can make certain speculations. The first group, who either did not accept that there were unbelievers in the Hausa region or chose not to declare *takfir* upon them could refer to scholars such as Muhammad al-Amīn al-Kānamī, who did not attribute unbelief to the traditional practices of the *Mai* of Bornu but rather defined it as *'urf* [local custom].[18] Equally, Usman may have had in mind scholars at the Hausa royal courts who did not recognise the rituals of the Hausa *sarakai* as unbelief. The second group – the *Ṭullāb* – is no doubt a reference to Usman's rivals in Hausaland who were also attempting to gather a following during this period. After all, Usman addressed *Ifhām al-munkirūn* to those who challenged him in his judgements on *takfir* and other matters. Abdullahi also wrote several satirical poems directed at local scholars who had criticised his elder brother, for example for allowing both men and women to listen to his preaching in the same space.[19] Usman would go on to use the same term to describe his later critics, including Abdullahi himself. As for the fourth group, those who followed the blameworthy practices of their fathers, in many other works Usman attributes these practices to the 'ignorant' among the Hausa.[20] Presumably, Usman had in mind the Hausa *mallam* class not attached to the royal court, as well as the *mallamai* in the communities he visited.

These speculations aside, the most important point here is not what these texts can tell us about the religious landscape of Hausaland but their implications for Usman's religious authority within it. Usman took care to place

[17] Bello, *Infāq al-maysūr fī ta'rīkh bilād al-Takrūr,* in Muhammad Shareef, 'Easy Expenditure' (2008) http://siiasi.org/digital-archive/sultan-muhammad-bello/infaql-maysuur [accessed 9 September 2020], Chapter 12, p. 2.

[18] See the exchange of letters between Bello and al-Kānamī in Shādhilī, *Infāq al-maysūr,* pp. 229–86.

[19] Usman, *Ifhām al-munkirīn,* pp. 6–10 (3-14 to 3-10); Hiskett, *Tazyīn al-Waraqāt,* pp. 86–7.

[20] See Usman, *Ḥukm juhhāl bilād al-Ḥawsa.*

himself in the middle ground between several extremes of thought, declaring his rivals to *fiqh* knowledge either apostates from Islam or immoral sinners. These judgements not only circulated among his growing community of followers but spread in the wider Sahel region, where Usman was making a name for himself as an expert on these matters.[21] His judgements served as a precedent that would later allow the Fodiawa to declare jihad upon the Hausa *sarakai* on the basis of *takfīr*, and for this judgement to be accepted or at least understood by other scholars in the region.

Leaving *takfir* and the *fiqh* tradition aside, other writings produced by Usman during this period drew on legitimising forces from a different element of the Sahelian discursive tradition. In one of his earliest works, *Tabshīr al-umma* [Bringing good news to the umma] dated 11 August 1794, Usman recounts the merits of the founder of the Qadiriyya, ʿAbd al-Qādir al-Jīlānī, but does not include a Qadiri *wird* or a *silsila* that would indicate his initiation into the Qadiri order. Three years later, in August or September of 1797, the Fodiawa were visited by Nūḥ ibn al-Ṭāhir, an emissary of the Kunta sent to Hausaland after reports of the growing strength of the *jamāʿa* [community] gathered around Usman. There is no record of what Ibn al-Ṭāhir and the Fodiawa discussed, but immediately after this visit, Usman commanded his followers to arm themselves for rebellion, and composed a poem announcing his initiation into the Qadiriyya, along with the *wird* of ʿAbd al-Qādir.[22] The poem, which he composed some five years before the start of the jihad, clearly pre-empts the conflict:

> Through the rank of one who is called ʿAbd al-Qādir
> Show me as a conqueror by your religion in these countries[23]

[21] See *Ajwiba muḥarrara*, Usman's response to questions put to him by one Shīṣumaṣ ibn Aḥmad, a Tuareg Shaykh who sought Usman's guidance on whether certain events in his community required the declaration of *takfir*. For example, Shīṣumaṣ mentioned a local man who complained that paying zakat caused the death of his cattle, as well as some people found practising the *Bori* possession ritual. Usman judges that both cases necessitated *takfir*. The work is undated.

[22] Hiskett, *Tazyīn al-Waraqāt*, pp. 104–7. Note parallels with Sharif ʿAbd Allāh Ḥannuna Gīwa. According to *Kashf al-liʿm*, a text purportedly authored by Abdullahi, this sharif arrived in Hausaland from a far-off land 'in answer to Usman's prayer'. He encouraged the *jamāʿa* and rendered them spiritual assistance through passing on his *silsila* connecting him to Prophet Muhammad. The text is dated *Shawwāl* AH 1220 (December 1805 – January 1806).

[23] *Ibid.*, p. 105.

Usman goes on to invoke the spiritual power of ʿAbd al-Qādir, and invites the saint to work through him as his intermediary on earth. By accepting the *wird* of the Qadiriyya through the Kunta, the Fodiawa established themselves within the principal politico-spiritual hierarchy of the wider Sahel region: the Qadiriyya Mukhtariyya.

A Discourse of Dissent (c.1804–1810)

According to Muhammad Bello, full-scale fighting between the jihadists and the Hausa *sarakai* first broke out on 21 June 1804, after Usman and his followers declared a 'hijra' from Gobir territory in February of that year.[24] But by the time the hostilities commenced, Usman had already produced a body of writings that legitimised such a conflict.[25] Building upon his earlier work on *takfir*, these texts focused narrowly on the elements of *fiqh* knowledge that would be relevant in the case of a jihad of the sword. Even though Usman did not mention the Hausa *sarakai* by name, the intent was clearly to provoke a popular, armed rebellion against the Hausa *sarakai*.[26] In short, a discourse of dissent.

Moving to the texts themselves, they affirmed – as Usman had already outlined in his previous works – that anyone committing an act that was opposed to the basic tenets of Islam, or who mixed Islam with pagan beliefs, was an unbeliever.[27] However, Usman made the vital (and, as we shall see, problematic) judgement that if a ruler engaged in non-Islamic practices, his territory would become *Dār al-Kufr* [a land of unbelief] irrespective of the religion of his subjects. Thus, Muslims who found themselves living in the lands of this ruler must emigrate to the *Dār al-Islām* and swear allegiance to a new and Muslim leader, the *Amīr al-muʾminīn*.[28] Obedience

[24] Last, *Sokoto Caliphate*, p. 27, using Bello's *Infāq al-maysūr*.

[25] Usman's work, *Masāʾil muhimma yaḥtāju ilā maʿrifatihā Ahl al-Sūdān* [Important matters that the Ahl al-Sūdān need to know], is the earliest of these writings and is dated 8 March 1803. *Wathīqa ilā jamīʿ Ahl al-Sūdān*, considered by Bivar to be the 'manifesto' of the jihad, could also date from this period. See H. Bivar, 'The Wathīqat Ahl Al-Sūdān: A Manifesto of the Fulani Jihād', *The Journal of African History,* 2:2 (1961), 235–43. Other works from the pre-jihad period such as *Iḥyāʾ al-Sunna*, *Ḥukm juhhāl bilād al-Ḥawsa* and *Tamyīz al-muslimīn min al-kāfirīn* also anticipate the conflict.

[26] Al-Hajj, 'Mahdist Tradition', p. 71.

[27] Usman, *Tamyīz al-muslimīn.*

[28] Usman, *Wathīqa ilā jamīʿ Ahl al-Sūdān* in Bivar, 'A Manifesto of the Fulani Jihād', p. 240.

to this leader was obligatory. Usman judged that any Muslims who did not emigrate to the *Dār al-Islām*, or who continued to maintain *muwālāt* [friendly relations] with the non-believers were non-believers also, and must be fought alongside them.[29] Usman went on to say that enslaving the children and wives of these erstwhile Muslims and appropriating their possessions was 'legal by consensus' of the scholars.[30]

None of these judgements were new to Islamic jurisprudence, nor at any point did Usman explicitly link them to the political context of Hausaland in the nineteenth century. Indeed, their authority derived from their repeated use throughout Islamic history, including – through al-Maghīlī – in the Sahel region.[31] However, these texts undoubtedly established the legal basis for declaring jihad and the terms of engagement in battle, as well as laws on emigration from non-Muslim lands, friendship with non-Muslims, the enslavement of non-believers during a jihad, and the appropriation of their property.

In parallel to the legal argument for jihad, Usman (or his followers) also spread a very different text suggesting that the mandate for jihad came from the highest echelons of the Qadiriyya spiritual hierarchy. As outlined above, Abdullahi recorded that Usman's initiation into the Qadiriyya occurred in 1797, the date he received the *wird* and *silsila* of the Qadiriyya Mukhtariyya from the Kunta. However, the document purportedly written by Usman recounts his initiation into the Qadiriyya via a different route, and at a time predating this period:[32]

> When I reached 36 years of age [c.1790], God removed the cover from my sight, the blockage from my ears and my nose, the film from my tastebuds, the seal from my hand, the stiffness from my legs and the heaviness from my belly. I could see the close as if it were the far and hear what was far

[29] Reiterated in *al-Amr bi-muwālāt al-mu'minīn wa-l-nahā 'an muwālāt al-kāfirīn* [Commanding friendship with the faithful and denying friendship with the infidels], dated 17 April 1805.

[30] Usman, *Masā'il muhimma*, Paris (BnF) Arabe 5678, f. 155a.

[31] Today, militant Islamic groups in the region deploy similar argumentation. See the speech of Muhammad Yusuf, the founder of Boko Haram, in Kassim, 'Defining and Understanding', p. 189: 'Working with the government that does not rule by the Sharı'ah is a lie; it is *Kufr*. Working with the security agencies is a lie; it is *Kufr*. For those who are ignorant, let them be aware that it is important for a Muslim to make hijrah from the institutions established by the *ṭawāghīt* [tyrants; despots]'.

[32] The document is known as *Lamma balaghtu* [Ar. When I reached…] because of its opening line, 'When I reached the age of thirty-six'.

> away as if it were close by. I could smell the sweetness of the slave of God and the foul stench of the sinner. I could taste the halal from the haram before swallowing. I could pick up with my hand what was far away while sitting down. I could walk on foot the distance a stallion could not cover in years. All this was by the grace of God who gives to whom He wills. I knew my body part by part, bone by bone, sinew by sinew and hair by hair, each in its proper place. On five of my ribs on my right side I found the words 'Praise be to God Lord of the Worlds' ten times, 'God pray for our master Muhammad and the family of our master Muhammad' ten times, and 'I seek forgiveness from God Almighty' ten times, all written with the divine pen. I was much surprised at that.[33]

As discussed in the previous chapter, to claim any experience of *kashf* was to assert an authority independent of regional politico-spiritual hierarchies.[34] But the text goes on to recount another vision that Usman received when he was forty years old, corresponding to the year 1794, and again before the Kunta's envoy had supposedly arrived in Hausaland. In this second vision, ʿAbd al-Qādir himself initiates Usman into the Qadiriyya, presenting Usman with a green robe and cap and pressing them to his chest, passing the garments between the Rashidun Caliphs Abu Bakr, Umar, Uthman and Ali as well as Prophet Yusuf, who is also present, before returning them to ʿAbd al-Qādir. ʿAbd al-Qādir then ceremoniously dresses Usman in the robe and cap and, as Usman states:

> declared me Imam of the Saints[35] and ordered me to hold the good and forbade me from the despicable actions. He girded me with the sword of truth[36] and bade me draw it against the enemies of God.[37]

ʿAbd al-Qādir goes on to instruct Usman in the *wird* of the Qadiriyya and granted him permission to spread this *wird* among his followers.

Before any analysis of this document, it is important to stress that within a rich Sufi tradition of *munājāt* [works recounting visions of God, Prophet Muhammad and the saints], Usman's account is highly formulaic. It also resembles actual initiation ceremonies of orders such as the

33 Usman, *Lamma balaghtu* (Zaria, Gaskiya Corp., n.d.), pp. 1–2.

34 Usman even refers to this term in the above citation when he says: 'God removed the cover from my sight' (Ar. *kashafa Allāh al-ghiṭāʾ ʿan baṣarī*). My emphasis.

35 Ar. امام الأولياء *imām al-awliyāʾ*.

36 Ar. سيف الحق *sayf al-haqq*.

37 Usman, *Lamma balaghtu*, p. 4.

Khalwatiyya, which Usman had joined through his teacher, Jibril ibn ʿUmar.[38] However, within the Sahelian discursive tradition, this inititation had significant implications. A vision of ʿAbd al-Qādir confirmed for Usman's followers that his spiritual authority had 'jumped the chain', bypassing the conventional hierarchy of the Qadiriyya Mukhtariyya and as such, reinforcing the legitimacy of his break with the established spiritual-political order in Hausaland.

That said, the text itself could simply be a forgery.[39] More fanatical elements of Usman's supporters could have fabricated the text after the jihad, attempting to re-energise the movement after Usman himself had denied receiving *kashf*. Alternatively, the text could have emerged during the *karāmāt* literature period of the 1820s and 1830s, in which hagiographies of Usman and Bello grew more extreme in their claims as Sokoto's hegemony over spiritual power declined. But while the precise dates of the visions do not match the chronology as we know it, other details make it likely that this text or a similar account was circulating in the Hausa region around the time of the jihad of 1804.[40]

After Usman's move to Sifawa around 1809 we know that people travelled great distances to receive the Qadiri *wird* from him; easily explained if, from what we understand in *Lamma balaghtu*, the *wird* came directly from ʿAbd al-Qādir.[41] Meanwhile, the 'sword of truth' motif – separating the good from the bad – could equally apply to Usman's earlier judgements on *takfir* and his call for a holy war against the Hausa *sarakai*. During his lifetime Usman's supporters addressed him as *walīy*, a clear indication that

[38] Moumouni, *Vie et œuvre du Cheikh Uthmân Dan Fodio (1754–1817): De l'islam au soufisme*, p. 106.

[39] The work has no formal title nor a standard introduction, and the conclusion speaks of Usman in the third person. This, as well as the discrepancy in dates discussed below, have led to questions over its authenticity (Last, 'The Book in the Sokoto Caliphate', p. 150). Unlike other works of questionable authenticity the text exists in a standardised form today and I noted no major discrepancies between the Zaria market edition (NU/Hunwick 122) and manuscript copies at NU/Hunwick 203 and two at Kaduna (NA), digitised as BL (EAP) 535 1/2/4/20; 535 1/2/25/3.

[40] Time references in *Lamma balaghtu* should not in any case be taken literally. Prophet Muhammad became aware of his prophethood in his fortieth year, and for this reason forty years is the traditional age at which important Muslim figures recognise their divine calling.

[41] Murray Last, 'Innovation in the Sokoto Caliphate', in H. Bobboyi and A. M. Yakubu (eds), *The Sokoto Caliphate: History and Legacies, 1804–2004* (2 vols, Kaduna, 2006), vol. 2, pp. 328–47, at p. 328.

they believed he had been granted *kashf* through ʿAbd al-Qādir. [42] Thus, whether or not this text is authentic, the idea that Usman had 'jumped the chain' and received *kashf* before the jihad certainly contributed to the discourse of dissent, in parallel to the more familiar literature making the legal case for jihad.

But we are also missing another important detail that helps to explain the enthusiasm for jihad. On 3 October 1808, the Gobir capital of Alkalawa fell to the jihadists, confirming the triumph of Usman's movement and the formation of the Sokoto state.[43] Less than a week after this momentous occasion, Usman finished the first of his works discussing the precise date for the end of the world.[44] With the jihadists still in the heat of battle, he composed three further works on the subject.[45] The timing of these compositions – and the care Usman took to chart his evolving views on the subject – strongly suggests that millenarianism also played an important role behind events of this period. In the texts themselves, Usman made repeated references to the works of ʿAbd al-Wahhāb al-Shaʿrānī, an Egyptian Sufi who spread the possibility that the Mahdi was already living on earth, citing a tradition from twelver Shi'ism.[46] Usman also quoted – and clearly believed – the prophecy that the Mahdi would arrive in the year AH 1200 or 1204.[47]

Alongside reports of Usman's personal connection to ʿAbd al-Qādir, the spread of al-Shaʿrānī's hidden Mahdi theory, as well as the millenarian expectations that Usman promoted in his writings, helps to explain the

[42] See Usman, *Taḥdhīr al-ikhwān* in Al-Hajj, 'Mahdist Tradition'. Usman was replying to a Tuareg leader who addressed him as *al-Walīy al-ʿārif bi-Allāh* 'the saint who has acquired the knowledge of God'. The text dates to 1814.

[43] Last, *Sokoto Caliphate*, p. 39.

[44] *Tanbīh al-fāhim ʿalā ḥukm muddat al-dunyā wa-khalq al-ʿālam* [Informing the learned of the verdict concerning the length of the world and the creation of the earth].

[45] *Tanbīh al-umma ʿalā qurb hujūm ashrāṭ al-sāʿa* [Informing the Umma about the imminent onset of the signs of the hour]; *Muddat al-dunyā* [The length of the world]; *Amr al-sāʿa wa-ashrāṭihā* [On the hour and its signs]. This last work is dated 23 July 1809. In it, Usman refers to the first two works, meaning that they must have been composed previously.

[46] ʿAbd al-Wahhāb al-Shaʿrānī (1492/3–1565) *al-Yawākīt wa-al-jawāhir*. According to Twelver Shias, the Mahdi is the son of eleventh Shia Imam, Al-Ḥasan ibn ʿAlī ibn Muḥammad (known as al-Ḥasan al-ʿAskarī). This 'hidden' twelfth Imam is waiting somewhere on earth to emerge on judgement day.

[47] Usman, *Amr al-sāʿa wa-ashrāṭihā*. See also his retraction in *Naṣīḥat ahl al-zamān*, discussed below.

appeal of the jihad on a popular level. Bello himself urged a gathering of Hausa rulers to accept Usman as *Amīr al-mu'minīn* precisely because he believed that Usman's rule would be followed by the Mahdi.[48] It also perhaps elucidates the answer that Richard Lander, a member of Hugh Clapperton's expedition, received from his Hausa travelling companions when he asked them to explain the success of the jihad, which had taken place some fifteen years previously:

> The Houssans have often declared to me that [during the jihad] the strength and inclination to 'shake the spear!' were denied them; they had no will of their own, – their hands fell powerless by their sides, and they felt as if they had been touched by the finger of a god, or were under the influence of an eastern talisman.[49]

Finally, during the jihad years, another discourse emerged that connected the Fodiawa's professed identity as Torobbe-Fulani with their legitimacy to rule. As Usman started to amass a following, Abdullahi composed a poem appealing directly to the Torobbe to join the *jamā'a*.[50] Although the poem mentioned nothing about the Torobbe's genealogy, it was an appeal for group solidarity, nonetheless. Similarly, when Usman discussed enslavement policy in his pre-jihad works he specifically emphasised caution when receiving Fulani captives, referring to the earlier judgement of Ahmad Baba that most of the Fulani clans were good Muslims and that enslaving them was against Islamic law.[51] Further, some of Usman's complaints against the Hausa *sarakai* seemed to be targeted at a Fulani audience, such as criticising the *jangali*, or cattle tax, which must have disproportionately affected pastoralist groups.[52]

[48] Last, *Sokoto Caliphate*, p. 36. The passage in Shādhilī, *Infāq al-maysūr*, p. 205 reads: 'I informed them [the Hausa rulers] of the glad tidings he [Usman] had brought them; of the approach of the Mahdi's appearance and that the *jamā'a* of the Shaykh are his harbingers'.
Ar. أخبرتهم بما بشرهم به من <قرب> المهدي وأن جماعة الشيخ طلائعه

[49] Lander, *Records of Captain Clapperton's Last Expedition to Africa with the Subsequent Adventures of the Author*, vol. 2, p. 29.

[50] Abdullahi, *Risālat al-naṣā'iḥ*, included in Hiskett, *Tazyīn al-Waraqāt*, pp. 98–101.

[51] Usman, *Masā'il muhimma,* Chapter 10, in MX Niamey (MARA) 280.

[52] See Mervyn Hiskett, '*Kitāb Al-Farq*: A Work on the Habe Kingdoms Attributed to 'Uthmān dan Fodio', *Bulletin of the School of Oriental and African Studies,* 23:03 (1960), 558–79, at p. 567.

By the outbreak of fighting in 1804, some Fulani clans were already militarised. With the exception of *Bā Arewa* leader Abd al-Salam and Aghali, a Tuareg, most of Usman's key supporters were Fulani.[53] All the flag-bearers whom Usman had appointed to extend the jihad to other regions were Fulani clan leaders.[54] Aside from Ya'qūb of Bauchi, all the emirs appointed by the Fodiawa to rule the territories gained in the jihad were Fulani. Ahmad Lobbo, at that time a flag-bearer for the jihad in Masina, was Fulani while Muhammad Bello, and probably Usman and Abdullahi too, were in communication with Fulani clan leaders from Futa Toro such as al-Ḥasan al-Bilbālī.[55]

To conclude, the discourse of dissent I have been describing, employed in the years prior to and during the jihad that began in 1804 and reached its end around 1810 had several components. First, a set of legal arguments allowed Usman to declare *takfir* on the Hausa *sarakai* and those who supported them; second, an alternative narrative of the Fodiawa's initiation into the Qadiriyya that bypassed current Sahelian hierarchies; third, claims that Usman was directly connected to the Mahdi figure and the end of days; and finally, an appeal to the Fulani clans of Hausaland based on group solidarity. While this discourse of dissent allowed the Fodiawa to overturn the established order, it also resulted in several negative consequences. Usman's rulings on *takfir*, specifically that the property of non-believers and Muslims who remained without allegiance could be taken legally,

[53] See Last, *Sokoto Caliphate*, pp. 16–22, who discusses the composition of the early *jamā'a* in some detail. According to Last, while the leadership of the movement was overwhelmingly Fulani, this was the case for only one third of the wider jihadist community gathered around Usman at Degel. The meaning of *Bā Arewa* will be discussed below.

[54] For a list of Fulani clans who joined the jihad and their areas of operations see Lovejoy, *Jihād in West Africa*, pp. 75–6. For a list of flag-bearers, see Last, *Sokoto Caliphate*, pp. 53–4.

[55] Bello mentions al-Ḥasan al-Bilbālī, a Tijani from Futa Toro, in several works. In *Ḥāshiya 'alā muqaddimat Īdā' al-nusūkh* he quotes al-Bilbālī as the source for his revised theory on Torobbe-Fulani origin. Bello makes a further reference to this person in *al-Qawl al-mukhtaṣar fī amr al-Imām al-Mahdī al-muntaẓar* [Short discourse concerning the expected Mahdi], stating that al-Bilbālī linked the Sokoto jihad to the imminent appearance of the Mahdi. See Minna, 'Intellectual Contribution', p. 331; Sabo Abdullahi Albasu, 'A Glimpse at Muhammad Bello's Views on the Mahdi and Mahdist Expectation', delivered at Seminar on Amirul-Mumin Muhammad Bello organised by Centre for Islamic Studies, University of Sokoto, Sokoto, Nigeria, 15–18 April 1985, p. 15.

swelled the ranks of the *jamā'a* with opportunistic raiders. This resulted in mass looting, killing and the taking of captives with apparently little regard to Usman's original rulings on the subject. Abdullahi described his own troops as 'sellers of free men on the market' and was almost killed when he tried to take back war spoils to divide them according to the Sharia.[56] Bello faced the same situation on his campaigns. Having also confiscated spoils he believed had been distributed incorrectly, his troops refused to resume fighting until he had given them back. Resigned, Bello is reported to have said: 'If I could find another people, I would wage jihad with them against you!'[57] Meanwhile, in an undated letter written by Usman and Abdullahi, they apologise to a Hausa Muslim leader for their messenger, who instead of inviting them to join the jihad had branded them unbelievers and subjected them to physical attack.[58]

Further, some Fulani clan leaders had evidently interpreted the Fodiawa's appeal to group solidarity as an invitation to overthrow their non-Fulani – but Muslim – overlords. By 1810, the jihad extended into the territories of the Kanem-Bornu Empire, an ancient Muslim power. Muhammad al-Amīn al-Kānamī, a noted Muslim scholar allied with the *Mai* of Bornu, wrote to Bello that the Fulani in his region believed that it was legal to attack any Muslims who had committed sin, and that they had learned this information from the works of Usman. Al-Kānamī used this situation to call into question the Fodiawa's authority as Muslim jurists. But as we have seen, *takfir* on the basis of sin was contrary to Usman's rulings. This, and Bello's surprised reaction to al-Kānamī's report, suggests that the Fodiawa's rulings either did not reach or were simply ignored by leaders of localised rebellions being fought in their name.[59]

In short, the Fodiawa seemed to have lost control of the discourse of dissent. The spark that was so vital to creating the jihadist movement had turned into a conflagration that the Fodiawa now needed to control. Louis Brenner suggests that al-Kānamī's challenge forced the Fodiawa to

[56] Hiskett, *Tazyīn al-Waraqāt*, p. 122.

[57] Al-Ḥājj Sa'īd, *Taqāyīd mimmā waṣala ilaynā*, Paris (BnF) Arabe 5422, f. 2a.

[58] *[Letter to a Hausa leader]*, Niamey (MARA) 3996.

[59] Louis Brenner, 'Religion and Politics in Bornu: The Case of Muhammad Al-Amin Al-Kanemi', in J. R. Willis (ed.), *Studies in West African Islamic History* (London, 1979), pp. 160–76; 'The Jihad Debate between Sokoto and Borno: An Historical Analysis of Islamic Political Discourse in Nigeria', in J. F. Ade Ajayi and J. D. Y. Peel (eds), *People and Empires in African History: Essays in Memory of Michael Crowder* (New York & London, 1992), pp. 21–43.

qualify and revise the legal means by which they had justified the jihad.[60] But this is only one part of the picture. The belief that Usman possessed supernatural powers evidently created a dangerous fanaticism among his supporters, as did his suggestion that the end of the world was at hand (so much so that Usman was later forced to retract these beliefs).[61] In less than a decade the Fodiawa had risen from dissenting Muslim rebels pushing radical social change to Muslim rulers seeking to buttress their control over a large population. Just as the Fodiawa had militated for a jihad of the sword using a well-established discourse of dissent, their victory and the desire to consolidate power required a shift to an alternative tradition of moderation, employed throughout Islamic history to explain and justify historical change.

A Discourse of Moderation (1810–c.1812)

In the years after 1810, Usman, Abdullahi and Muhammad Bello wrote histories of the jihad and its background.[62] This was because the challenge of al-Kānamī and others forced them to revisit and explain the reasons behind the conflict and to justify and excuse the violence that had taken place on its account. But a broader problem was that the ideals of the jihad needed to be moderated to reflect the compromises necessary to govern the conquered territories effectively. This entailed revisiting some of the harsh judgements that had helped to galvanise support for Usman's movement. In fact, when

[60] *Jihad Debate between Sokoto and Borno.* Last and Al-Hajj, 'Attempts at Defining a Muslim', p. 240, argue it is more a case of genre. While Usman's earlier writings were intended as educational works to 'instruct people without perplexing them', the responsibilities attached to their victory led to the Fodiawa to explore the complexity of legal rulings when 'more precise knowledge was necessary'.

[61] Usman, *Tanbīh al-umma* in Muhammad Shareef, 'The Signs of the End of Time' (1998) http://siiasi.org/wp-content/uploads/2014/12/Tanbeeh.pdf [accessed 9 September 2020], p. 36: 'I have seen these times and I have not yet seen the appearance of the al-Mahdi. For this reason I have [now] judged these traditions to be false'.

[62] Usman's *Tanbīh al-ikhwān* [Admonition to the brothers], dated 11 November 1811, combined sections of what would become Bello's famous *Infāq al-maysūr* and Abdullahi's *Tazyīn al-waraqāt* to produce a single narrative explaining the reasons for the jihad. Completed sections of Bello's *Infāq al-maysūr* (1812) and Abdullahi's *Tazyīn al-waraqāt* (1813) must therefore have existed in 1811. Usman dedicated a second work to this subject, *Taʿlīm al-ikhwān* [Instruction to the brothers], dated 7 December 1813.

we compare these writings with those discussed in the previous section, we find some striking differences. I argue that these differences amount to a wholly new discursive mode which I am calling a discourse of moderation. Here, we will examine these differences in detail.

As we recall, the legality of the jihad depended upon the *takfir* of the Hausa *sarakai* and the judgement that Hausaland consequently was *Dār al-Kufr*. But in fact, the issue was far more complex. The problem was that two contradictory statements on this question were known to the Fodiawa, and presumably to other scholars in the region. Ahmad Baba's famous fatwa dating to 1614 mentioned 'lands whose people have been established to be Muslims, such as Bornu, ʿAfnū, Kano, Gao and Katsina', which in effect meant that he considered the whole of Hausaland and Bornu lay within the *Dār al-Islām*.[63] However, Baba's statement was in contradiction to the Kunta, who ruled much later, in the early 1790s, that the majority of the inhabitants of the *Bilād al-Sūdān* and all of their rulers were non-Muslims.[64]

Because of their pedigree, these judgements carried significant authority in the Sahelian *fiqh* tradition. Usman's writings on this subject are, in effect, a lengthy attempt to make these two judgements mutually compatible. In *Bayān wujūb al-hijra* [Declaring the obligation of emigration], written in 1806, Usman tried to justify his declaration of *takfir* upon the rulers of Hausaland and Bornu by combining the two judgements together: 'These, too, are lands of unbelief without any doubt, since the spread of Islam there is [only] among the masses but as for their sultans, they are unbelievers [...] even though they profess Islam'.[65] However, in November of 1811 (and

[63] Ahmad Baba, *al-Kashf wa-l-bayān* (also known as *Miʿrāj al-suʿūd*) in Hunwick and Harrak, *Miʿrāj al-Suʿūd: Ahmad Baba's Replies on Slavery*, p. 22. Ahmad Baba was in fact repeating the question of Saʿīd ibn Ibrāhīm al-Jirārī, for whom he wrote the fatwa. He replied that indeed the people of these lands were Muslim except for ʿAfnū, which he had not heard of. This term is also absent from the Fodiawa's references to Ahmad Baba's statement.

[64] Al-Mukhtār ibn Aḥmad al-Kuntī, *al-Jurʿa al-ṣāfiya wa-l-nafḥa al-kāfiya* in El-Masri, *Bayān wujūb al-hijra ʿalā al-ʿibād*, p. 51: 'the Sudan is a land where unbelief prevails among the majority of its people and all the Muslims there are under the domination of the unbelievers whom they have recognised as rulers'. John O. Hunwick, Ousmane Kane and Bernard Salvaing, *Arabic Literature of Africa Volume 4: The Writings of Western Sudanic Africa* (Boston, 2003), pp. 76–7, date the text to 1792–3.

[65] El-Masri, *Bayān wujūb al-hijra ʿalā al-ʿibād*, p. 50.

perhaps under the scrutiny of al-Kānamī) Usman was forced to clarify that he had reached this conclusion based on his own observations:

> Every learned man judges according to the knowledge of his age. Conditions change with the times and the cure changes with the disease. It is well known that in our time Islam has become widespread in the land of Hausa among other than kings. [But] the kings are unbelievers and nothing else.[66]

A statement he repeated, two years later, with reference to the inhabitants of Bornu: 'As far as our own times are concerned, the people in question are no longer what they used to be [i.e. no longer Muslim].'[67] These statements demonstrate that the argument for jihad, framed within what appeared to be a watertight legal argument derived from Sahelian *fiqh* tradition, in fact came from conjecture. After the jihad, Usman overturned his ruling on Hausaland based on the reality that the Hausa *sarakai* were no longer in charge: 'The above description was applicable to the condition of the Hausa peoples as we found them, before the Jihad [...] We have [now] appointed Muslim Governors over this land and it has become a land of Islam without doubt.'[68] While Usman's change in judgement may seem reasonable enough, it also had a secondary implication. If Hausaland had become part of the *Dār al-Islām*, rebellion against its new, Muslim rulers would be tantamount to apostasy, an argument Bello would in fact use in the early years of his rule.[69] This new judgement was one of many that sought to enforce a new status quo in which obedience to the ruler, not dissent, was the correct legal action for Muslims to take.

To properly justify their jihad against the Hausa *sarakai* the Fodiawa also required a historical precedent. Usman had conceptualised the jihad as an extension of the work of his teacher, Jibril ibn ʿUmar.[70] However,

[66] Usman, *Tanbīh al-ikhwān* in Palmer, 'Early Fulani Conception (Continued)', p. 53.

[67] Usman, *Taʿlīm al-ikhwān* in Bradford G. Martin, 'Unbelief in the Western Sudan: 'Uthman Dan Fodio's "Ta'lim Al-Ikhwan"', *Middle Eastern Studies*, 4:1 (1967), 50–97, at p. 88.

[68] Usman, *Tanbīh al-ikhwān* in Palmer, 'Early Fulani Conception (Continued)', p. 54.

[69] See Chapter 4.

[70] Usman, *Naṣāʾiḥ al-umma* in Hiskett, *An Islamic Tradition of Reform*, p. 591: 'The beginning of the destruction of these blameworthy customs in our Sudanese towns [Ar. *bilādnā al-Sūdānīya*] was by his hands, and the completion of that was by our hands'.

he found a more authoritative precedent in the example of Askiya Muhammad's seizure of power from the descendants of Sonni Ali. It is for this reason that al-Maghīlī and his text, the *Ajwiba*, assumes a prominence in works written after the jihad that it did not have previously.[71] *Sirāj al-ikhwān*, dated September 1811, is essentially a paraphrase of the *Ajwiba*, while *Tanbīh al-ikhwān*, written some two months later, reproduces the whole text of al-Maghīlī's *Tāj al-dīn* as well as Ahmad Baba's biography of him. In January 1812, Abdullahi wrote a commentary on al-Maghīlī's works, explicitly linking the legacy of al-Maghīlī in the Sahel to the Fodiawa's own actions in Hausaland:

> If you believe what was said regarding Sonni Ali and his officials and the judgement made in their regard, then you know without a doubt that this is what we found with most of the Hausa kings and their officials and their allies from the south and west. The judgements on the former apply equally to the latter. If you know this, then you know that our jihad against them and our taking of their power was the correct path.[72]

But while it was possible for Usman to revise and strengthen some of the juridical underpinnings of the jihad, it was impossible to deny the looting, enslavement and loss of Muslim life that had occurred on its account. In the years after the jihad, the Fodiawa developed a new legal framework that served both to complicate the clear and dogmatic *fiqh* rulings of the doctrine of dissent and to excuse the actions – pragmatic, rash or heinous – that jihadist troops on the ground had taken on account of such rulings. Usman's aim was to maintain legal authority at a time when it was being threatened both from the outside (by scholars such as al-Kānamī) and the inside (by the actions of his own supporters who did not receive or refused to listen to his commands). This framework rested on the legal maxim known as *inkār al-ḥarām*: that one cannot categorically allow or forbid any action that is subject to *iktilāf* [difference of opinion] among legal scholars.

[71] *Iḥyā' al-Sunna* mentions al-Maghīlī only once and *Masā'il muhimma* on only a couple of occasions. Some passages of al-Maghīlī appear verbatim in *Kitāb al-farq* and *Nūr al-albāb* but Usman does not reference them to their source.

[72] Abdullahi, *Ḍiyā' al-sulṭān wa-ghayrihi min al-ikhwān fī ahamm mā yuṭlabu ʿilmuhu fī umūr al-zamān,* Paris (BI) 205, p. 39. Note that the pagination of Arabic MSS in Paris (BI) is so confused that I begin page numbers from the *basmala*.

In Usman's earlier works setting out the 'code of conduct' for jihad, his position had been very clear: Muslims must undertake hijra to the nearest Muslim region, pledge allegiance to the *Amīr al-muʾminīn* and wage war on the infidels and apostates. Any Muslim who remained with the infidels was an infidel, and the possessions of any Muslim who stayed in the lands of the infidels could be counted as war booty. While these rulings achieved their aim – dissent against the Hausa *sarakai* – they also caused widespread confusion, violence and displacement. Usman's post-jihad works complicated and at times contradicted these earlier judgements. In the preface to *Naṣīḥat ahl al-zamān* [Advice for the people of this time], which he wrote in 1811, Usman explained that he wished to 'warn the people against judging others for actions about which the scholars are not in agreement'.[73] But before the jihad, Usman had claimed that the judgement on several of these actions was clear 'by consensus of the scholars'. For example, let us compare the ruling on Muslims abiding in the land of the infidel by choice:

1803 taking the possessions of such Muslims is legal by consensus if they fall within the booty taken from the polytheists, even if they had been set apart.[74]

1811 we do not outlaw categorically confiscating and consuming their property, even if it is in the way of caution not to do so since this is a subject that is in dispute among the scholars.[75]

Similarly, regarding whether it was permissible to enslave apostates from Islam:

1803 their men cannot be enslaved, and their women cannot be taken as concubines.[76]

1811 we do not outlaw categorically their enslavement and that of their children and their families, even though the common opinion is that this is not permissible, since this is a subject that is in dispute among the scholars.[77]

[73] Usman, *Naṣīḥat ahl al-zamān*, Sokoto (n.d.), p. 2. The full title of this work is *Naṣīḥat ahl al-zamān li-Ahl al-Sūdān [wa-li-man shāʾa Allāh min al-Ikhwān] min al-ʿArab wa-l-ʿajam fī jamīʿ al-buldān* 'Advice for the people of this time – to the Ahl al-Sūdān and to whomever God wills from the brothers whether Arab or non-Arab in all the lands'.

[74] Usman, *Masāʾil muhimma*, f. 155a. My emphasis.

[75] Usman, *Naṣīḥat ahl al-zamān*, pp. 17–18. My emphasis.

[76] Usman, *Masāʾil muhimma*, f. 158a. My emphasis.

[77] Usman, *Naṣīḥat ahl al-zamān*, pp. 17–18. My emphasis.

It was not that Usman's judgements had become stricter or laxer. Rather, his claim was that the Fodiawa did not mention them to encourage a discourse of dissent but *only because other scholars had likewise mentioned them* – the very model of taqlid. But the Fodiawa had not discussed taqlid, *ikhtilāf* or *inkār al-ḥarām* before the jihad. On the contrary, they presented their judgements as if they were the prevailing legal opinion. Arguably such an action amounted to *ijtihad*, even if Usman had never described it as such.

Another challenge to Usman came from his speculations about the Mahdi, which had evidently spread across the Sahel region. As we recall, Usman had quoted al-Shaʿrānī's theory of a hidden Mahdi on earth, as well as al-Suyūṭī's prediction that the world would end in AH 1200 or 1204, which he was forced to retract when these had passed. Some of Usman's followers also believed that he himself was the chosen Mahdi. After the jihad, Usman continued to claim that he had special knowledge of the Mahdi through his initiation into a Sufi order connected with al-Shaʿrānī by his former teacher, Jibril ibn ʿUmar.[78] Pointing out that he shared certain 'conditions which agree with the conditions of the Imam Mahdi',[79] Usman reinterpreted the hadith of the twelve caliphs, commenting: 'I hope that I am the first of them [i.e. the eleventh successor] and that the awaited Mahdi is the second'.[80] The aim was to maintain Mahdist expectation while quelling speculation that he himself was the expected figure.

However, in 1814, Usman was forced to clarify the situation further. That year, a Tuareg leader wrote to Usman asking for his judgement concerning one Hamma, a member of his community who claimed to be the Mahdi. Usman's response illustrated that, regardless of his earlier writings, some still believed that he was the Mahdi:

> I am not the imam-mahdī, and [...] I have not claimed the *mahdiyya*, albeit that is heard from the tongues of other men. Verily, I have striven beyond measure in warning them to desist and explicitly rejected their claim in my Arabic and ʿajamī writings.[81]

Just as al-Kānamī had questioned Usman's legal rulings on the jihad, it seems that some scholars also questioned Usman's theory of a hidden Mahdi on earth which he took from al-Shaʿrānī. To deal with this criticism, Usman likewise retreated to the safety of taqlid:

[78] Usman, *Naṣīḥat ahl al-zamān*, Chapter 7.

[79] Usman, *al-Khabar al-hādī ilā umūr al-imām al-Mahdī* in Al-Hajj, 'Mahdist Tradition', p. 223.

[80] Usman, *Naṣīḥat ahl al-zamān*, p. 37.

[81] Usman, *Taḥdhīr al-ikhwān* in Al-Hajj, 'Mahdist Tradition', p. 229.

> We are not quoting these works [...] to support the statement of ʿAbd al-Wahhāb [*al-Shaʿrānī*] because we do not rely on anything other than the evidence of the *Sharīʿa*. On the other hand, we are not quoting them to refute them because we have not come across any evidence in the *Sharīʿa* which rules out the possibility of [the Mahdi] being of eternal existence.[82]

Here too, Usman made his excuse based on *inkār al-ḥarām*: his reason for mentioning al-Shaʿrānī's words on the hidden Mahdi was not to signal his agreement with them. Rather, by quoting the works of previous scholars on a given topic he was only following the principles of taqlid. To support this conclusion, Usman went on to propose 'a just scale for the verification of the *mahdiyya*', a classic exercise of taqlid in which he methodically listed the qualities of the Mahdi as revealed in accepted hadiths to demonstrate that his own circumstances did not correspond. He judged that Hamma should be executed by crucifixion for deigning to claim knowledge of the end of days.[83] Still, this did not settle the matter. In 1815, Ahmad Lobbo wrote to Abdullahi dan Fodio wanting to know:

> Firstly, is the correct name of the father of the expected Mahdi ʿAbd Allāh[84] or al-Ḥasan al-ʿAskarī, as al-Shaʿrānī took from Ibn ʿArabī? [Secondly, I] request a work by *Amīr al-muʾminīn* Usman [dan Fodio] about the Mahdi, his physical appearance and his character. [Lastly], is all that ʿAbd al-Wahhāb [al-Shaʿrānī] described in *al-Yawāqīt [waʾl-Jawāhir]* correct, or is there some that is faulty?[85]

The alleged meeting between Usman and ʿAbd al-Qādir also created a spiritual and political problem in the Sahel. As discussed above, the implication that Usman had 'broken the chain' and bypassed Sahelian spiritual hierarchies unleashed a fanaticism that was difficult to control. Although we do not know whether the Kunta learned of this vision, and if so what their reaction to it could have been, we can imagine that it constituted an impediment to the acceptance of Sokoto within a wider region that considered the Kunta as the established *muqaddams* of the Qadiriyya. In 1813, Usman ended his work on the reasons for the jihad by presenting his *silsila*

[82] *Ibid*., p. 241.

[83] Last, 'From Dissent to Dissidence', p. 37.

[84] Prophet Muhammad stated that the Mahdi's name would be Muḥammad ibn ʿAbd Allāh.

[85] Abdullahi *[al-Ajwiba li-ʿAbd Allāh ibn Fūdī ʿalā asʾilat Aḥmad Lubbu]*, Niamey (MARA) 1716. Abdullahi replied that he had never heard of such a tradition in any of the reliable hadith collections.

to ʿAbd al-Qādir. Usman clearly demonstrated that the connection to ʿAbd al-Qādir he sought was through the accepted route of the Kunta (Figure 1). The reason for the inclusion of this *silsila* was to demonstrate Fodiawa's close connection to al-Maghīlī, reinforcing the link between their jihad of 1804 and al-Maghīlī's own reformist mission in the Sahel.[86] However, it also contradicted the vision presented in *Lamma balaghtu* that would have Usman receiving the Qadiri *wird* from ʿAbd al-Qādir himself.

God
Muhammad
*al-Aqṭāb**
ʿAbd al-Qādir al-Jīlānī (founder)
[earlier *muqaddams* of the Qadiriyya]
Jalāl al-Dīn al-Suyūṭī
ʿAbd al-Karīm al-Maghīlī (*muqaddam* of West Africa)
the Kunta family (local *muqaddams*)
Nūḥ ibn al-Ṭāhir (Kunta agent in Hausaland)
Usman dan Fodio

* Ar. "poles", mystical figures who gained kashf directly from God and form a conduit through which this divine knowledge passes to others

Figure 1 Usman's *silsila* of the Qadiriyya Mukhtariyya. Usman dan Fodio, *Taʿlīm al-ikhwān*. Adapted from Bradford G. Martin, 'Unbelief in the Western Sudan: 'Uthman Dan Fodio's "Ta'lim Al-Ikhwan"', Middle Eastern Studies, 4:1 (1967), 50–97, at p. 93

But the following year, in the same work in which he denied – again – that he was the Mahdi, Usman had to return to the nature of his connection with ʿAbd al-Qādir, and whether he had in fact experienced *kashf*:

> It is heard from the tongues of other men that I can fly in the air and walk on water, that the earth is folded up for me in such a way as to enable me to walk to Mecca and Medina, that the jins serve me as they serve the most perfect saints, and that I can guide the people not only on the path of piety and righteousness but also on the path of mystical knowledge [*kashf*].[87]

[86] Usman, *Taʿlīm al-ikhwān* in Martin, 'Unbelief in the Western Sudan', p. 77.
[87] Usman, *Taḥdhīr al-ikhwān*, in Al-Hajj, 'Mahdist Tradition', pp. 224–72. In Islamic tradition, jin (or jinn) are powerful beings living in parallel with

In this work he presented another version of his encounter that had quite different implications than the first:

> God placed me in a spiritual state (*wāridāt al-aḥwāl*) during my youth, until I reached the age of thirty one years [c. AD 1785]. Then I was pulled up by a transitory spiritual power (*jadhba*) emanating from the light of the Messenger of God and generated by prayer to him, till I found myself in front of the Messenger of God.[88]

In the vision, Prophet Muhammad told Usman: 'I am your guide on the path of religion, you will not go astray'. In other words, Usman had not 'broken the chain' to receive *kashf* from a more important source than that allowed by the Qadiriyya Mukhtariyya. While his vision certainly distinguished him among his followers, it did not make him a *walīy* able to guide people on the path of *kashf*.[89]

The last notable difference between the discourses of dissent and moderation is the growing importance of the Torobbe origin story. While the Fodiawa had appealed directly to the Fulani clans before and during the conflict, their call for jihad was grounded in *takfir* of the actions of the Hausa *sarakai*, rather than their identity as Hausa. The Fodiawa's narratives of the jihad, which they wrote after the conquest, sought to justify their newly acquired dominance over the Hausa majority through a retelling of Sahelian history. According to Muhammad Bello, the inhabitants of the *Hausa bakwai* [the seven Hausa states] descended from the seven slaves of the *Mai* of Bornu;[90] *Kanta*, the first ruler of Kebbi, was 'a slave of the Fulani'.[91] Meanwhile, in his account of the conflict, written in 1813, Usman explicitly stated that it was persecution of the Fulani that had first led to the war with Bornu:

---

the human world. Certain individuals are able see and interact with these beings, but they are otherwise unperceived.

[88] *Ibid.*

[89] *Ibid.*

[90] Shādhilī, *Infāq al-maysūr*, Chapter 7. Except for the Gobirawa, whom Bello says descend from the Copts of Egypt. See also Abdulkadiri dan Tafa, *Rawḍāt al*-afkār. Zehnle, *A Geography of Jihad*, pp. 255–6, suggests that Bello deliberately confused the Bayajidda legend of the Hausa. He stated that it was Bayajidda's son, Bawo, rather than Bayajidda himself, who came from Bornu. This may have been because of Bawo sounding similar to the Hausa term *bawa* [slave].

[91] Shādhilī, *Infāq al-maysūr*, Chapter 8.

> as to the cause of the fighting against the Muslim communities who were in their towns, and the battles which took place between us and our neighbours, its cause was that [Mai Ahmed's] Galadima [chief minister] went to his Dayāma (The ruler of Daya, South West Bornu) and told him falsely that the Amir had ordered him to kill the Fallatiya (Fulani), so he had begun to slaughter them. That was why disorder had broken out in our towns.[92]

In the years after the jihad, Abdullahi also worked to highlight the Arab genealogy (*nasab*) of the Torobbe-Fulani.[93] The theory of Fulani origin espoused by Abdullahi – and relayed non-critically by Muhammad Bello in *Infāq al-maysūr* – was that the Fulani descended from the union of the descendants of Ishmael (the Arabs) and Isaac (the Byzantines and Jews), the two sides of the Abrahamic family.[94] This union took place during the early Muslim conquests in the region of Mount Sinai (Tūr Sīnā'), from whence the Torobbe gained their name:

> The warrior 'Uqba ibn 'Āmir, who conquered the lands of the west in the time of 'Umar bin al-'Āṣ in Egypt, reached them [the Torobbe] when they were one of the *qabā'il* of the Byzantines. Their king converted to Islam without a fight and 'Uqba married the daughter of their king, called *Baju Maghu*, and all the Fulani came into being.[95]

If we follow this story correctly, the Torobbe were not – as was believed in Futa Toro – originally clients or even slaves of the Fulani, but in fact the source of all the Fulani clans and the first speakers of the Fulfulde language.[96] What is more, the Torobbe also had an ancient territorial claim on Hausaland:

> Musa [Jokollo][97] he it was who came with our clan from the country of the west, which is Futa Toro, according to what we have heard, and he was

[92] Usman, *Ta'līm al-ikhwān* in Martin, 'Unbelief in the Western Sudan', p. 90.

[93] Abdullahi's *Īdā' al-nusūkh* (1812) contains a summary of the origin of the Torobbe, as does *Tazyīn al-waraqāt* (1813), *Kitāb al-nasab* (after 1817) and the undated *Aṣl al-Fulātiyyīn.*

[94] See Naylor, 'Abdullahi Dan Fodio and Muhammad Bello's Debate over the Torobbe-Fulani'. Salau, *Plantation Slavery in the Sokoto Caliphate*, pp. 33–8 suggests Hausa claims to Arab origin were common knowledge at the time of the jihad but provides no evidence.

[95] Abdullahi, *Kitāb al-nasab*, NU/Wilks 115, p. 1.

[96] See Abdullahi, *Īdā' al-nusūkh.*

[97] In *Kitāb al-nasab* Abdullahi lists ten generations between his father and Musa Jokollo while in *Aṣl al-Fulātiyyīn* he states that there are 39 generations

> one of their chief men until he came with them to the country of Kunni [Konni],[98] and they were the first who lived in it before the Hausas and the Touareg, until subsequently they spread through the country of the Hausas. They were the origin of the Fulani, and their language was the language of the Fulani. They preceded all the Fulani in Hausaland by seven years, according to what we have heard.[99]

We can perhaps understand this origin story as a mix of the ʿUqba myth common to Sahelian knowledge elites and the *yan kasa* [sons of the land] motif that formed the basis for many Hausa origin stories.[100] But whatever the material used to construct it, the implication was that by arriving in Hausaland before any other group and naming some localities there, the Torobbe were Hausaland's rightful rulers. The jihad was thus not the sharp break with the past as Abdullahi had characterised it in his earlier writings, but a return to things 'as they should be', perhaps seeking to reverse the prevalent belief among the Hausa that the Fulani were a 'foreign' group. Like the other elements in the discourse of moderation, this Torobbe origin story arguably had the same role: normalising the Fodiawa's rule and justifying it using innovative reworkings of historical precedents.

Between around 1811, when the Fodiawa's rule of Hausaland was fully assured, up to the last few years of Usman's life, Usman and Muhammad Bello sought to stem the tide of rebellion that had brought them to power and instead cultivate an acceptance of the status quo. To do so, they injected caution and doubt into many of the forceful arguments they had used for the jihad, seeking to prevent them being used by others. They also found creative ways to make the jihadists' otherwise reprehensible actions during the conflict comprehensible within Islamic discursive tradition. By downplaying his links to the Mahdi and revising his experience of *kashf,*

---

between Prophet Abraham and ʿUqba and nine generations between ʿUqba and Musa Jokollo.

[98] In *Aṣl al-Fulātiyyīn*, Abdullahi specifies that this emigration occurred in the fifth century AH (corresponding to the eleventh or twelfth century AD). He states that Musa Jokollo had three sons. He sent his first son, Adam, to the Benue river where he founded the Adamawa. A second, Jugu, he sent to Kulwa where he founded the Jegawa. A third, Ayyūb, stayed with him in Konni. The Fodiawa descend from Ayyūb.

[99] Abdullahi, *Īdāʿ al-nusūkh* in Hiskett, 'Material Relating to the State of Learning among the Fulani before Their Jihād', p. 560.

[100] For the ʿUqba myth see Nobili, 'Back to Saharan Myths: Preliminary Notes on 'Uqba Al-Mustajab'. For more on *yan kasa* see Guy Nicolas, *Dynamique sociale et appréhension du monde au sein d'une société hausa* (Paris, 1975).

Usman also sought to reaffirm the traditional politico-spiritual hierarchy of the region, thus extinguishing – or rather, delaying – the Mahdist fervour spreading in Hausaland. Through an exercise in creative genealogy, the Fodiawa also suggested that their rule was the natural result of their identity as Torobbe-Fulani, a group with historical claims to the Hausa region. These actions I call, collectively, a discourse of moderation.

The Intellectual Challenge of Abdullahi dan Fodio (c.1812–1817)

> When the Shaykh [Usman] realised that the enemy of God was coming, he ordered those with him to consult together and elect an Imam […] saying: 'God has made jihad obligatory upon you due to the desire of the infidel to poison the Islam of these lands. But do not appoint me, for I am excused. I am not able'. So, they deliberated, and some pointed to Abdullahi while others said, 'No. He pits people against one another'.[101]

At the end of this tale, related by Al-Ḥājj Saʿīd, Usman reluctantly accepts the leadership of the *jamāʿa*. No doubt, as Last suggests, this apocryphal story was intended to demonstrate Usman's humility and his lack of interest in political power.[102] However, it is telling with regard to how Abdullahi was portrayed within the jihadist movement. The remainder of this chapter narrates Abdullahi's role in the early *jamāʿa* and his growing dissatisfaction with the jihad campaign. It then follows in detail the direct criticisms he made of his elder brother, which began around 1810, and Usman's responses. These debates exposed the inconsistencies between the harsh judgements required in the discourse of dissent and the more pragmatic views that Usman had adopted in the discourse of moderation. Abdullahi re-examined the circumstances of the jihad of 1804 and the rulings that were made to justify it, while also criticising the questionable logic Usman used to defend the actions of the jihadists after the conflict. In short, his works constituted an intellectual challenge to the Sokoto project as envisioned by Usman, and now Muhammad Bello as well.

Some fifteen years before the preparation of Usman's community for war, Abdullahi's poems already had a markedly militaristic bent. In 1789, shortly after he and Usman had celebrated Eid al-Adha with *Sarkin*

[101] Al-Ḥājj Saʿīd, *Taqāyīd mimmā waṣala ilaynā*, Paris (BnF) Arabe 5484, f. 110b. Ar. يحمله بعضا عن بعض *yaḥmalahu baʿḍan ʿan baʿḍ.*

[102] Last, *Sokoto Caliphate*, p. 24.

Gobir Bāwa, Abdullahi composed the following lines on the veneration of Prophet Muhammad:

> He is the lion, and they are the lion cubs
> They cut off at a blow the heads of the unbelievers
> With swords the blades of which are bright.
> Whetted arrows, transfixing, assist them,
> While under them are fine horses.[103]

Abdullahi was the first to pledge allegiance to Usman as *Amīr al-mu'minīn*.[104] In *Tazyīn al-waraqāt*, his account of the conflict, he plainly stated that Usman did not call for an armed uprising for the purposes of defence but rather because of 'the greatness of the community, and their desire to break away from the unbelievers'.[105] He supported the jihad wholeheartedly and turned his pen to glorifying the conflict:

> O community of Islam, strive and wage Holy War
> And do not be weak, for patience comes home to victory!
> Your slain are in Paradise for ever,
> And he who returns returns with glory and wealth.[106]

In these poems, Abdullahi frequently compared the jihad to battles of the early Muslims under Muhammad.[107] He depicted the Hausa *sarakai* and their armies as corrupted, proud and tyrannical. In his poems they invariably appear besotted with fine living, clothed in rich and luxurious gowns and riding decorated horses. He presented the jihad as an allegorical punishment from God for their sins.[108] To replace their rule, Abdullahi envisioned a perfect Islamic state in the model of the Rashidun Caliphs, an imamate in which confusion and oppression would fall away before the clarity of the Sharia.

While offering the jihadists moral support though his poems, Abdullahi also fought extensively in the campaigns. He led the first raids in the Konni region and the first siege of Alkalawa, oversaw the fall of Zamfara in 1805 and made more than twenty offensive raids while the jihadists

[103] Hiskett, *Tazyīn al-Waraqāt*, p. 89. Abdullahi composed this poem around 1789.
[104] See Abdullahi, *Tazyīn al-waraqāt*; Bello, *Infāq al-maysūr*.
[105] Hiskett, *Tazyīn al-Waraqāt*, p. 105.
[106] *Ibid.*, p. 111.
[107] *Ibid.*, p. 110.
[108] *Ibid.*, p. 112.

were camped at Sabon Gari.[109] Abdullahi's conduct in battle seems to have matched the heroism of his poems. Even Al-Ḥājj Saʿīd, who as an ally of Bello showed a marked bias against Abdullahi, vividly captures his bravado during a surprise attack against the jihadists at Argungu:[110]

> The infidels descended on them after the [Muslim] armies had gone in search of provisions. They came across [Usman's] brother Abdullahi during his study session and killed students and teachers from that group. Abdullahi fought them off alone, killing five of the armoured men.[111]

In October 1805, Usman tasked Abdullahi with leading the jihadist troops at the battle of Alwasa. The battle was a big defeat for the jihadists, resulting in major loss of life.[112] There were many scholars among the dead, and Abdullahi must have lost many friends and teachers. This experience may have put some distance between Abdullahi and his beloved elder brother, who never actively participated in the jihad that he sanctioned.[113] Surveying the scene after Alwasa, Abdullahi began to show the first signs of doubt about the motivations of the jihadists:

> I have been left among a remnant who neglect their prayers
> And obey, in procuring pleasures, their own souls.
> And the majority of them have traded their faith for the world.
> Preferring what they desire; and the heart wheedles,
> Bold for forbidden food, and the eating of it,
> As the beasts eat, they eat the tree of Hell.
> They do not listen to orders, they disobey their imam
> And whosoever stands and forbids them from evil, it is as if
> he spoke foul language![114]

Despite Abdullahi's complaints, in the following years the fortunes of the jihadists improved with the rising star of Muhammad Bello. Under his supervision, Gwandu became a permanent fortified base from which the jihadists launched successful attacks as far as Yauri, Borgu and Dendi.

[109] *Ibid.*, pp. 115–16.

[110] Dated in Bello, *Infāq*, to between 1807 and 1808.

[111] Al-Ḥājj Saʿīd, *Taqāyīd mimmā waṣala ilaynā*, Arabe 5484, f. 111b. Ar. أصحاب اللبود *aṣḥāb al-lubūd*, a reference to *lifidi*, the padded cotton armour worn by the Hausa troops.

[112] Accounts of Alwasa can also be found in Bello's *Infāq al-maysūr* and Abdulkadiri dan Tafa's *Rawḍāt al-afkār*.

[113] See Mahibou, *Théorie du gouvernement*, pp. 197–8.

[114] Hiskett, *Tazyīn al-Waraqāt*, p. 118.

Through his diplomatic efforts at the meeting in Magami, the Hausa kingdoms of Zamfara, Katsina, Daura and Kano pledged allegiance to the growing jihadist state.[115] It is notable that, in *Tazyīn al-waraqāt*, Abdullahi makes scant reference to these events.

In October 1807, Usman chose Bello to lead a second attack on Gobir's capital, Alkalawa. On the night of 4 October, as Abdullahi marched towards Alkalawa along with the jihadist army he had an abrupt change of heart. He and five companions abandoned the jihadist army, resolving to journey far from Hausaland to undertake a pilgrimage to Mecca: 'Then there came to me from God the sudden thought to shun the homelands… I left the army and occupied myself with my own (affairs) and faced towards the East, towards the Chosen One'.[116]

Abdullahi first stopped at Kano where he was, in his own words, 'preoccupied, and at a loss what to do'.[117] In Kano, things were no better. Abdullahi stated that, 'I saw among them that from which I had fled in my own country'.[118] Instead of continuing his journey eastwards to Mecca, the people of Kano persuaded Abdullahi to stay and write for them something 'by which they might be enlightened regarding the judgements of the Sharia and its application'.[119] Abdullahi's stay in Kano gave him the mental space to develop, in writing, a detailed vision for Islamic governance in Hausaland, a vision that was in reality already slipping away. The result was *Ḍiyāʾ al-ḥukkām*, one of Abdullahi's first works on Muslim statecraft.[120]

In *Ḍiyāʾ al-ḥukkām*, Abdullahi explained how to found and govern a 'proper' Islamic state, and looked in detail at the legal rulings around jihad and the taking of war booty.[121] While these topics were clearly a response to

[115] Last, *Sokoto Caliphate*, p. 36; Shādhilī, *Infāq al-maysūr*, p. 205.

[116] Hiskett, *Tazyīn al-Waraqāt*, p. 120.

[117] Abdullahi, *Ḍiyāʾ al-ḥukkām fī-mā la-hum wa-ʿalayhim min al-aḥkām*, Paris (BI) 175, p. 5.

[118] Hiskett, *Tazyīn al-Waraqāt*, p. 121.

[119] Abdullahi, *Ḍiyāʾ al-ḥukkām*, pp. 4–5.

[120] I hesitate to say 'the first' – as Mahibou (2010) claims – because in an undated work entitled *Ḍiyāʾ al-muqtadīn*, Abdullahi states that there should be no obedience shown to one who rules contrary to the Sharia and consequently, 'there is no remaining under the kings of *al-Sūdān*'. This statement, and the fact that the content is largely lifted from al-Suyūst's *Taʾrīkh al-khulafāʾ* without any input from Abdullahi, suggests that he wrote it prior to *Ḍiyāʾ al-ḥukkām*. See Abdullahi, *Ḍiyāʾ al-muqtadīn li-l-khulafāʾ al-rāshidīn*, Paris (BI) 192, f. 2b.

[121] See Abubakar Aliyu Gwandu, 'Abdullahi B. Fodio as a Muslim Jurist' (Unpublished PhD dissertation, Durham University, 1977), p. 108.

the concerns Abdullahi had at that time, he was perhaps looking further ahead, to the direction of the Sokoto project in the longer term. Among the conditions for the appointment of a ruler, he stated that it would be improper for a son to succeed his father.[122] It is possible that he had Muhammad Bello in mind.

Whatever Abdullahi's sentiments at this stage, he soon decided to rejoin the jihad campaign. Under Muhammad Bello, the jihadists finally took Alkalawa the following year and killed *Sarkin Gobir* Yunfa, dissolving the state against which they had initially gone to war. Abdullahi was given command of an army to make raids into Gurma, and continued to write triumphalist poetry about their victories, as he had done in the first years of the jihad. Around December 1809, Usman made the decision to move north-east to Sifawa along with Muhammad Bello and most of his followers, ordering Abdullahi to remain in the west and continue the jihad there.[123] Abdullahi was evidently upset at this arrangement:

> I set out with a small army because most of the people had turned towards the place of emigration in order to acquire houses, and in order to make productive the unworked lands, and they were unwilling to fight Holy War at that time, in that area.[124]

By 1811, Abdullahi returned to Bodinga, a few miles south-west of Sifawa, to be closer to Usman. Meanwhile, Bello led military campaigns in Gwari and began the construction of Sokoto as a new capital for the jihadist state.[125] The following year, Usman divided the territory gained in the jihad among his most senior commanders.[126] He gave the western half to Abdullahi, the east to Bello and the north to military commander ʿAlī Jedo, dividing the

[122] Minna, 'Intellectual Contribution'. Murray Last states that, according to Waziri Junaidu, this moment reflected the division between the older generation – as represented by Abdullahi – and the younger generation, who looked to Bello as their future leader. See Last, *Sokoto Caliphate*, p. 65.

[123] S. A. Balogun, 'Succession Tradition in Gwandu History', *Journal of the Historical Society of Nigeria,* 7:1 (1973), 17–33, at p. 19.

[124] Hiskett, *Tazyīn al-Waraqāt*, p. 127.

[125] Balogun, 'Succession Tradition', p. 19; Hiskett, *Tazyīn al-Waraqāt*, pp. 129–30.

[126] Balogun convincingly argues that the date of 1812 given in Saʿd b. ʿAbd al-Raḥmān's *Tarṭīb al-aṣḥāb* is more likely than local accounts giving a date of 1809. Since Bodinga (only a few miles south-west of Sifawa) fell inside the western portion of the territory granted to Abdullahi, logically the division must have been made when Abdullahi was at Bodinga, that is, after 1810. See Balogun, 'Succession Tradition'; 'The Place of Argungu in Gwandu History', *Journal of the Historical Society of Nigeria,* 7:3 (1974), 403–15.

south between another of his sons, Al-Bukhāri, and the *Bā Arewa* leader Abd al-Salam.[127] Retrospectively, it seems that Bello gained the greatest amount of territory from this division, although were Ahmad Lobbo to have remained Sokoto's regional Emir in Masina, the western half of the division may have been the more prestigious.[128] In any case, the division plainly showed that by 1812 Usman was treating both Abdullahi and Bello as senior figures in the *jamāʿa*. Around the time of the division of 1812, Abdullahi completed his *magnum opus*, *Tazyīn al-waraqāt* [Adornment of Papers], a history of the jihad that collected together the best of his poems. Strikingly, in the preface Abdullahi announced that he would cease composing poems because 'there was no benefit in them … as regards religion'.[129] In the following years, he would instead continue his series of works on correct Islamic governance.

When reviewing the clash between Usman and Abdullahi, we are fortunate that both men took the care to date various works relating to their conflict. This allows us to place the debate between them within a precise chronological period and document how their views changed. Abdullahi's first criticism of his fellow jihadists, although not citing Usman directly, was *Ḍiyāʾ ūlī-l-amr* [Guidance for the responsible], which he completed on 28 December 1810. In *Ḍiyāʾ al-sulṭān*, completed on 19 January 1812, Abdullahi took aim at Usman directly, critically commenting on *Miṣbāḥ li-ahl hadhā-l-zamān* (1808) and *Sirāj al-ikhwān* (1811), precisely those works in which Usman began to use *inkār al-ḥarām* as discussed previously. Usman responded to these criticisms in *Najm al-ikhwān*, which he completed the following year. After this period of conflict, both men continued to produce works on Islamic governance and legal practice, but without explicit reference to the other.[130]

[127] 'Succession Tradition', p. 18. As Balogun is right to point out, Usman's division of 1812 was probably intended as a temporary arrangement under which the administrative responsibilities of this vast amount of land were divided between 'Senior Wazirs', each man organising separate forces to extend the jihad in his area of command.

[128] See Lovejoy, *Jihād in West Africa*, pp. 93–4. For the Hausa, the east-west division between Bello and Abdullahi likely had a deeper historical significance, marking the division between the *Hausa bakwai* that would become the Sokoto Caliphate (Biram, Daura, Gobir, Kano, Katsina, Rano, Zaria), and the *Banza bakwai* that would form the Emirate of Gwandu (Zamfara, Kebbi, Yauri, Gwari, Nupe, Kororofa [Jukun], Yoruba), with some important consequences for their rule.

[129] Hiskett, *Tazyīn al-Waraqāt*, p. 84.

[130] Usman, *Tawqīf al-muslimīn* (1813); *Shams al-ikhwān* (1813); Abdullahi, *Ḍiyāʾ al-umarāʾ* (1813); *Ḍiyāʾ al-wilāyāt* (1815).

It is important to note that during these four or so years Abdullahi was not solely occupied with criticising his brother.[131] Neither did he wish to undermine the Sokoto project as a whole: both he and Bello sought to calm people who were misinterpreting the conflict.[132] However, that Abdullahi raised his objections in this period makes sense. As we have seen, 1810 to 1812 was exactly the period in which Usman (and increasingly, Muhammad Bello) began a discourse of moderation that excused the excesses of the jihad while normalising the Fodiawa's rule of Hausaland. This conflict also reflects the fact that, as the jihad expanded outwards, the *jamāʿa* was becoming increasingly divided geographically and, as its members began to digest and interpret the events of the jihad years, more ideologically fractious. It was also a precursor to the nascent dispute between Abdullahi and Muhammad Bello over the succession, discussed in the next chapter.

First let us examine the conflict between Usman and Abdullahi concerning the nature of correct Islamic governance and the necessary qualities of a Muslim ruler. As outlined in Chapter 1, Prophet Muhammad made very few statements about who should lead the Muslim community after his death. Usman and Abdullahi – like many Muslims before and after them – adopted radically different interpretations of these hadith which attested to their very different visions of Muslim governance in Hausaland after the jihad. The exact point of contention was over the concept of *mulk* [kingship], a term mentioned by Muhammad in two hadiths on the question of Muslim governance:

1 This matter began with prophethood and grace. After that, caliphate and grace. After that, rapacious kingship. After that, tyranny and corruption.[133]

2 The caliphate in my Umma is thirty years and then kingship after that.[134]

Abdullahi's interpretation of the hadith was that the age of the Rashidun Caliphs was over and that there could be no more caliphs after them.[135]

[131] Other works from this period include *Ḍiyāʾ al-mujāhidīn* (a summary of Jaʿfar al-Naḥḥās's treaty on jihad) and *Ḍiyāʾ al-umma* (a summary of al-Shaʿrānī's primer on *uṣūl al-fiqh* entitled *Kashf al-ghumma ʿan jamīʿ al-umma*).

[132] Abdullahi, *Kaff al-ikhwān ʿan al-taʿarruḍ bi-al-inkār ʿalā ahl al-īmān* [Restraining the brothers from antagonising those who are believers]; Bello, *Kaff al-ikhwān ʿan ittibāʿ khuṭuwāt al-shayṭān* [Restraining the brothers from following the steps of Satan]. I was unable to consult either of these works.

[133] Abdullahi, *Ḍiyāʾ al-sulṭān*, p. 3. My emphasis. It closely resembles *Sunan Abū Dāwūd*, Hadith no. 222.

[134] *Jāmiʿ al-Tirmidhī*, Hadith no. 2226. My emphasis.

[135] See Abdullahi, *Ḍiyāʾ ūlī-l-amr*, f.2a, in which he calls Caliph ʿUmar ibn

At the time that he was writing, some twelve hundred years later, the only correct path open to a Muslim leader was to imitate the ways of the Rashidun Caliphs in every aspect. While the Rashidun Caliphate was no more, other forms of Muslim statecraft such as an imamate (*imāma*) or an emirate (*imāra*) offered acceptable alternatives. But Abdullahi made a strong distinction between a Muslim state led by an imam or emir and the kingship or *mulk* mentioned by Prophet Muhammad:

> [The imam should i]mprove the religion and the livelihood of the populace following the Sunna of the Messenger of God. He should act as a deputy for the Messenger of God to the Muslims and as their emir. He should not come to his position through inheritance and lord over the people by force to obtain the riches of the world, with complete freedom to do as he wishes and take pleasure in fine foods, clothing and living quarters, for [all] that is *mulk* [kingship].[136]

From the above we understand that, for Abdullahi, *mulk* pertained to any form of government that contrasted with Muslim statecraft. He depicted a *malik* [king] as an un-Islamic and tyrannical ruler who 'lords over his people like a master over his slaves'[137] and, importantly, one whose power was hereditary.[138] For Abdullahi, it was the confusion between these terms that had led to the tyrannical government of the Hausa *sarakai*: 'Our ignorant ones believe that kingship is praiseworthy in Islam and in fact is a duty. They do not distinguish between it and the praiseworthy caliphate and emirate.'[139] Further, Abdullahi did not believe that the jihad had rid Hausaland of the *mulk* of the Hausa *sarakai*. He worried that, with their own lust for power, land and possessions, the jihadists were simply replicating it. He reasoned that to clearly differentiate Muslim from non-Muslim leadership required a clear differentiation of terms. He declared that Prophet Muhammad had meant *mulk* and *malik* to refer only to a

---

'Abd al-'Azīz 'the seal of the Caliphs'. Significantly, Abdullahi makes no reference to the narration of *Musnad Aḥmad ibn Ḥanbal*, Hadith no. 18406, discussed on p. 38 n. 23, in which tyrannical kingship is followed by 'Caliphate in the way of Prophethood'.

136 Abdullahi, *Ḍiyāʾ ūlī-l-amr*, f. 2b. My emphasis.

137 Abdullahi, *Ḍiyāʾ al-sulṭān*, p. 4. He is referring to al-Maghīlī's definition of a king in *Ajwiba*.

138 See Mahibou, *Théorie du gouvernement*, pp. 206–8. He cites Abdullahi, *Ḍiyāʾ al-ḥukkām*; *Ḍiyāʾ al-sulṭān*.

139 Abdullahi, *Ḍiyāʾ ūlī-l-amr*, f. 2b.

non-Muslim ruler, and that al-Maghīlī had also made this point clear in his influential works on Islamic governance:

> He [al-Maghīlī] specified *imāra* and *emir* because it is the Islamic, praiseworthy name and more precise than 'Caliph without kingship'. And [he specified] *mulk* because it is the term applied to the kings of the world before Islam. As the Prophet said, 'This matter began with prophethood and grace. After that, caliphate and grace. After that, rapacious kingship. After that, tyranny and corruption'.[140]

Abdullahi's censure of *malik* and *mulk* had clear repercussions in the *jamā'a*, as Usman explained in a particularly revealing passage from *Najm al-ikwhān* which he wrote in response to Abdullahi's criticisms:

> The reason why I have dwelt so long on this matter [of kingship] is that the people have inundated me with questions about it and asked me for a response on the truth of it. Some of the students having heard the censure of the word 'king' [...] in *Ḍiyā' al-sulṭān* and *Ḍiyā' ūlī-l-amr* written by my brother, Abdullahi, think that they should censor the use of the word 'king' in this Umma. One of them even told me, 'We will not use the word "king" to describe the ruler, but rather "imam"'.[141]

For his part, Usman had a very different standpoint on the terminology of a Muslim ruler. Like Abdullahi, this also reflected his vision for the government of Hausaland post-jihad:

> There is no harm in applying the terms *khilāfa, imāma, imāra, wilāya, sulṭana* and *mulk*[142] to the leaders of Islam because they are found in the Sharia. If their utterance was not merited, it would not have been found in the Sharia. None of them imply censure or praise in themselves, but only in their manifestations.[143]

As to Abdullahi's interpretation of the hadith in question: 'the censure of "rapacious kingship" is due to the *rapaciousness* [...] not to uttering the word "king"'.[144]

Usman's rejoinder to Abdullahi was not merely a dispute over terminology. It pointed to a deep division between the two men as to the objective

140 Abdullahi, *Ḍiyā' al-sulṭān*, p. 3.
141 Usman, *Najm al-ikhwān*, Niamey, Collection of Seyni Moumouni, p. 33.
142 These terms equate to 'caliphate', 'imamate', 'emirate', 'state/sovereignty', 'sultanate' and 'kingship' respectively.
143 Usman, *Najm al-ikhwān*, p. 28. My emphasis.
144 Usman, *Najm al-ikhwān*, p. 30. My emphasis.

of Muslim governance. Abdullahi considered that the only period of *true* Islamic governance was the thirty-year rule of the Rashidun Caliphs. After this period, the only legitimate pursuit of Muslim governance was 'to cultivate the Sunna and do what the Prophet of God and his Rightly Guided Caliphs did'.[145] But Usman suggested otherwise:

> 'King' can be applied to the kings of the infidels and the kings of Islam from the time of Muʿāwiya[146] to judgement day because of the Prophet's words, 'The caliphate in my Umma is thirty years and then kingship after that'. His words should not be taken literally[147] but rather by the specific understanding that he means the kingship of the infidels, namely, the king who 'lords over his people like a master over his slaves'.[148]

In Usman's interpretation of the hadith, it was possible for kingship to be Muslim so long as it was not *rapacious* kingship. This logic allowed Usman – and later, Muhammad Bello – to create a more pragmatic Muslim statecraft specific to the context of nineteenth-century Hausaland, which Abdullahi's strict interpretation of the hadith did not allow.

The second point of contention between Usman and Abdullahi involved the legal basis for declaring *takfir* upon the Hausa *sarakai*. As we recall from the previous section, both Usman and Bello had quoted the parallel Abdullahi had made between the Hausa *sarakai* and Sonni Ali in *Ḍiyāʾ al-sulṭān* to back up their claims that the jihad in Hausaland had been legitimate.[149] However, they overlooked the fact that Abdullahi had dedicated a significant portion of this same work to undermining Usman's judgement of *takfir* and, implicitly, the justification for the jihad.

145 Abdullahi, *Ḍiyāʾ al-sulṭān,* p. 7.

146 Muʿāwiya ibn Abī Sufyān (AD 602–680) was a prominent member of the Meccan elite. Initially hostile to Muhammad and his Companions, he converted to Islam and led Muslim military campaigns, becoming Governor of Damascus. He disputed the appointment of the Prophet's nephew, ʿAlī ibn Abī Ṭālib, as fourth Caliph and after ʿAlī's assassination declared himself Caliph, ruling from Damascus. His seizure of power marked the end of the Rashidun Caliphate and the beginning of the hereditary Umayyad dynasty. Muʿāwiya as a historical precedent for the Fodiawa's rule will be discussed in subsequent chapters.

147 Ar. على ظاهره المذكورة *ʿalā ẓāhirihi al-madhkūra.*

148 Usman, *Najm al-ikhwān*, pp. 30; 35.

149 Abdullahi, *Ḍiyāʾ al-sulṭān,* p. 39. Quoted in Usman, *Najm al-ikhwān;* Bello, *Miftāḥ al-sadād.*

In *Sirāj al-ikhwān* (1811), Usman reiterated his judgement of *takfir* on those who claimed to be Muslim but performed none of the acts of Islam, or else mixed Islamic and non-Islamic rituals. In this he claimed to be following the judgements of al-Maghīlī in the *Ajwiba*.[150] Abdullahi, perhaps informed by his own experiences during the jihad campaign, emphasised the negative consequences of such a blanket ruling: 'the Shaykh's judgement that those infidels could be killed or captured without differentiating between them may be misinterpreted'.[151] He went on to argue that additional considerations should have been made before declaring *takfir* on self-proclaimed Muslims. That such a judgement should not in any case be made unilaterally, but only on a case by case basis: 'the act that confirms the infidelity must undoubtedly be defined as one that has infidelity as its intention. Therefore, only actions that pertain exclusively to acts of infidelity can be a reason for anathematisation.'[152] As an example, he pointed to some initiation ceremonies of the Fulani, which Usman had criticised in previous writings.[153] Abdullahi ruled that these actions could not be grounds for *takfir* since the Fulani were not engaging in them for a purpose that would specifically negate their belief in Islam, such as presenting offerings at a shrine.[154]

But Usman had claimed that the Hausa *sarakai*'s maintenance of *muwālāt* [friendly relations] with the infidels – i.e. with *Sarkin Gobir* – and the assistance they had granted him against the jihadists were grounds enough for *takfir*:

> They assist and support the unbelievers, and even aid their forces against the Muslim armies not from [motives] which might be interpreted, indirectly at least, to bring some advantage to the Muslims, but purely for the sake of consolidating their own domains.[155]

As was also the case for the *Mai* of Bornu: 'We fought them only because they began to attack us; they were the first to commit aggression against us.

[150] See Usman, *Sirāj al-ikhwān* in Muhammad Shareef, 'The Guiding Light of the Brethren' (2000) http://siiasi.org/wp-content/uploads/2014/12/Siraajl-Ikhwaan-2.pdf [accessed 9 September 2020], Chapters 3–4.

[151] Ar. فيه ما فيه *fī-hi mā-fī-hi*. Abdullahi, *Ḍiyāʾ al-sulṭān*, p. 55.

[152] *Ibid.*, p. 56.

[153] See Usman, *Nūr al-albāb* in Ismail Hamet, 'Nour-el-Eulbab (Lumière des cœurs) de Cheïkh Otmane ben Mohammed ben Otmane dit Ibn-Foudiou', *Revue africaine*, 41:227 (1897), 297–320.

[154] Abdullahi, *Ḍiyāʾ al-sulṭān*, p. 57.

[155] Usman, *Taʿlīm al-ikhwān* in Martin, 'Unbelief in the Western Sudan', p. 87.

What led them to commit such aggression was their co-operation with the unbelievers.'[156] Usman's basis for this judgement hinged on al-Maghīlī's interpretation that *muwālāt* was mentioned in the Qur'an with the sense of helping the infidels in battle, and as such constituting apostasy from Islam.[157] But in *Ḍiyā' al-sulṭān*, Abdullahi questioned al-Maghīlī's logic:

> as for him placing infidelity on someone who helps the infidels in their armies against the armies of the Muslims, this is not evident for me because the Qur'anic verse that al-Maghīlī used as evidence in fact pertained to aiding [the infidels] in their infidelity. This is an action of the hypocrites for whom this verse was meant, as scholars of *tafsīr* have made clear.[158]

That is to say, the verse was meant for the 'hypocrites' within Muhammad's own community who accepted his message while continuing their interactions with the pagan Meccans for personal or financial benefit, thus 'aiding them in their infidelity'. It did not necessarily mean 'aiding them' in battle against the Muslims. Abdullahi goes on:

> Al-Maghīlī spoke of *naṣr* [aid], but he did not define it. He equated 'aiding them' in general terms with 'infidelity', not 'sin'. Now, aiding them in infidelity is infidelity. However, aiding them in committing sin is not infidelity at all, but rather it is sin. If the act is not in itself infidelity, then how can the action be infidelity by default?[159]

In essence, Abdullahi's point was that 'aiding the infidels' was not sufficient in and of itself to warrant the judgement of *takfir* such as al-Maghīlī had made. Usman himself pointed out that Abdullahi's literalist interpretation risked invalidating the very basis of the jihad:

> His [Abdullahi's] interpretation suggests that [the act of] waging war on Muslims is not judged to be infidelity, even after they have made *muwālāt* with the infidels (i.e. procuring their help and assistance against the Muslims, agreeing jointly to fight the Muslims, and supporting actions that contravene the Sharia). This is absolutely not the case. Rather, fighting

[156] *Ibid.*, p. 89.

[157] Al-Maghīlī, *Miṣbāḥ li-l-arwāḥ*. The verse in question is Qur'an 5:80 'Thou seest many of them making friends with those who disbelieve [Ar. يتولّون الذين كفروا *yatawallūna alladhīna kafarū*]. Surely ill for them is that which they themselves send on before them: that Allah will be wroth with them and in the doom they will abide'.

[158] Abdullahi, *Ḍiyā' al-sulṭān,* p. 59.

[159] *Ibid.*

[Muslims] having made *muwālāt* with the infidels is infidelity, as al-Maghīlī has pointed out.[160]

As with the question of whether there could be Muslim kingship, Abdullahi grounded his critiques of *takfir* on a close and literalist reading of the Sahelian *fiqh* tradition. However, his plea for the *jamāʿa* to look more closely into each case before making the judgement of *takfir* clearly went against the spirit of an aggressive jihad campaign with a simple message of 'with us or against us'. In his summary of the conflict between Usman and Abdullahi, a fervent supporter of Usman named Abdulkadiri dan Tafa defended the harsh judgements of the early 1800s by presenting them as a necessary evil, given the context in which they had been made: 'In his judgements, the Shaykh had taken into consideration the circumstances of time and place. He adopted the path of rigour and severity in order to intimidate those who might adopt similar behaviour.'[161] Later in the work, dan Tafa speaks of those in the *jamāʿa* who 'condemned Abdullahi because he was not in agreement with the Shaykh [...] going as far as to brand him ignorant and lost'.[162] However, that dan Tafa felt compelled to write a defence of Usman suggests that Abdullahi had received support from those '*Ṭullāb*' who shared his more rigorous, literalist approach to the Sharia.

Another subject of dispute between Usman and Abdullahi that we can link more closely to Abdullahi's experience on the front lines of battle concerned the treatment of Muslims who remained in the *Dār al-Ḥarb* (meaning in this case the lands of the Hausa *sarakai*) after the declaration of jihad. Just as blanket rulings on *takfir* had caused many Muslims to be killed or taken captive, blanket rulings that allowed raiders to claim possessions of Muslims who remained in the *Dār al-Ḥarb* as war booty resulted in wholesale looting: 'Some of them who claimed to be Muslim before this jihad of ours presumed that the possessions they had consumed were *halal* since they heard that we did [not] object to that. But this was not the case.'[163] We saw earlier how Usman attempted to excuse responsibility for these rulings by adopting the cautious approach of *inkār al-ḥarām*: he modified his judgement to say that, while looting was not outlawed, it was better not to do so because it was a subject of *ikhtilaf*. Of course, his

160 Usman, *Najm al-ikhwān*, p. 64.

161 Abdulkadiri dan Tafa, *ʿAshr masāʾil fī-l-khilāf* in Mahibou, *Théorie du gouvernement*, p. 258.

162 *Ibid.*, p. 259.

163 Abdullahi, *Ḍiyāʾ al-sulṭān*, p. 42.

objective here was not to address the issue of stolen property, but rather to preserve his legal authority in the eyes of the *jamāʿa*.

However, in *Ḍiyāʾ al-sulṭān*, Abdullahi again compromised Usman's efforts to shift focus away from these inconsistencies. He argued that Muslims whose possessions were taken in the jihad could reclaim them if they had sufficient proof, even if their possessions had ended up in the *bayt al-māl* [state treasury].[164] Using Usman's pragmatic judgements of 1811, Abdullahi reported that judges on the ground had concocted an elaborate argument to prevent Muslims from pursuing such claims: supposing that the fall of Alkalawa marked the transition of Hausaland from *Dār al-Kufr* to *Dār al-Islām*, a Muslim only had legal recourse to recover possessions taken *after* the fall of Alkalawa. For Abdullahi, this chicanery was unacceptable:

> It is plain to see that the fall of Alkalawa is not a date upon which to base correct legal judgements. What was before it and what is after it is the same. This is what we know from the books [of law]. Whoever claims otherwise, let him come to us with clear evidence and if we find such then we will follow it, if God wills, and if not, then we shall rely on what we know.[165]

The 1804 jihad was meant to liberate the Muslims of Hausaland from an oppressive pagan rule. However, Abdullahi depicted Hausaland post-jihad as a place in which Muslims were actually living at a disadvantage:

> They judge that all the Muslim possessions consumed before the fall of Alkalawa by the infidels who had a peace settlement with us, or a passage of safe conduct, or who claimed to be Muslim, should not be enquired after. If a [Muslim] owner comes across [his possessions], all he can do is either buy them [back] or abandon them. Even if they had taken a free Muslim from us or bought him before [the fall of Alkalawa], the [judges] say that they will not enquire about the matter and they leave [the infidels] to do what they will with the possessions of the Muslims and their womenfolk,[166] to consume their goods and have sexual intercourse with

[164] Abdullahi, *Ḍiyāʾ al-sulṭān,* pp. 41–2. This argument did not apply to those judged to be *muḥāribūn*, such as many nomadic groups, the argument being that whatever possessions they had were likely to have been stolen from others first. For more on this topic see Chapter 4, p. 137.

[165] *Ibid.*, p. 42.

[166] Ar. حريم *ḥarīm*. This may refer to female concubines or female family members.

> their women [...] and what heinous act of Islam is greater than putting free men into servitude and making [Muslim women] sexually available for the infidels and immoral folk![167]

These highly emotive and fantastical claims must have generated considerable unease among the *jamāʿa*. Further, Abdullahi's quip that he and his followers would 'rely on what [they] know' was a clear challenge to the status quo enforced or at least permitted on Usman's authority. Indeed, while Abdullahi at no point referred to his elder brother by name, we gather by Usman's response to his assertions in *Najm al-ikhwān* that he had indeed endorsed such a pragmatic policy when it came to Muslim captives:

> What he [Abdullahi] said was well and good, but I want to inform you all about some points in regard to these issues. In the situation [he] mentioned, if *ḥarbiyyīn* [raiders] present us with a passage of safe conduct and have in their party Muslims whom they took as booty from us, they are not obliged to release them but can instead return with them to their land, whether the captives are male or female, freemen or slaves.[168]

The judgement that Muslims had no right to recover their relatives, their slaves or their possessions lost in war cannot have been the most popular and would surely have been abhorrent for dogmatists such as Abdullahi. However, it was surely the most pragmatic standpoint to take. Hausaland had witnessed some eight years of constant warfare and pillaging. Innumerable captives had been taken on both sides, and many enslaved or forced into concubinage. The fighting also resulted in mass migration. Some settlements and rural areas became depopulated, while others swelled with refugees. The practicalities of locating lost relatives, slaves and possessions in such circumstances would be monumental. Abdullahi, however, was not a pragmatist. He saw his duty as upholding the legal stipulations of the Sharia and rooting out those judgements that did not have a firm precedent within it.

During his early teaching tours, Usman would no doubt have said the same thing. Even in *Tanbīh al-ikhwān*, dated 1811, Usman claimed to make rulings by the maxim 'prefer the usual to the unusual'.[169] In his criticisms of Usman's use of *inkār al-ḥarām*, Abdullahi stuck to this maxim, arguing that a true *muqallid* should always adopt the majority view. Although their disputes were framed in reference to longstanding legal questions,

167 Abdullahi, *Ḍiyāʾ al-sulṭān*, p. 43.

168 Usman, *Najm al-ikhwān*, p. 72. My emphasis.

169 Usman, *Tanbīh al-ikhwān* in Palmer, 'Early Fulani Conception (Continued)', p. 54.

we will see that this exchange was directly relevant both to events on the battlefield and to the authority of Usman as leader.

First, let us examine Usman's judgement on wearing gold. Prophet Muhammad clearly stated that Muslim men were not permitted to wear gold, silk or other fineries. However, faced with many jihadist troops displaying their captured war booty, Usman referred to the story of Surāqa ibn Mālik[170] to rule that they were simply showing 'gratitude to God' for their victory. While the majority of scholars ruled against wearing gold, citing this single hadith allowed Usman to claim that, following the logic of *inkār al-ḥarām*, it was 'one of the subjects over which the scholars are in dispute' and thus could not be forbidden. As we recall, the covetousness and lavish displays of the jihadist troops was one of the reasons Abdullahi left the jihad. In this context, his opposition is not surprising:

> To cite the story of Surāqa as evidence for the permissibility of wearing gold and silver 'out of gratitude to God' does not appear correct to me. The writer of *al-Mi'yār*[171] did not mention this and I did not find any of our Maliki scholars saying anything to this effect. Making Surāqa wear those things was to validate the miracle of the Prophet [...] how can wearing them be showing gratitude [to God] when that is one of the things He has forbidden of us?[172]

Secondly, we come to Usman's judgement on playing musical instruments. Again, the majority of scholars ruled that playing musical instruments was forbidden unless to encourage troops in battle or to celebrate a marriage. Usman cited a single hadith that Prophet Muhammad allowed a drum to be beaten in his honour to rule that musical accompaniment was permitted on other occasions. Abdullahi, who had singled out the playing of musical instruments as one of the outrages he encountered in Kano and claimed to have turned the city's drums into feed troughs[173] naturally

[170] Surāqa ibn Mālik was a member of the Quraysh elite of Mecca. Initially hostile to Muhammad, whom he attempted to assassinate, he later converted to Islam. According to the hadith, Muhammad promised Surāqa that he would one day wear the gold and silver bangles of the Persian king, Khosrow. Years later, after the successful campaign in Persia, Caliph Umar adorned Surāqa, who lay on his deathbed, with the plundered robes of the Persian king, fulfilling the words of the Prophet.

[171] *al-Mi'yār al-mu'rib*, the noted fatwa collection of North African Maliki jurist Aḥmad al-Wansharīsī (1430/1–1508).

[172] Abdullahi, *Ḍiyā' al-sulṭān*, p. 61.

[173] Hiskett, *Tazyīn al-Waraqāt*, p. 121.

disagreed: 'This hadith was either equivocal, inauthentic or abrogated [...] otherwise why else would all the scholars have abandoned it?'[174]

Thirdly, we examine Usman's ruling on dressing in richly decorated clothing. As stated above, the majority of scholars considered this forbidden. However, Usman ruled that it was acceptable for Muslim rulers to wear fine, expensive clothing to gain respect in non-Muslim lands, where people expected their rulers to dress extravagantly. Again, his ruling was based on a single historical anecdote in which Caliph Umar accepted the excuses of Mu'āwiya, Governor of Syria, for having adopted the local Christian dress. As such, it was also 'one of the subjects over which the scholars are in dispute' and thus not forbidden. For Abdullahi, lavish robes were a symbol of the *mulk*, or pagan kingship, discussed above. But his criticism in this case was subtler:

> From the above [words of Usman], we have understood that it is not required for Imams to dress differently to the Companions of the Prophet except under necessity and 'the necessities have rulings of their own'.[175] A situation of 'necessity' results from the breakdown of Islamic law and the absence of respect for religion. Such [a practice] is demanded of every Imam who lives among a nation where the people do not glorify religion so as he does not lose advantage. But as for [the Imam] who differs in dress from the Companions but lives among a nation of people who glorify religion over clothes and other such fineries, his actions are not based on the Sharia but on worldly concerns, so beware of this satanic conspiracy. Know that our community today – God be praised – needs only that its Imam be pious and follow the Sunna. For the most part, its system has not broken down, may God preserve us from that.[176]

Abdullahi's argument was that in a place such as Hausaland where Islam had already been well established, there was no need for a ruler to impress his subjects with fine clothes. In Muslim lands, a Muslim ruler gained respect by following the Sharia and the actions of the Rashidun Caliphs, not by acting like a pagan king. As Usman had said himself, Hausaland after the jihad had become a land of Islam.[177] Therefore, if Usman's excuse was that Hausaland was not 'a nation of people who glorify religion' he was surely contradicting himself. As we saw previously, Usman had changed his mind over the status of Hausaland several times, reflecting

[174] Abdullahi, *Ḍiyā' al-sulṭān*, p. 64.
[175] Ar. فالضرورات لها أحكام آخر, an established legal maxim.
[176] Abdullahi, *Ḍiyā' al-sulṭān*, p. 65.
[177] See Chapter 2, p. 65.

his shift between discourses of dissent and discourses of moderation after the jihad was won. Again, Abdullahi was frustrating Usman's efforts to smooth over the contradictions between them.

Conclusion: From *Ijtihad* to Taqlid

How to view Usman's shifting doctrinal positions depended upon the interpretation of *ijtihad* and taqlid, two terms that have been discussed above. Usman claimed that in invoking *inkār al-ḥarām* he was simply following taqlid in a particularly scrupulous manner. However, Abdullahi and his followers suggested that using minority positions to justify otherwise illegal acts equated to *ijtihad* which, like many of their contemporaries, both Usman and Abdullahi considered appropriate only for the greatest of legal scholars. The following passage from *Najm al-ikhwān* nicely captures this difference of opinion: 'If you said, "What you have done is *ijtihad* […] so how can that be?" the answer is: "This is not *ijtihad*, but rather joining like with like and that is praiseworthy"'.[178]

To complicate matters, Usman's loyal followers such as Abdulkadiri dan Tafa also considered that his actions amounted to *ijtihad*. However, far from undermining his authority as a scholar, it enhanced it:

> [In these judgements] the Shaykh acted as a *mujtahid* and was successful in his *ijtihad*. The singular place that the Shaykh occupies – and his superiority over all the scholars of his age – appeared in a shining light. This *ijtihad* of Shaykh Usman is in and of itself proof of his shared qualities with the Mahdi. It is said that one of the distinctive characteristics of the Mahdi is that in his judgements he will disagree with the majority of scholars.[179]

Thus, while certain members of the *jamāʿa* believed that through *ijtihad* Usman had overstepped the boundaries of the Sahelian knowledge tradition, there were evidently many others whose adherence to the Sokoto project in fact depended on the view that Usman had surpassed all scholars in *fiqh* knowledge.

In an attempt to bring the two sides together, Usman reminded the *jamāʿa* that they should be seeking agreement, not division. In what would seem to be a veiled critique of Abdullahi, he suggested that *ikhtilaf* was no basis to raise a dispute within the Muslim community:

178 Usman, *Najm al-ikhwān*, p. 60.

179 Abdulkadiri dan Tafa, *ʿAshr masāʾil fī-l-khilāf* in Mahibou, *Théorie du gouvernement*, p. 258. Usman had in fact highlighted this similarity with the Mahdi in *al-Khabar al-hādī*, written in 1811.

> The Prophet said: 'The Sharia has three hundred and thirteen ways, and of these ways there is not one by which the servant of God will meet his Lord other than entering paradise'. Thus, only someone who were to know all these paths and find one that does not accord with any of the others has [the right] to dispute. But if he is ignorant of even one path, he does not.[180]

The argument here was that the *fiqh* tradition is so voluminous and so diverse that man cannot possibly grasp it all at once. Thus, any judgement found within an accepted legal school is correct and cannot be disputed. The taqlid that Usman speaks of here is a long way from the blind imitation of legal norms. Rather, it allows for considerable volition on the part of the *muqallid*, who could follow one madhab for a particular issue and a different madhab for another, depending on the need.[181]

Instead of comparing Sokoto with the age of the perfect Rashidun Caliphate, Usman encouraged the *jamāʿa* to reflect on the good things that his rule had brought them:

> Know my brothers that thankfulness is a duty, given what God has bestowed upon you in your time both in religion and in worldly comforts. If it is lacking with respect to what God bestowed upon those ancestors who came before, this is because you are in the end of days and all matters are lacking in the end of days. But despite this, religion endures, and truth is manifest.[182]

Rather than scouring *fiqh* tradition for inconsistencies between the actions of their own leaders and the Rashidun, Usman orders the *jamāʿa* to simply accept what they are told:

> My brothers: occupy yourselves with reading the works of the scholars of your age, because they are the ones who know what is most important in your time. Their works explain what is most beautiful from the works of scholars.[183]

In the final part of *Najm al-ikhwān*, the last work Usman would write that referenced his conflict with Abdullahi directly, he reframed their entire dispute in a positive light, presenting Abdullahi's criticisms as contributions to a shared body of literature:

[180] Usman, *Najm al-ikhwān*, pp. 6–8.
[181] Usman, *Tawqīf al-Muslimīn ʿala ḥukm madhāhib al-mujtahidīn* (Sokoto, n.d.), pp. 40–2, quoting *al-Durar al-multaqaṭa* of ʿAbd al-ʿAzīz al-Damīrī, among other sources.
[182] Usman, *Najm al-ikhwān*, p. 22.
[183] Usman, *Najm al-ikhwān*, pp. 84–5.

> Occupy yourselves with reading the works of my brother, Abdullahi, because he is concerned most often with maintaining the manifest aspects of the Sharia. Occupy yourselves with reading the works of my son, Muhammad Bello, because he is concerned principally with maintaining the knowledge of the policies of the Umma regarding people, goals, times, places and circumstances. Occupy yourselves also with reading my own works, because I am principally concerned with maintaining the two aspects. All of our works explain what is most beautiful in the works of the scholars who have preceded us, and the works of the scholars who have preceded us explain what is most beautiful in the Qur'an and the Sunna.[184]

The notion of the Fodiawa as a 'triumvirate' of scholars, now standard in Sokoto historiography, may first have been conceived in this very paragraph. But knowing what we know, it was far from an accurate reflection of things as they stood at that moment. Rather, it was an attempt by Usman to project the unity of the *jamāʿa* and monopolise his preferred interpretation of the jihad and its future legacy. In his earliest works on *takfir*, Usman had presented himself as the middle ground between extremist students of theology and the *laissez-faire* scholars of the Hausa royal court. Now, he placed himself in the middle ground between the literalist Abdullahi and the more pragmatic Bello.

In a sense, the later works of Usman served to bring the doctrine of moderation to its intended conclusion. If we accept Usman's arguments, his authority no longer came from knowledge and selective deployment of the Sahelian *fiqh* tradition, but from the undeniable fact that he had been victorious in the jihad of 1804 and now held unrivalled control of a growing territorial entity, soon to be known as Sokoto. Curtailing discussion over the legal justification for the Fodiawa's rule allowed Usman – and soon, Muhammad Bello – to create a Muslim state that could nevertheless absorb local traditions of political power. But while the compromises this entailed were vital to assuring the state's survival, they left deep divisions in the *jamāʿa* and foreshadowed the conflict between Bello on the one hand and Abdullahi on the other over the intellectual and political leadership of the Sokoto project.

[184] Usman, *Najm al-ikhwān*, p. 85.

CHAPTER 3

'Lesser of two evils': The Succession of Muhammad Bello

On 20 April 1817, Usman dan Fodio died after a long illness.[1] According to the popular version recounted by Murray Last and others, Abdullahi set off to Sokoto to pay his respects, and expected to discuss the appointment of a new leader. But when he arrived, he found the city gates locked and was told that Muhammad Bello had been appointed Usman's successor.[2] While many different versions of this event exist, including Bello's own telling to Ahmad Lobbo, discussed below, what is clear is that Bello had quickly become *Amīr al-mu'minīn* in mysterious circumstances.

The immediate challenge to Bello's rule came from Abdullahi, who wrote a document contesting the succession. But more broadly, the period 1817–1821 was a difficult time both for Muhammad Bello and the legitimacy of the Sokoto project. Bello continued Usman's work to dismantle the discourse of dissent and framed his rise to power pragmatically as the 'lesser of two evils'. However, copies of those early texts circulated

[1] Last, *Sokoto Caliphate*, p. 60 n.67.

[2] *Ibid.*, p. 65 citing John A. Burdon, *Northern Nigeria: Historical Notes on Certain Emirates and Tribes* (London, 1909) and noting a resemblance to the account given by Wazir of Sokoto Muḥammad al-Bukhārī in Ta'nīs al-ikhwān, written in 1905. Other accounts of the succession exist, although likewise written significantly after the event. See Sa'd ibn 'Abd al-Raḥmān, *Tartīb al-aṣḥāb* (1840–1841); Al-Ḥājj Sa'īd, *Taqāyid* (c.1854); Ahmad b. Sa'd, *Lubāb mā-fī Tazyīn al-waraqāt* (1908); the anonymous *History of Gando* (translated in 1909) as well as an account by Alhaji Umaru recorded in the early twentieth century in Stanisław Piłaszewicz, *Hausa Prose Writings in Ajami by Alhaji Umaru from A. Mischlich/H. Sölken's Collection* (Berlin, 2000). When Clapperton passed through Sokoto in the 1820s he heard that Atiku, another son of Usman, had tried unsuccessfully to claim the succession. See Denham and Clapperton, *Narrative of Travels and Discoveries*, pp. 97–8.

across the Sahel where various actors employed their own 'discourses of dissent' to delegitimise his new regime. This chapter gives a summary of the threats facing Muhammad Bello and how he dealt with them through both military action and discursive argument.

Defending the Succession (1817)

While Usman was alive, the Fodiawa had repeatedly emphasised the need for a Muslim ruler to lead the community – the *Amīr al-mu'minīn* – and discussed at length the qualities he should possess. Before the jihad, they had contrasted this promised ruler to the corruption of the Hausa *sarakai*. Afterwards, Usman and Abdullahi argued over the precise authority held by the ruler and the terms by which he should be addressed. However, Usman had seemingly failed to name a successor before his death and left little clarity as to how the community should appoint their next leader.

Three weeks after Usman died, Abdullahi wrote *Sabīl al-salāma*, a text challenging the legal basis of the succession. Bello, now addressing himself as *Amīr al-mu'minīn*, wrote his response, *al-Inṣāf*, some nine and a half weeks later. The two texts are remarkably similar because both Abdullahi and Bello relied on the same set of Islamic legal sources on the election of a ruler: the well-known *al-Aḥkam al-sulṭāniyya* [The ordinances of government] by Abū al-Ḥasan al-Māwardī (972–1058), who served as a diplomat to two Abbasid Caliphs, as well as later writers such as Abū 'Abd Allāh al-Qurṭubī (1214–1273) and Muḥammad Mayyāra (1591–1662). We have discussed previously the link between quoting and authority in Sahelian knowledge elites. Given the gravity of the situation, it makes sense that both texts consist almost entirely of direct quotations. However, both Abdullahi and Bello skilfully worked with this material to argue that historical precedent was on their side.

As we recall, Abdullahi equated hereditary rule with pagan kingship (*mulk*). He first made this assertion in *Ḍiyā' al-ḥukkām*, which as we recall he composed in Kano during his temporary abandonment of the jihad. He later ruled that the imam should not come to power 'through force, subjugation or inheritance'.[3] A year later, referring to the cautionary words of al-Maghīlī on hereditary succession, he urged his readers to 'reflect carefully [...] it is often for this reason that the relation between a ruler and his subject deteriorates'.[4] Now, in *Sabīl al-salāma*, Abdullahi repeated

[3] Abdullahi, *Ḍiyā' ūlī-l-amr*, f. 2b.

[4] Abdullahi, *Ḍiyā' al-sulṭān* in Mahibou, *Théorie du gouvernement*, p. 76.

al-Māwardī's ruling that upon the death of a ruler the community should form an electoral council to choose the most suitable candidate to replace him.[5] A successor chosen by the previous ruler – that is, Usman – *could* trump the council's decision, unless that choice was 'a son or the father' of the ruler.[6]

If Abdullahi's argument against hereditary succession was not sufficiently clear at this point, he moved to a study of the origins and negative consequences of hereditary rule in Islamic history. Abdullahi cited Muʿāwiya, discussed above, as the first Muslim ruler that had appointed a son to succeed him.[7] As founder of the hereditary Umayyad dynasty, Muʿāwiya declared that he was 'the first of the kings'. As we recall, Abdullahi associated this term with non-Muslim tyrants.[8] Abdullahi demonstrated, through quoting established Muslim histories, that many early Muslims also considered Muʿāwiya's actions illegitimate:

> Muʿāwiya was the first [caliph] to pledge the caliphate to his son. He wrote to Marwān [ibn ʿAbd al-Ḥakām] in Medina, demanding he honour the appointment. Marwān proclaimed [to the Medinans], 'The *Amīr al-muʾminīn* [Muʿāwiya] thinks that to appoint his son Yazid over you is following the Sunna of [Rashidun Caliphs] Abu Bakr and Umar'. ʿAbd al-Raḥmān, son of Abu Bakr, stood up and said, 'This is rather the Sunna of Khosrow and Caesar! Abu Bakr and Umar did not pass [the caliphate] to their sons or to any member of their families'.[9]

What is more, Abdullahi claimed that Muʿāwiya's decision to appoint his son a successor caused a permanent *fitna* of the Umma, divided between those who accepted the rule of Muʿāwiya and his son (who would become the Sunnis) and those who upheld the claim of ʿAli and his son Ḥusayn on the basis of their direct descent from Muhammad (who would become the

[5] Ar. أهل الحل والعقد *ahl al-ḥal wa-l-ʿaqd.*

[6] Abdullahi, *Sabīl al-salāma fī-l-*imāma, NU/Paden 244, p. 2, quoting Mayyāra's *Sharḥ al-Zaqqāq*. Mayyāra gives three schools of thought, two of which rule against hereditary succession from father to son.

[7] Relatively early in his reign, Muʿāwiya appointed his son, Yazīd, as prince regent. Yazīd assumed power after Muʿāwiya's death in AD 680, beginning the hereditary rule of the Umayyad dynasty.

[8] See Usman, *Najm al-ikhwān*, pp. 30, 35, discussed above.

[9] Abdullahi, *Sabīl al-salāma*, NU/Paden 244, p. 9, quoting al-Suyūṭī's *Taʾrīkh al-khulafāʾ*.

Shia): 'had it not been for them appointing their sons, there would have been good counsel between the Muslims until judgement day'.[10]

Having given the example of a proverbially bad ruler, Muʿāwiya, Abdullahi moved on to a proverbially good one, ʿUmar ibn ʿAbd al-ʿAzīz.[11] In previous works, Abdullahi had referred to this ʿUmar as the 'seal of the caliphs'. As opposed to Muʿāwiya, who famously stated that he was unable to follow the path set by the Rashidun, ʿUmar ibn ʿAbd al-ʿAzīz declared upon his accession to power that he would 'return things to how they were in the time of the Messenger of God'. Furthermore, he did not engage in *ijtihad*, humbly stating that he was 'not a lawmaker but an implementer, not an innovator but a follower'.[12]

In Abdullahi's mind, the situation in 1817 offered a clear historical parallel to the circumstances of Muʿāwiya's accession to power: Bello's succession would result in a schism of the *jamāʿa* between those who accepted the succession and those who did not, whereas his own rule would implicitly resemble that of ʿUmar II, in which 'the land filled with justice, iniquities were repelled and the true Sunna was followed'.[13] But given that Bello had already declared himself *Amīr al-muʾminīn*, should the community pay him allegiance? Not unless the ruler 'was like ʿUmar ibn ʿAbd al-ʿAzīz', said Abdullahi.[14] Further, 'if the Imam is unjust, then rebelling against him is just and just rebellion is obligatory until God's religion is made manifest'.[15]

Bello's *Inṣāf* is almost three times as long as *Sabīl al-salāma*. Despite relying on the same set of legal texts as Abdullahi, his depiction of a good Muslim ruler, his duties and the obligations of the community towards him were very different to those of his uncle. While Abdullahi's ideal leader was 'not an innovator but a follower', Bello's was 'a *mujtahid*, not needing anyone else to make fatwas based on hadith'. For Abdullahi,

[10] *Ibid.*, p. 9, quoting from the works of al-Ḥasan al-Baṣrī.

[11] ʿUmar ibn ʿAbd al-ʿAzīz (AD 682–720), also known as ʿUmar II, was an Umayyad Caliph. Because of his attempts to return Islamic governance to what it had been under the Rashidun Caliphs, he is often referred to as the 'fifth' of the Rashidun.

[12] Abdullahi, *Sabīl al-salāma*, NU/Paden 244, p. 10, quoting al-Suyūṭī's *Taʾrīkh al-khulafāʾ*.

[13] *Ibid.*, p. 10, quoting *Sunan Abū Dāwūd*.

[14] Abdullahi, *Sabīl al-salāma* in Minna, 'Intellectual Contribution', pp. 53–5.

[15] Abdullahi, *Sabīl al-salāma*, NU/Paden 244, p. 3. Whether Abdullahi meant this as a threat or not, subsequent rebellions against Bello, discussed below, rested on the accusation that he was an unjust, oppressive ruler.

the singular condition of a good Muslim ruler was that he should know and correctly follow the Sharia. But Bello stated that knowledge in a host of more practical matters such as 'experience and sound judgement in matters of war, the management of armies and the securing of forts' was equally important.[16]

When it came to the election of a ruler, Bello quoted the same passage as Abdullahi concerning the necessity of forming an electoral council. He even conceded that most jurists ruled against hereditary succession. However, he had something of his own to add:

> We have been informed from some of our learned shaykhs that [the imamate] can come together through a third means – that is, through having superior force and might of arms. Opposition [in this case] is forbidden due to committing the lesser of two evils.[17]

Bello's point was that if the most powerful contender came to power through hereditary succession, he should be accepted by all (the lesser evil) to avoid the loss of Muslim life that may arise from challenging him (the greater evil). As Bello put it: 'Even if a slave is appointed by [only] some of the imams, or overturns the country with his power and the strength of his following, he should be heard and obeyed.'[18] In this case, blame for any *fitna* that followed from a succession predicated on 'the lesser of two evils' lay not with the ruler himself, but with those who opposed him. As Bello stated, 'whomever causes dissent among you and divides your community, kill him'.[19]

The hereditary transfer of power to Muhammad Bello carried many negative connotations, both in Islamic tradition and through association with the hereditary rule of the Hausa *sarakai*, whom the Fodiawa had overthrown. Bello made no claims that his ascent to power corresponded to any actions from the Rashidun period, which the Fodiawa had put forward as a model for how Hausaland should be governed after the jihad. Rather, he plainly stated that his rule represented 'the lesser of two evils'. While Abdullahi himself did not contest the succession again (at least in the written sources that are preserved today), the period following their

16 Bello, *al-Inṣāf fī dhikr mā-fī masāʾil al-khilāfa min wifāq wa-khilāf,* Paris (BI) 206, pp. 4–5, quoting al-Qurṭubī.

17 *Ibid.*, p. 32 and adapted from Minna, 'Intellectual Contribution', p. 58. My emphasis.

18 Bello, *al-Inṣāf,* p. 31, quoting al-Nawawī's (*Minhāj al-ṭālibīn*) interpretation of the hadith, 'Hear and obey [your ruler], even if he is a slave'.

19 *Ibid.*, pp. 32–3, quoting Mayyāra. This is a Prophetic hadith.

exchange saw widespread dissent from Bello's rule. Some members of the *jamāʿa* used Abdullahi's arguments from *Sabīl al-salāma* – among his other writings – to claim that Bello had come to power through illegitimate means. Whether Bello meant his harsh words on dissenters as a direct threat to his uncle, he soon engaged militarily – and killed – some members of the *jamāʿa* who had disputed the succession.

A Second Jihad (1817–1821)

After the death of Usman, many of the territories gained in the jihad shook off Bello's attempts to consolidate them under his rule. Bello was forced to reconquer them in what amounted to a 'second jihad'. In reference to those Hausa populations who sought to return their rulers to power, these events are known as the Tawaye Rebellions.[20] But in truth, rebellion against Bello's rule came from many parties besides the Hausa. While our primary interest is in Bello's intellectual response to the rebellions in the form of written texts, we must first review the threats to Bello's rule in this period, and his responses.

First, let us examine the situation in Hausaland. Contrary to popular assumptions, the fall of Alkalawa did not lead to the dissolution of the Hausa state of Gobir. The *sarauta* remained near their erstwhile capital and in 1814, under *Sarki* Gonki dan Kaura Gado, the Gobirawa expelled the governor that the Fodiawa had put in place and were in open rebellion upon Bello's accession to power.[21] Rebellion also raged in much of Katsina and Zamfara as communities restored the power structures that had existed before the jihad. Meanwhile, closer to Sokoto, the *Bā Arewa* leader Abd al-Salam, one of the only non-Fulani to play a prominent role in the jihad, rebelled against Bello after having initially pledged allegiance.[22] Abd al-Salam's attacks on trade caravans bound for Sokoto prevented the Fodiawa from communicating with many of the newly established emirates, as well as Masina.

Not long after his failed succession bid, Abdullahi returned to Gwandu, a town south-east of Sokoto which the *jamāʿa* had fortified during the jihad. He refused to recognise Bello as *Amīr al-muʾminīn* and likewise cut

[20] From Hausa *yan tawaye* [rebel].

[21] See History of Gobir in Moïse A. Landeroin, 'Notice historique', in J. Tilho (ed.), *Documents scientifiques de la mission Tilho, 1906–1909* (3 vols, Paris, 1909), vol. 2, pp. 309–552. English translation in Jean Boyd Papers, SOAS special collections.

[22] See Bello, *Sard al-kalām*, analysed in Last, '"Injustice" and Legitimacy'; 'From Dissent to Dissidence'.

off communications with Sokoto.[23] He did nothing to help Bello against the Tawaye. Soon after Usman's death, Abdullahi asked Ahmad Lobbo to pledge allegiance to him and not Bello, addressing himself as *Amīr al-mu'minīn*. He subsequently accepted Lobbo's arguments for independence from Sokoto at a time when Bello adamantly refused them.[24]

To the east, in Bornu, the power of al-Amīn al-Kānamī, whose missives against the jihad had caused the Fodiawa so much anxiety, was growing ever stronger. Al-Kānamī wished to restore Bornu's western territories that the Fulani had captured in the jihad, including the old Bornu capital of Birni Gazagamu, also known as Ngazargamu. In 1814 he built his own capital, Kukawa, and his authority quickly came to overshadow that of the *Mai*.[25] To the west, in Masina, was Ahmad Lobbo. Lobbo had earlier pledged allegiance to Usman in return for the latter's endorsement of his jihad against Ségou.[26] After Usman's death, Bello requested that Lobbo pledge allegiance to him as Usman's successor. Buoyed by his victory at Noukouma in 1818, Lobbo refused.[27]

In the north, *aneslem* Ait Awari Tuareg leader, Muhammad al-Jaylānī, had established a reformist community inspired by Usman's *jamā'a* at his stronghold east of Tahoua. From there, between 1809 and 1815 al-Jaylānī and his followers raided *imajeghen* Tuareg clans such as the Kel Gress, Itesen, Kel Away and Iwellemmedan in Ader and Air, whom they branded non-believers. However, al-Jaylānī's new regime proved unpopular.[28] An alliance of Temezgidda and Kel Gress defeated al-Jaylānī, and in 1816 he

[23] *Sokoto Caliphate*, p. 42. Last, '"Injustice" and Legitimacy', suggests Abdullahi's seclusion in Gwandu was an 'exile option' offered to him by Bello.

[24] See [Abu Bakr 'Atīq MS] analysed in Ahmad M. Kani and Charles C. Stewart, 'Sokoto-Masina Diplomatic Correspondence', *Research Bulletin, Centre of Arabic Documentation, University of Ibadan*, 11 (1975), 1–12. This correspondence will be discussed below.

[25] Brenner, *Religion and Politics in Bornu: The Case of Muhammad Al-Amin Al-Kanemi*, p. 166.

[26] See Amadou Hampaté Bâ and J. Daget, *L'empire peul du Macina* (Paris, 1962), p. 36; *[Abū Bakr 'Atīq MS]*.

[27] See Kani and Stewart, 'Sokoto-Masina Diplomatic Correspondence', discussed below. On Ahmad Lobbo and Masina, see William A. Brown, 'The Caliphate of Hamdullahi, ca. 1818–1864: A Study in African History and Tradition' (Unpublished PhD dissertation, University of Wisconsin, 1969) and Nobili, *Sultan, Caliph, and the Renewer of the Faith*.

[28] Benedetta Rossi, *From Slavery to Aid: Politics, Labour, and Ecology in the Nigerien Sahel, 1800–2000* (New York, 2015), p. 51.

fled to Sokoto.[29] The alliance, headed by a fellow *aneslem*, Ibra of the Temezgidda, now took their raids to Sokoto's northern territories, allying with the Hausa Tawaye. Despite Bello offering him sanctuary in Sokoto, al-Jaylānī wavered in his allegiance, accusing Bello of hypocrisy when the latter had rebuked him for his raids against the Tuareg.[30]

Beyond Masina were the Kunta of Azawad. As we recall, the Kunta lent considerable spiritual support to the jihad of 1804 by granting Usman the Qadiri *wird*. Although no record exists of how the Kunta viewed Bello's succession, they did not share his enthusiasm for al-Jaylānī, whose Islamic revivalism damaged their relations with the Tuareg and compromised their own missionary activity in the region.[31] Given the scarcity of sources, at this point in time their position regarding Ahmad Lobbo is unclear.[32] However, the Kunta later supported Lobbo enthusiastically and backed his caliphal claims.[33]

In sum, in the period 1817–1821 Bello faced rebellions from the irredentist Hausa *sarauta*, many of the non-Fulani supporters of the jihad, as well as attacks from the Tuareg. Borno threatened invasion[34] and Ahmad Lobbo of Masina refused to pledge allegiance to him, as did his own uncle, Abdullahi. The Kunta were supportive in word, but their pragmatism and, perhaps, clerical pacifism prevented them from taking any practical steps to assist him.[35] The *jamāʿa* also remained divided due to the longstanding

[29] Harry T. Norris, *The Tuaregs: Their Islamic Legacy and its Diffusion in the Sahel* (Warminster, 1975), p. 154; Rossi, *From Slavery to Aid*, pp. 50–1.

[30] See Norris, *The Tuaregs*, pp. 156–7.

[31] *Ibid.*, p. 158.

[32] Ahmad Lobbo's aggressive forays into Fittuga threatened to disrupt grain imports to Timbuktu as well as salt and tobacco exports to Gwandu and Sokoto. Kani and Stewart in 'Sokoto-Masina Diplomatic Correspondence' argue that, like Bello, the Kunta also refused to accept Lobbo's independence from Sokoto and even supported unsuccessful rebellions against Lobbo's rule in Fittuga. However, Nobili in *Sultan, Caliph, and the Renewer of the Faith* suggests that their attitude was one of pragmatism, containment and compromise, and that the Kunta only expressed hostility to Lobbo after he invaded Timbuktu in 1826.

[33] See al-Mukhtār ibn Muḥammad al-Kuntī, *[Poem in nūn: advice to the Fulani]*, Timbuktu (BMH) 23201; *[Poem in praise of Ahmad Lobbo]*, Timbuktu (BMH) 20897. Both texts are accessible online via www.vhmml.org/readingRoom.

[34] See exchange in the *Infaq* between Bello and al-Kānamī in Shādhilī, *Infāq al-maysūr*, pp. 229–86.

[35] For example, Bâ and Daget, *L'empire peul du Macina*, p. 109, assert that during Al-Bakkā'ī's visit to Sokoto, Bello asked him to help defend

disagreements between Usman and Bello on the one hand and Abdullahi and his followers on the other. Still, Bello had the Fulani elite in Sokoto on his side, and those Fulani emirs who had not been deposed by the Tawaye remained loyal to him.[36]

The reasons for rejecting Bello's authority to rule were as numerous as the rebellions facing him. Evidently, the irredentist Hausa never recognised the new regime in Sokoto. They wished to reclaim the territory they had lost in the jihad and wreak vengeance on the Fulani specifically for raiding their towns and taking their dependents captive. Abd al-Salam, who did fight on the jihadist side, clearly stated that his desertion of Bello stemmed from his disappointment at the share of the territory he received after the jihad, and his belief that this was a result of his being non-Fulani.[37] The jihad's non-Fulani supporters had already witnessed the excesses of Fulani mercenaries fighting in the jihadist armies. Usman's appointments to the new emirates had been exclusively Fulani, while the 1812 division of territories – Abd al-Salam's paltry share excepted – was between the Fodiawa's inner circle of Fulani clan leaders. Bello's appointment as *Amīr al-mu'minīn* confirmed suspicions that the jihad had turned into a 'family affair' in which non-Fulani were not welcome. Thus, as Murray Last reasons, 'the Sudani element in the jihad movement began to detach itself from the leadership' and sought to rule their own territories independently.[38]

Tuareg resistance to the jihad meanwhile was never ideological, but rather driven by internal clan divisions. *Ineslemen* Tuareg such as al-Jaylānī were more likely to support the jihad, while most *imajeghen* would oppose it.[39] Given that Bello was a vocal supporter of al-Jaylānī's movement and provided shelter for him in Sokoto, it made sense that those *imajeghen* Tuareg who wished to avenge themselves of the latter's

Sokoto's trade routes from Tuareg incursions. Al-Bakkā'ī replied that his 'religious preferences and family status and traditions' would contradict such a course of action.

36 For a list of these emirs see Shādhilī, *Infāq al-maysūr*, p. 309.

37 Bello, *Sard al-kalām*. See Minna, 'Intellectual Contribution', pp. 413–20; Zehnle, *A Geography of Jihad*, pp. 441–4. In Alhaji Umaru's account of the 1812 division of territories (Piłaszewicz, *Hausa Prose Writings*) Abd al-Salam is tricked out of his share by a conspiracy between the Fodiawa.

38 Last, '"Injustice" and Legitimacy', p. 48. See analysis of *Sard al-kalām*, below.

39 *Sokoto Caliphate*, p. ix; Minna, 'Intellectual Contribution', p. 98.

raids would ally with the Tawaye and attack Sokoto.[40] As for Ahmad Lobbo, he may well have been genuinely at a loss for what to do, given the demands of allegiance from both Abdullahi and Bello and the loss of contact with Sokoto. However, his continued refusal to recognise Bello as *Amīr al-muʾminīn,* even after Bello had suppressed the Tawaye and reconciled with Abdullahi, suggests that he had sought to rule independently of Sokoto all along.[41]

By 1821, Bello had removed most of the immediate challenges to his rule through military means. In 1817, he launched several attacks on the Gobirawa, killing *Sarki* Gonki and forcing his followers to flee further north under Ali dan Yakubu, who suffered several more defeats before suing for peace in 1823.[42] In January 1818, Bello's forces attacked the community of Abd al-Salam, who was wounded and later died in Zamfara.[43] Al-Ḥājj Saʿīd reports a rumour that after defeating Abd al-Salam in 1817, Bello planned to turn his attentions to his uncle, explaining Abdullahi's hurried move from Bodinga to Gwandu around eight months after the succession.[44] For several years, a group of Tawaye led by Dan Boya held Gwandu under siege from their base at Kalambayna.[45] In 1821, Bello sent his Wazir, Gidado dan Layma, to negotiate with the rebels.[46] After the negotiations broke down, the combined forces of Sokoto and Gwandu sacked Kalambayna.[47] With this victory complete, so the story goes, Abdullahi recognised Bello as *Amīr al-muʾminīn* and Bello, for his part, recognised Abdullahi as Emir of *Gwandu.*[48] Separately, in 1820, al-Kānamī sent Bello

[40] 'Intellectual Contribution', p. 96.

[41] Inferred in Bello, *Jawāb shāfin li-l-murīd.* See Table 1, p. 114.

[42] See History of Gobir in Landeroin, 'Notice historique'.

[43] Last, '"Injustice" and Legitimacy', p. 55.

[44] Minna, 'Intellectual Contribution', p. 61, citing al-Ḥāj Saʿīd, *Taqāyīd mimmā waṣala ilaynā* in Charles E. Whitting, *History of Sokoto* (Kano, n.d.), p. 190.

[45] Gwandu, 'Abdullahi B. Fodio as a Muslim Jurist', pp. 56–7.

[46] Muhammad S. Zahradeen, ''Abd Allāh ibn Fodio's Contributions to the Fulani Jihad in Nineteenth Century Hausaland' (Unpublished PhD dissertation, McGill, 1976), p. 185. It is unclear whether Abdullahi asked for Bello's assistance directly, or Bello came of his own accord having heard that Gwandu was in danger of falling. According to *Tartīb al-aṣḥāb,* a source otherwise favourable to Abdullahi, assistance from Bello came only after a desperate appeal from a wife of Abdullahi. See Gwandu, 'Abdullahi B. Fodio as a Muslim Jurist', p. 85.

[47] 'Abdullahi B. Fodio as a Muslim Jurist', p. 85. See also Balogun, 'The Place of Argungu'.

[48] Balogun, 'Succession Tradition', p. 20; *History of Gando,* p. 8. While the

a letter establishing the border between their two territories, leading to a temporary peace between Sokoto and Bornu.[49] Ahmad Lobbo continued to assert his independence but did not threaten Bello territorially. With time, Sokoto-Masina relations became cordial.[50] Meanwhile, the Tuareg leader Ibra continued to cause problems for Bello, but with the Tawaye Rebellion suppressed, Bello had greater freedom to deal with the Tuareg threat in isolation.[51] The Kunta increased their friendly relations, crowned by the visit of Aḥmad al-Bakkāʾī, grandson of al-Mukhtār ibn Aḥmad al-Kuntī, to Sokoto in the late 1820s.[52]

'Fear them not, but fear me': Enforcing Obedience to Bello's Rule

Bello compared the rebellions against him to the situation facing Caliph Abu Bakr after the death of Prophet Muhammad, which led him to reconquer much of the early caliphate by force in what are known as the Ridda Wars.[53] The comparison was apt. Various actors in the Sahel region – both Muslim and non-Muslim – had used Usman's death as an excuse to renege on their promises of allegiance. A 'second jihad' was the most immediate way to enforce obedience to him as ruler. However, in a series of works precisely dated to this same historical period, Bello also set out the intellectual grounds through which he could demand such obedience from his sceptical or outright rebellious subjects.

In what follows, we will investigate these arguments in detail. First, the rebellion of Abd al-Salam, which occurred soon after the succession,

---

story is probably apocryphal, it nevertheless served to illustrate the rapprochement between Sokoto and Gwandu, confirmed by Lobbo's comments in his exchange with Bello, discussed below.

[49] Minna, 'Intellectual Contribution', pp. 137–8, citing a letter from al-Kānamī reproduced in Landeroin, 'Notice historique'.

[50] Bello *[Maktūb fī radd masāʾil ʿan Aḥmad Lubbu]*. In the absence of a formal title I adopt the title devised by Nobili, *Sultan, Caliph, and the Renewer of the Faith.*

[51] See Minna, 'Intellectual Contribution', pp. 94–9.

[52] See Bâ and Daget, *L'empire peul du Macina*; Abdelkader Zebadia, 'The Career and Correspondence of Ahmad Al-Bakkay of Timbuctu: An Historical Study of His Political and Religious Role from 1847 to 1866' (Unpublished PhD, SOAS, University of London, 1974). Bello later set out a vision of mutually beneficial relations with the Kunta in *[Letter to al-Mukhtār ibn Muḥammad ibn al-Mukhtār al-Kuntī]*, which he wrote in 1825–6. This document is analysed in Minna, 'Intellectual Contribution', pp. 361–3.

[53] See Bello, *Miftāḥ al-sadād.*

and Bello's own account of these events, *Sard al-kalām fī-mā jarā baynī wa-bayn Abd al-Salam* [The dialogue that passed between me and Abd al-Salam]. As outlined above, Abd al-Salam was one of the Fodiawa's few prominent non-Fulani supporters. Bello described him as the leader of the *Bā Arewa* or 'Northerners', a reference to the Mawri people centred around Dogondoutchi in present-day Niger.[54] Like Usman, Abd al-Salam had been a well-known teacher and reformer before the jihad. Prior to the hijra of Usman, Abd al-Salam had already made his own hijra from Gobir territory to Kebbi, building a settlement and attracting many followers. Most histories of the jihad point to the Gobirawa's attack on this settlement, Gimbana, and the jihadists' forcible release of those they had taken captive as the starting point of the jihad itself.[55]

In 1817, Abd al-Salam swore allegiance to Bello after some hesitation. During the Tawaye Rebellions, Bello commanded Abd al-Salam – like other regional rulers – to send him troops and cease communications with the rebels. Instead, Abd al-Salam sent a reply declaring Bello a *ẓālim* [oppressor] and cut off contact, arguing that the unity of the Muslims was no longer desirable if it resulted in the harm of one party.[56] This was a clear reference to the perceived injustices towards non-Fulani under Usman, and now under Bello. To prove his point, Abd al-Salam drew a map for Bello demonstrating his paltry share of the 1812 division of territories compared with that given to the Fodiawa and other Fulani.[57] In conscious imitation of Usman's actions vis-à-vis the ruler of Gobir, Abd al-Salam declared his settlement, just outside of Sokoto, a sanctuary for refugees fleeing Bello's suppression of the Tawaye. He also opened his gates to traders from non-Muslim territories. His justification, again, was that obedience was not due to an oppressor who 'transgressed the right [course]'.[58]

[54] See Bello, *Sard al-kalām fī-mā jarā baynī wa-bayn Abd al-Salam,* Kaduna (NA), f. 1a. Ar. من قبيلة أريو *min qabīlat Arīwa*. Historically, the *Arewa* lived between areas of Hausa and Songhay influence, and speak the Zarma language. See Marc H. Piault, *Histoire Mawri: introduction à l'étude des processus constitutifs d'un État* (Paris, 1970).

[55] For more on the history of Abd al-Salam before 1817 see Bello, *Sard al-kalām*; Last, '"Injustice" and Legitimacy'; Zehnle, *A Geography of Jihad*, pp. 329–30.

[56] Bello, *Sard al-kalām*, Kaduna (NA), unpublished English translation by Hermann G. Harris, pp. 9–14; Minna, 'Intellectual Contribution', pp. 413–20.

[57] See analysis in Zehnle, *A Geography of Jihad*, pp. 441–4.

[58] Bello, *Sard al-kalām* in Harris, pp. 17–19. As we recall, Abdullahi invoked this argument in *Sabīl al-salāma*, discussed above, on p. 98.

After Bello learned that Abd al-Salam had welcomed the Emir of Kore – a non-Muslim – to his community, he wrote to Abd al-Salam demanding that he hand the Emir and his entourage over to Sokoto. Abd al-Salam suspected that Bello considered the people of Kore – as non-Muslims – to be enslavable, replying, 'I deem it best not to send them because I am like one of themselves'.[59] In response, Bello summoned the Emir's brother and supported his takeover of Kore if he converted to Islam. Meanwhile, the by then erstwhile Emir of Kore, with the help of Abd al-Salam, returned to Kore to restore his rule. Because the new Emir installed by Sokoto had become a Muslim, Abd al-Salam was, in effect, helping a pagan king regain his throne.

As we recall, Usman's judgement was that *naṣr* [help] given to infidels against Muslims constituted *takfir*. By sticking by this judgement, Bello could argue that Abd al-Salam's actions amounted to apostasy.[60] While apostasy justified Bello's military intervention against him,[61] what is more striking is that Bello went on to conflate this apostasy with the refusal to pay him allegiance:

> Those who were with him acknowledged him as their prince and he proclaimed the word '*tawaye*' [...] it is a word that has been appointed by the Infidels and the warriors as a mark of entrance into their path and of admission into their religion.[62]

Yet not all the 'Tawaye' resisting Muhammad Bello's succession were non-Muslim. Furthermore, it is highly unlikely that Abd al-Salam renounced his Muslim faith given that in Bello's own account he framed his refusal to pay allegiance within Islamic legal tradition. His support of the Emir of Kore had more to do with ethnic solidarity in the face of perceived Fulani injustices than any change of faith. But as he had done with the

[59] Bello, *Sard al-kalām* in Harris, p. 19.

[60] Bello even included this precise definition of *muwālāt* in the title of his treatise on the subject written in September 1819, *Kashf al-ghiṭā' wa-l-sitr fī muwālāt al-kuffār (bi-ma'nā al-naṣr)* [Revealing the cover and the veil concerning friendship with the infidels (meaning aiding them)].

[61] Based on his reading of *Sard al-kalām*, Last, '"Injustice" and Legitimacy', suggests that Bello formulated a 'strategy' for dealing with dissent. This strategy forced the dissenters into committing an act of apostasy, justifying military action against them. He cites Bello sending a 'tempting' caravan past Gimbana, which Abd al-Salam raided. I think this may be reading too much into the case.

[62] Bello, *Sard al-kalām* in Harris, p. 21.

Hausa *sarakai* in *Infāq al-maysūr*, Bello entrenched the association of Abd al-Salam's rebellion with unbelief by using racialised language to set him apart from others in the *jamāʿa*, decribing Abd al-Salam as 'a man from the blacks'.[63] The implication was that all who resisted Bello's rule whether directly or by assisting the rebels were unbelievers. This undoubtedly closed the ranks of the *jamāʿa* behind Muhammad Bello. His victory over Abd al-Salam in battle strengthened the argument that he had made to Abdullahi: 'might makes right' and that obeying him was the 'lesser of two evils'.

But Abd al-Salam's community was not the only one to consider Bello an unjust ruler. During the same period, Muhammad al-Jaylānī told Bello that since he had taken power many considered him 'an oppressor'. In his response, Bello turned al-Jaylānī's statement on its head to argue that 'oppression' does not come from power, but rather from its absence:

> Even a perfect Caliph will be incapable of establishing justice if he can find no assistance. Religion, if not raised up by consensus, will descend into warring factions. In this manner, [a ruler] is strengthened by his people and weakened for lack of them.[64]

Following Bello's logic, his so-called 'oppression' was in fact his assertiveness in establishing the right and removing the iniquitous:

> It is no sin that God Almighty commanded us to promote the good and forbid the bad, to enter into allegiance and to wage jihad, to establish mosques, appoint judges [...] and implement many of the rulings of the Sharia.[65]

True oppression was thus a result of the *fitna* that accompanied a lack of firm governance. It followed that people who were obedient to their leader would be free from *fitna*. It was in this spirit that Bello felt able to order his emirs to conduct jihad against the Tawaye 'because of the

[63] Ar. *Rajul min Ahl al-Sūdān* in Bello, *Sard al-kalām*, f. 1. *Kanz al-awlād* describes Abd al-Salam and his followers as *Nūbī* [Nubian] and *Zanj*, pejorative terms commonly used further west in Masina and Timbuktu, where Sambo Kulwa claimed to have studied.

[64] Bello *[Risāla ilā Muḥammad al-Jaylānī]*, Niamey (MARA) 1744, pp. 5; 8. Note that there is some confusion between this document and another of Bello's responses to al-Jaylānī, *Jawāb shāfin wa-khiṭāb minnā kāfin*. While Hunwick & O'Fahey (*ALA 2*, p. 121) say that this text is the same as the *[Risāla]* quoted here, MX Niamey 1744 is a different document.

[65] *Ibid.*, p. 9.

obligation of obedience to the leader'[66] rather than as a religious duty to help oppressed Muslims, which had been the prevailing argument during the jihad of 1804.[67]

Another legitimacy problem for Bello was the *Ṭullāb*, that is, those followers of Abdullahi who equated the rulings Usman made after the jihad in works such as *Naṣīḥat ahl al-zamān* with *ijtihad*. The *Ṭullāb* only increased their attacks once Bello became *Amīr al-mu'minīn*. But in defending Usman, Bello adopted a different legal approach than Usman's doctrine of *inkār al-ḥarām*. His leadership of the *jamā'a* assured, Bello stated that he would abandon *ẓāhir al-fiqh* – that is, the literal or outward meaning of Islamic law – in favour of *legal principles* whose applications changed according to the needs of the community and, of course, the needs of its ruler.[68] In *Najm al-ikhwān*, Usman had stated that *ẓāhir al-fiqh* was the principal merit of Abdullahi's works. Now, working with legal principles and not literal meanings meant that as leader, Bello would have a far greater command of the law than either Usman did or Abdullahi would have done. The new principle of *rifq* [tolerance][69] in legal interpretation when it came to upholding the 'common good'[70] allowed Bello the flexibility to make new policy decisions specific to the local context without reference to standard works of Islamic law.[71] As we will see in the

[66] Bello, *Risāla li-l-amrāḍ shāfiya fīhā naṣīḥa li-l-aghrāḍ kāfiya* (quoting al-Qurṭubī) in Muhammad Shareef, 'A Letter of Healing' (1995) http://siiasi.org/wp-content/uploads/2014/12/Risaalat-LilAmraad.pdf [accessed 9 September 2020], p. 108.

[67] See Bello *[Letter to Emir Ya'qūb]*.

[68] Bello, *Shifā' al-asqām fī dhikr madārik al-aḥkām*. This is a summary of a longer work, *al-Taḥrīr fī qawā'id al-tabṣīr*. The text is undated, but Minna, 'Intellectual Contribution', p. 184n, suggests that Bello wrote it after his succession or shortly before Usman's death when he was leader 'but in name'. Bello wrote another related text: *Shams al-ẓahīra fī minhāj ahl al-'ilm wa-l-baṣīra*. I was unable to consult a copy of this work and I am basing my understanding of its content on the summary given in Minna, 'Intellectual Contribution', pp. 185–92.

[69] See Bello, *The Political Thought of Muhammad Bello*, pp. 213–20. See also Muhammad Bello's reply to Ahmad Lobbo concerning his misunderstanding of these policies in *[Abū Bakr 'Atīq MS]*.

[70] Ar. *al-maṣāliḥ al-mursala*. For an explanation of this concept see Gwandu, 'Abdullahi B. Fodio as a Muslim Jurist', pp. 172–89.

[71] For more on tools of flexibility in Islamic law in the Sahelian tradition see Charles C. Stewart, *Islam and Social Order in Mauritania: A Case Study from the Nineteenth Century* (Oxford, 1973), especially pp. 69–70.

following chapter, Bello grounded these rulings not on Islamic authorities of the past, but on his own authority as the established Muslim ruler of a large and powerful territory.

The *Ṭullāb* (as well as al-Kanemi and Ahmad Lobbo) also questioned whether Bello – then in his thirties – had the necessary experience and legal know-how to assume leadership of the *jamāʿa*. Bello had already released some details about his education, written in direct response to Abdullahi's *Īdāʿ al-nusūkh* and therefore, although the work is undated, at some point after 1812.[72] There, his aim had been to demonstrate that he too had studied widely, under a range of teachers. In this text, Bello dedicated only a single paragraph to his father, Usman, as the first of his teachers, while the list of works he cited was a modest: twenty-nine, comparable to Abdullahi's thirty-eight.[73] Faced with the undeniable fact of his age and – in comparison with his uncle – relatively limited legal education, Bello nevertheless found a way to use his hereditary succession, which would otherwise count against him, to his bolster his claims to authority in Islamic law.

In *Shifāʾ al-asqām fī dhikr madārik al-aḥkām* [Cure for sickness by mentioning faculties of judgement], Bello's response to many of the *Ṭullāb*'s criticisms against him, he claimed to have read 'innumerable numbers of books. I even counted them over some days, getting to 20,300 books'.[74] The subjects he listed covered all areas of the Sahelian 'core curriculum' of Islamic learning but especially the areas of *tafsīr*, *fiqh* and hadith interpretation – all areas in which his judgement was being challenged. However, Bello did not place the emphasis on the works themselves, but on the unlikely and contradictory assertion that he had studied the majority of them at the feet of his father. The *jamāʿa* recognised Usman as the *Nūr al-zamān* [Light of the Age], the foremost scholar of his time. The idea that he had been consciously tutoring Bello made a strong case for the hereditary succession so excoriated by Abdullahi and other Muslim authorities in the region.

A close connection to Usman also helped Bello to energise and channel the more popular Mahdist sentiments circulating in the *jamāʿa*. Like Usman before him, Bello was in the awkward position of both needing to

[72] Bello, *Ḥāshiya ʿalā muqaddimat Īdāʿ al-nusūkh*. The question of when exactly Bello wrote this text is discussed in Naylor, 'Abdullahi Dan Fodio and Muhammad Bello's Debate over the Torobbe-Fulani'.

[73] Bello, *Ḥāshiya ʿalā muqaddimat Īdāʿ al-nusūkh*.

[74] Bello, *Shifāʾ al-asqām fī dhikr madārik al-aḥkām*, Niamey (MARA) uncatalogued, f. 5a.

demonstrate Mahdist knowledge while finding a means to delay or redirect radical millenarianism that could threaten his rule. In *Qawl al-mukhtaṣar*, written in 1820, Bello stated that the Mahdi would appear in AH 1280 [AD 1863], in effect leaving his successors to deal with the problem.[75] Similarly, in an undated letter written to Modibbo Adamu, who had been a flag-bearer of the jihad in Adamawa, Bello instructed him to

> dispatch troops to the south of Wadai, the south of [Dar]fur and to the banks of the Nile because our Shaykh told us that his community would reach these parts by the time of the Mahdi's appearance to join him and pledge allegiance to him.[76]

By pro-actively preparing for the Mahdi's appearance at a point in time after his rule, and at a location conveniently far from Sokoto, Bello could conceivably rally to his side those who would otherwise have joined a more anarchic Mahdist movement.[77] But Bello's predictions were only believed because of his close connection to Usman and his repeated hints that Usman had entrusted him with some kind of secret knowledge before he died.[78]

When attempting to summarise Bello's various justifications for his succession and his demands of obedience we need look no further than the first chapter of Bello's kingship manual, *al-Ghayth al-wabl fī sīrat al-imām al-ʿadl* [Abundant downpour concerning the conduct of the just leader].[79] In the text, Bello affirmed what was implied in his earlier

[75] Albasu, 'Bello's Views on the Mahdi', p. 16.

[76] Bello, *[Majmūʿ baʿḍ al-rasāʾil]*, pp. 12–16.

[77] Minna, 'Intellectual Contribution', p. 337, considers Bello's works on the Mahdi during the period of succession crisis a 'weapon for political control'. Meanwhile Albasu, 'Bello's Views on the Mahdi', p. 14, suggests that he was also influenced by the millenarian theories of al-Ḥasan al-Bilbālī.

[78] See *Wathīqa ilā jamāʿat al-muslimīn*, Niamey (MARA) uncatalogued, f. 2b: 'the Shaykh did not pass away until he had made rulings and ensured I had inherited understanding' and *Shifāʾ al-asqām*, f. 6b: 'he [Usman] acquainted me with the finest points of his knowledge and made me aware of the strange aspects of his hidden things [Ar. *gharāʾib maknūnātihi*]'. Bello's reliance on Usman when it came to *kashf* is confirmed by Gidado dan Layma's hagiographic biography of Bello, *al-Kashf wa-l-bayān ʿan baʿḍ aḥwāl al-sayyid Muḥammad Bello b. al-shaykh ʿUthmān*. Bello's successor, Atiku, would also rely heavily on the possession of secret knowledge from Usman to bolster his rule.

[79] Written in 1820 or 1821, the text is a summary of Bello's previous words of advice to regional emirs. See O. S. Ismail and A. Y. Aliyu, 'Bello and the Tradition of Manuals of Advice to Rulers', in *Nigerian Administration Research Project, Second Interim Report* (Zaria, 1975), pp. 54–73.

correspondences: that obedience to the ruler is obligatory even if the ruler is unjust. He went as far as to say that:

> Verily by means of the corrupt ruler [*al-fājir*] Allah protects the roads, jihad is undertaken by him against the enemies, the dead lands are revived, the prescribed punitive punishments are established, pilgrimage is made to the House [Mecca] and by means of him the Muslim worships Allah safely until his appointed time comes.[80]

The discourse of dissent against the Hausa *sarakai* was founded on the notion that an unjust and corrupt ruler deserved no allegiance. Indeed, the Fodiawa had relied upon the precedent set by al-Maghīlī when he told the *Askiya* that unjust rulers ought to be designated unbelievers.[81] After the succession went to Bello, Abdullahi commented that rebellion against an unjust ruler was not only lawful but the correct course of action. But now Bello used a Qur'anic injunction to demand that the *jamāʿa* pay unwavering loyalty to him as *Amīr al-muʾminīn* regardless of his critics: 'In order to make it easier to accept what I am telling you, if you are people of good sense[82] then "save such of them as do injustice – Fear them not, but fear Me!"'[83] While Bello framed the obligation of obedience within Islamic history and legal traditions, he also relied increasingly on the power bestowed by his succession through 'might of arms' and the example of his violent repression of the Tawaye.

Creating a Caliphate: Bello's Exchanges with Ahmad Lobbo

Throughout the first four tumultuous years of Bello's reign there was a steady exchange of correspondence between Muhammad Bello in Sokoto and Ahmad Lobbo in Masina. As we recall, it seems that Lobbo had originally expanded the jihad to the west under Usman's flag but after Usman's death reneged on his pledge. Instead, he embarked upon his own project of

[80] Bello, *al-Ghayth al-wabl*, adapted from Muhammad Shareef, 'The Abundant Downpour' (2002) http://siiasi.org/wp-content/uploads/2014/12/Chapter-1-_Ghayth_.pdf [accessed 9 September 2020], p. 15, quoting the words of ʿAlī ibn Abī Ṭālib as related by Imām al-Bayhaqī.

[81] Usman, *Sirāj al-ikhwān*, Chapter 5, quoting al-Maghīlī's *Ajwiba*.

[82] Ar. *Ahl al-rushd wa-l-falāḥ*.

[83] Bello, *Shifāʾ al-asqām*, f. 4b. The quoted text is Qur'an 2:150 and is addressed by God to Muslims fearing recrimination from those in the Umma who contested Muhammad's decision to change the direction of prayer from Jerusalem to Mecca.

state creation in what is today the Mopti region of Mali, known as Masina or by the name of its principal town, Hamdallahi. Too far away for Bello to repress militarily, the two men instead engaged in a tense intellectual conflict, most of which was collated by Bello's successors and survives today. An analysis of these exchanges allows us to capture Bello's aspirations for Sokoto, both regarding the exact land area that it was to control directly and the precise authority he wished it to hold relative to other Muslim powers in the region. In broader terms, Bello moved beyond the discourses of dissent and moderation that had characterised the period immediately before and after the jihad. He crafted a new sort of authority for himself that depended less on the various legitimations grounded in the textual world of the Sahelian tradition and instead on the reality that he now represented a nascent and powerful Muslim state.

During their communications, Bello defeated those rebellions against him that were closer to home and silenced his critics in Sokoto. It is therefore no surprise that Bello explained his succession to Lobbo in a far more direct manner than he had to Abdullahi:

> The imamate is achieved by two means. The first is by *ikhtiyār* [free choice], to which many conditions are attached depending on the time and the ability. The second is by *iḍṭirār* [compulsion], for which none of the above conditions need apply but belief in Islam and that the majority of people flock to [the claimant] on account of the superiority of his power.[84]

As we recall, Abdullahi vilified Caliph Muʿāwiya was a tyrant who permanently divided the Umma and brought about the end of the Rashidun Caliphate by appointing his own son as successor. In his correspondence with Lobbo, Bello created a different view of Muʿāwiya informed not by *fiqh* standards such as al-Māwardī but by his own interpretations of historical works such as *al-Bidāya wa-l-nihāya* [The Beginning and the End] of Ibn Kathīr. For Bello, Muʿāwiya's succession as described by Ibn Kathīr represented the first instance of the 'lesser of two evils' argument by which Bello had defended his own succession: 'In this instance, allowing the transfer of power to him who is not permitted to take it is less damaging than allowing *fitna* to emerge, for which there is no cure

[84] Bello, *Jawāb shāfin li-l-murīd,* MS Kaduna (NA), digitised as BL (EAP) 535 1/2/1/10, pp. 2–3. Although Bello mentions that this information can be found in the works of '[Abu Bakr] al-Khaffāf and others', the rendering is his own. This response to Ahmad Lobbo has escaped attention, not appearing in *ALA 2*. It may have been confused with Bello's response to al-Jaylānī, *Jawāb shāfin wa-khiṭāb minnā kāfin.*

Table 1 Pertinent Written Exchanges between the Fodiawa and Ahmad Lobbo c. 1817–1821. In collaboration with Mauro Nobili. Adapted from Ahmad M. Kani and Charles C. Stewart, 'Sokoto-Masina Diplomatic Correspondence', Research Bulletin, Centre of Arabic Documentation, University of Ibadan, 11 (1975), 1–12

No.	Date	Source/Title	Correspondence			Purpose
1	1817*	Mentioned in [*Abū Bakr ʿAtīq MS*]	Lobbo	→	Usman	Offering allegiance and requesting authority for his jihad
2	c.1817	Mentioned in [*Abū Bakr ʿAtīq MS*]	Abdullahi	→	Lobbo	Requesting allegiance to him as Amīr al-muʾminīn
3	c.1817	Mentioned in [*Abū Bakr ʿAtīq MS*]	Bello	→	Lobbo	Requesting allegiance to him as Amīr al-muʾminīn
4	after 1817	Cited in [*Abū Bakr ʿAtīq MS*]	Lobbo	→	Abdullahi	Explaining his refusal to pay allegiance
5	after 1817	Mentioned in [*Abū Bakr ʿAtīq MS*]	Abdullahi	→	Lobbo	Accepting his break in allegiance
6	c.1821**	Cited in [*Abū Bakr ʿAtīq MS*]	Lobbo	→	Bello	Explaining his refusal to pay allegiance
7	c.1821	Cited in [*Abū Bakr ʿAtīq MS*]	Bello	→	Lobbo	Rejecting his break in allegiance
8	c.1821	Mentioned in Jawāb shāfin li-l-murīd	Lobbo	→	Bello ***	Asking for clarification
9	c.1821†	*Jawāb shāfin li-l-murīd*	Bello	→	Lobbo	Expanding on the reasons for rejection
10	1821–1828‡	[*Maktūb fī radd masāʾil ʿan Aḥmad Lubbu*]	Bello	→	Lobbo	Summarising Lobbo's arguments and his responses

* According to Ba & Daget (1962), Lobbo sent a delegation to Sokoto to seek support for the battle of Noukouma, which took place in 1818, in the form of a flag from Usman. That Usman gave a flag suggests that the delegation had pledged allegiance to him. Usman died in April 1817 and thus the pledge will probably have been made earlier that year. That such a pledge was made is proven by some comments in *Jawāb shāfin li-l-murīd* and *[Abū Bakr ʿAtīq MS]*.

** See *[Abū Bakr ʿAtīq MS]*, MX Kaduna (NA) p .13: 'and as for our continuing [not to pledge allegiance] <u>after</u> we heard of the resolution of the issue between you [Bello and Abdullahi]'. My emphasis. Therefore, Lobbo probably wrote his reply after the battle of Kalambayna had taken place in 1821.

*** The existence of this letter is assumed by Bello's comment in *Jawāb shāfin li-l-murīd*, discussed in †.

† See *Jawāb shāfin li-l-murīd*, p. 1: "[Your messenger explained] that you were obliged to withhold [allegiance] for the second [time?] […] We consider our [first] answer [i.e. Letter no. 7?] to be sufficient […] but when you requested even more [in way of an answer], we wrote to you what came to mind […]". A reference to rebellions closing the road between Sokoto and Masina suggests that Bello wrote this second reply soon after his first – after his reconciliation with Abdullahi but before he had entirely suppressed the "second jihad" following his succession.

‡ Written before the death of Abdullahi but after the above correspondences, all of which are summarised therein. Probably never sent to Masina.

and no salvation.'[85] He invited Lobbo to 'follow the histories' to see that from eleventh-century Al-Andalus to the Ottoman Empire, the principles of 'the lesser of two evils' were always followed. Bello paid no attention to Caliph ʿUmar ibn ʿAbd al-ʿAzīz, so revered by Abdullahi for his attempts to return Umayyad government to the standards set by the Rashidun. Instead, he focused on later rulers of largely hereditary dynasties, such as the Ottoman Caliph Suleiman the Magnificent. What appealed to Bello was not the extent to which these later rulers followed the ways of the Rashidun, but the degree of authority they wielded and the reach of their territorial power.[86] These historical examples reflected Bello's ambitions to expand his own territories. They also confirmed his earlier argument that the candidate with the greatest power would best serve the Umma.

The main purpose of Bello's exchanges with Ahmad Lobbo was to demand Lobbo's obedience to him as *Amīr al-muʾminīn*, as he had done with other regional figures discussed above. For this, Bello engaged another legal maxim – *al-Awwal fa-l-awwal* [Preference to the first] – to argue that since Lobbo had pledged allegiance to Usman and that Usman had chosen Bello as his successor, Lobbo owed Bello allegiance as well. However, this argument depended upon Bello producing evidence that Usman had explicitly chosen him as a successor. This point was not raised in the dispute between Bello and his uncle, and Lobbo flatly dismissed the event as a fabrication. Bello countered that in fact Usman *had* made a written pledge to this effect in front of the Sokoto elite:

> Know that I am surprised when he [Ahmad Lobbo] said so. If he was far away when the covenant was written [*katb al-ʿahd*], those present wrote to him about that while giving him their excuse for not waiting for him, and to the effect that the covenant had been confirmed.[87]

He went on to say that Lobbo must respect Usman's choice and 'maintain the pledge as it should be', making clear that the consequences of reneging on such a pledge would be severe:

[85] *Ibid.*, pp. 3–4.

[86] Bello, citing al-Suyūṭī's *Taʾrīkh al-khulafāʾ*, noted (*ibid.*, p. 14) that 'the majority of lands of Islam were under his [Caliph Suleiman's] obedience such as Iraq, *al-Sham* [the Levant], Yemen, Egypt, *al-Ḥaramayn* [Mecca and Medina], *Ifrīqiyya* [Tunisia], *Barqa* [Eastern Libya], *al-Jazāʾir* [Algeria] and more besides'.

[87] Bello *[Maktūb fī radd]*, translation in Minna, 'Intellectual Contribution', p. 109.

> It is plain to see from the outset that you did indeed pledge allegiance and hesitation after all doubt has been eliminated is not acceptable.[88] Not showing allegiance to one to whom it is due is judged to be rebellion [*khurūj*].[89]

But regardless of the existence (or not) of a written pledge, Ahmad Lobbo revealed that the true reason for reneging on his allegiance to Sokoto was because he did not think that Bello's rule should apply to Masina:

> Look upon this with a just eye: did your ruling [jurisdiction] reach us since the death of our Shaikh, the late 'Uthmān, up to the present date? If you are certain that your rule did not reach us, on this basis is it not then permissible to have more than one ruler?[90]

Quoting from Abdullahi's *Ḍiyā' al-ḥukkām*, Lobbo reasoned that it was permissible to have more than one Muslim ruler if the *Dār al-Islām* grew so large that communication between distant regions became impossible. In reference to Bello's claim over Masina, Lobbo retorted that if he expected allegiance from regions where his rule could not reach, Bello might as well claim that Al-Andalus and Khorasan (regions at opposite ends of the classical Muslim world) belonged to him as well. Bello's response was that 'the reaching of their [Masina's] books on *bay'a* is enough for unity and necessitates his obedience to what I order'.[91] However, Lobbo's reference to Al-Andalus and Khorasan prompted a lengthy argument between the two men in which each sought to outcompete the other in geographical knowledge.

The clearest takeaway from their exchange is that the Muslim scholarly elite of the nineteenth-century Sahel had formed no consensus as to what the nearest Muslim power to their region was, or what degree of allegiance they might owe it. The nearest representatives of the Ottoman Caliphate to the Sahel region were Yusuf Karamanli, Pasha of Tripoli, and Muhammad Ali, Pasha of Egypt, although by the early nineteenth century the latter ruled independently of Istanbul. The Alaouite dynasty of Morocco also claimed the *khilāfa* due to their alleged descent from 'Alī ibn Abī Ṭālib, Prophet

[88] Presumably, Bello is referring to the confusion over whether Lobbo should pledge allegiance to himself or to Abdullahi.
[89] Bello, *Jawāb shāfin li-l-murīd*, p. 25.
[90] *[Abū Bakr 'Atīq MS]* in Charles C. Stewart, 'Frontier Disputes and Problems of Legitimation: Sokoto–Masina Relations 1817–1837', *The Journal of African History*, 17:04 (1976), 497–514, at p. 504.
[91] Bello *[Maktūb fī radd]*, Kaduna (NA), digitised as BL (EAP) 535 1/4/1/9, f. 2b.

Muhammad's cousin and son-in-law.[92] In fact, Bello made clear that while Usman was alive, paying allegiance to a greater Muslim state was never in doubt, although the question of which one remained unanswered:

> He [Usman] ordered me to write letters of allegiance to the Caliph in Istanbul and send him a gift. I told him, 'Shouldn't the letter be written to the one who is in Fez? For he is a Qurayshi, while the one in Istanbul is a Turk'. However, Usman said, '[No,] he is the one who is in the line of communication and the majority of the Muslims are with him'. Therefore, I wrote letters and had them sent to the Lord of Tripoli [Pasha Yusuf Karamanli] who sent them on to him. However, it was not possible for me to send the gift.[93]

Returning to the argument between Bello and Lobbo, the latter's point was that because a superior Muslim authority existed in another part of the world – whether in Tripoli, Fez, Cairo or Istanbul – the Fodiawa were at best only regional emirs to these larger Muslim states. As such, they did not have the authority to appoint emirs themselves, or demand allegiance from other regions.[94] However, using geographical works such as Ibn Wardī's *Kharīdat al-ʿajāʾib* [Pearl of wonders], Bello argued that Sokoto and Masina were sufficiently close to have a common ruler:

[92] Representatives of the Alaouite Sultan were also aware of and supported the jihad of 1804, which they had heard about through Muḥammad al-Bāqirī, Sultan of Agadez. A Moroccan representative urged al-Bāqirī to join the jihadists and sent a separate letter to Usman supporting his jihad. See Stewart, 'Frontier Disputes', pp. 512–13; Minna, 'Intellectual Contribution', pp. 123–6, citing *Infāq al-maysūr* in which these letters appear. According to Stewart, the Alaouite Sultan named Usman his representative [Ar. *nāʾib*] in the Bilād al-Sūdān, a region he considered part of his territories although Minna (cited above) disputes this interpretation.

[93] Bello, *Jawāb shāfin li-l-murīd*, pp. 35–6. Bello continued his correspondence with Yusuf Karamanli, who referred to Bello as *Ṣāḥib wilāyat al-Sūdān* [Lord of the Province of *al-Sūdān*] just as Bello referred to Karamanli as *Ṣāḥib (wilāyat?) Ṭarābulus* [Lord of the Province of Tripoli]. This terminology suggests that the two men considered the Ottoman Caliph as a common superior, but the evidence is far from conclusive. See Adrian D. H. Bivar, 'Arabic Documents of Northern Nigeria', *Bulletin of the School of Oriental and African Studies,* 22:1 (1959), 324–49, at pp. 344–8.

[94] See Lobbo *[Maktūb fī radd]*, ff. 2b–3a: 'as you are well aware, all that was mentioned concerns caliphs and not regional emirs [*umarāʾ al-bilād*] such as we have'.

> It should be obvious to the likes of you that this region in which both you and I live is one country. The issue of a distance the like of that between Khorasan and Al-Andalus does not figure. This south-western, *Sūdānī*, *Takrūrī* region forms some parts of the province [*iqlīm*] of Egypt.[95]

As outlined above, Bello understood Egypt to be only a representative of the Ottoman Caliphate in Istanbul. He observed that Istanbul was very far from Sokoto and Masina such that '[t]he news of its ruler or his jurisdiction does not reach us'.[96] As such, Bello concluded that 'if the seat of the Imam is so removed that he cannot enforce his rule in some far-off lands, it is permissible to appoint someone else [to govern] that region.[97] In sum, Sokoto and Masina –while far enough away from other Muslim polities to necessitate the establishment of an independent Muslim state – were close enough to allow for only one Muslim ruler to govern it, himself. This was because his predecessor, Usman, 'was the first to show *imāma* in this region'.[98]

The assertion that Usman was 'the first' to establish Muslim statecraft in the region raised certain issues. Leading up to the jihad, the Fodiawa had made no such claims. In fact, citing the precedent of *Askiya* Muhammad of Songhay was what connected the Sokoto project to the region's longstanding traditions of Muslim governance.[99] What is more, the terminology of leadership was important. During his lifetime, Usman allowed himself to be known as *Shaykh* or *Amīr al-Mu'minīn* but abstained from using terms that suggested anything more than a very localised authority.[100] A 'Sokoto Caliphate' would therefore have been incongruous at this time. But in his exchange with Lobbo, Bello contested that Usman had been more than, in Lobbo's words, a 'regional emir':

95 Bello, *Jawāb shāfin li-l-murīd*, p. 18.

96 Bello *[Maktūb fī radd]*, translation in Minna, 'Intellectual Contribution', p. 108.

97 Bello, *Jawāb shāfin li-l-murīd*, p. 20.

98 *Ibid.*, p. 34. Here *imāma* is meant with the sense of commanding Muslim leadership.

99 Lobbo himself referenced this tradition, replying (*ibid*, p.34): 'this point is not obvious to me, for he [Usman] was preceded by the just Amir *Askiya* who waged jihad and thereafter undertook the Hajj. Al-Maghīlī composed for him his famous *Ajwiba* and likewise al-Suyūṭī'.

100 Although interestingly, the History of Gobir in Landeroin, 'Notice historique', states that after the fall of Alkalawa, Muḥammad al-Bāqirī conferred the title of *Sarkin Gobir* on Muhammad Bello. However, the Fulani insisted on the more significant title of *Sarkin Musulmi* [Chief of Muslims].

> Our Shaykh was chosen for the caliphal office […] and if he was a Caliph, after his appointment it is not permissible for anyone in this region to claim that office. Those [who live] in this region can do nothing but pay allegiance to him.[101]

As evidence, Bello cited a familiar passage of *Naṣīḥat ahl al-zamān* in which Usman says – in reference to al-Suyūṭī's interpretation of the hadith of the twelve caliphs – 'I hope that I am the first of them and the awaited Mahdi the second'.[102] If Bello's interpretation seems surprising to us, Lobbo was also taken aback: 'I never heard such words, nor did he put it in any book – and it was not in his nature to conceal.'[103] Lobbo's incredulity suggests that Usman's limited geographical claims, as well as the fact that 'caliph' was a title that could be conferred only in specific circumstances, was common knowledge in the wider region.[104] However, the issue is more complex than this. A letter circulated by Lobbo's supporter, Nūḥ ibn al-Ṭāhir, claimed *Ahmad Lobbo* was the heralded twelfth caliph in the aforementioned hadith.[105] If the letter (or at least the ideas it contained) was in circulation at this time, it would certainly explain Lobbo's reticence to accept a 'caliph' in Sokoto.

The exchange between Muhammad Bello and Ahmad Lobbo did not result in any significant geopolitical changes. Lobbo continued to rule independently of Sokoto, and during Bello's reign relations between Sokoto and Masina became open and relatively cordial.[106] However, what

[101] Bello *[Maktūb fī radd]*, f. 3a.

[102] This passage has been discussed above in Chapter 2, p. 68.

[103] Bello *[Maktūb fī radd]*, f. 6a.

[104] See Lobbo in *Jawāb shāfin li-l-murīd*, p. 34: 'God alone knows what the writer [Bello] intended [by these words] for it is not permissible for anybody to be appointed to caliphal office […] rather there are narrowly defined procedures'.

[105] See Mauro Nobili, 'A Propaganda Document in Support of the 19th Century Caliphate of Ḥamdallāhi: Nūḥ b. al-Ṭāhir al-Fulānī's "Letter on the Appearance of the Twelfth Caliph"(Risāla fī ẓuhūr al-khalīfa al-thānī 'ashar)', *Afriques*, 7 (2016), although Nobili estimates that it was composed after the date of these exchanges. The letter proclaims Lobbo to be the twelfth caliph after *Askiya* Muhammad, with no mention of the Mahdi. This may explain the lack of comparable Mahdist agitation in Masina during the early nineteenth century.

[106] Bello, for example, wrote to Lobbo informing him of Hugh Clapperton's arrival and his desire to travel westwards into Masina territory. From *[Abū Bakr 'Atīq MS]* we understand that Bello soon apologised to Lobbo for the views he expressed during this earlier dispute.

is noteworthy is that Bello and his successors carefully maintained this correspondence and even produced fresh summaries that in all likelihood were never sent to Masina.[107] This suggests a domestic use of such texts, namely, creating and maintaining the authority of Muhammad Bello and his successors as rulers of a Muslim state, Sokoto.

Conclusion

The promise of correct Islamic governance inspired by Prophet Muhammad's early community lent considerable legitimacy to the jihadist movement. However, the hereditary succession of Muhammad Bello and his demands of obedience led some in the jamāʿa to return to the discourse of dissent, branding him another 'oppressive' ruler who must be toppled to preserve Muslim lives. But Abdullahi's fruitless attempts to overturn the succession effectively ended that intellectual challenge to Bello's rule. With the mandate provided by his victory over the Tawaye and the continued expansion of the jihadist state, Bello emphasised that when it came to political power, 'might makes right'. Although he did not generate the same spiritual fervour as his father, with the widespread belief among the *jamāʿa* that Usman had experienced *kashf*, Bello nevertheless reaffirmed and repurposed these beliefs to justify his own rule, emphasising his personal connection to Usman not just as his preferred son but as an inheritor of both *zahir* and *batin* knowledge. In converting the problematic aspects of his succession into a source of legitimacy for his rule, Bello was also aided by a rich tradition of Muslim historiography that had sought to make sense of turbulent political change and justify the rise of powerful family dynasties that seemed to transgress the ideals of Muslim statecraft.

Bello envisioned Sokoto as a Muslim state on a par with established powers in the region such as Alaouite Morocco, Agadez, and even the Ottoman Caliphate, which required him to subtely change Usman's legacy and, in effect, 'create' a caliphate. That he faced such resistance from Ahmad Lobbo shows the extent to which Sahelian elites kept a careful eye on the written output of their contemporaries. It also demonstrates that Usman's Arabic writings had already become a touchstone for debates over authority and legitimacy.

In his future writings, Bello largely dispensed with the kinds of legitimacy devices required for the discourses of dissent and moderation, which

[107] *[Maktūb fī radd]* was probably compiled by Bello between 1821–8. *[Abū Bakr ʿAtīq MS]* was produced by Bello's successor, Atiku, in the years 1837–42.

ultimately rested on emphasising different 'modes' existing within Islamic legal and spiritual traditions. Instead, he came to rely principally on his own authority as a Muslim ruler to be 'feared and obeyed'. In Bello's parting words to Lobbo, he warned that 'by withdrawing your hand from obedience comes the corruption of your religion'.[108] Although he was unable to force Masina to return to Sokoto's control, by equating his own rule with 'Islam' and all resistance to him as *fitna*, the sort of power Bello claimed for himself was becoming less the power to define right from wrong claimed by a scholar and more the monopoly on violence claimed by the state.

[108] Bello, *Jawāb shāfin li-l-murīd*, p. 37.

CHAPTER 4

'God has subjugated this land for me': Bello's Rule of Sokoto 1821–1837

> To announce to the people any public measure [...] the city crier is sent round, who first proclaims, 'This is the will of the sultan;' the people replying 'Whatever the sultan does, is good; we will do it'.
>
> – Records of Captain Clapperton during his first visit to Sokoto, March 1824[1]

Sokoto is typically written about as a coherent political and cultural system. Power radiated out from the *Amīr al-muʾminīn* through a system of emirates and sub-emirates who paid yearly taxes and in-kind tributes to the capital. Titled officials in the large and complex courts of the Amirs managed all aspects of day-to-day administration, from the operation of the law courts, to tax collection, the supervision of markets and the design of streets and sanitation systems.[2] Forts, palaces, city walls and gates were constructed in a unique architectural style, while manufacturing centres such as Kano produced a rich material culture of clothing, textiles, leather goods and handicrafts.[3] The system was fuelled by the labours of the approximately one quarter to one half of Sokoto's inhabitants who were

[1] Denham and Clapperton, *Narrative of Travels and Discoveries*, p. 97.

[2] See Sa'ad Abubakar, 'The Emirate-Type Government in the Sokoto Caliphate', *Journal of the Historical Society of Nigeria*, 7:2 (1974), 211–29.

[3] See Colleen Kriger, 'Textile Production and Gender in the Sokoto Caliphate', *The Journal of African History*, 34:3 (1993), 361–401; Mark D. DeLancey, 'The Spread of the Sooro: Symbols of Power in the Sokoto Caliphate', *Journal of the Society of Architectural Historians*, 71:2 (2012), 168–85; 'Moving East, Facing West'; Hakim and Ahmed, 'Rules for the Built Environment'; Murray Last, 'Contradictions in Creating a Jihadi Capital: Sokoto in the Nineteenth Century and Its Legacy', *African Studies Review*, 56:2 (2013), 1–20.

enslaved in the *gandu* [plantation] system or performing other forms of unfree labour in the homes of the wealthy.[4]

In this stable (and atemporal) depiction, the Sokoto state was legitimate because it competently performed the vital functions of governance, such as securing borders and delivering justice, as well as presiding over an economic system that generated adequate wealth and status for the free inhabitants, while ensuring that the enslaved remained in bondage. This was in addition to functions specific to Muslim statecraft such as the construction of mosques and schools, the management and distribution of zakat and the furtherance of jihad to expand the borders of the state and replenish its supply of captive labour.[5]

The kind of legitimacy associated with states and the good performance of state functions (akin to the bureaucracy which, according to Weber, represented 'the purest type of legal authority') came to full fruition under Sokoto's later rulers, and as such will not be discussed here.[6] However, Muhammad Bello's unchallenged rule from 1821 until his death in 1837 set many of them in motion. The records of British explorer Hugh Clapperton, who visited Bello's court in 1824 and again in 1826, capture this period of Sokoto's history in vivid detail.[7] The system of ribats as well as the planned cities of Sokoto and Wurno are the lasting physical manifestations of Bello's grand vision.[8] But many of the distinctive features of Sokoto

[4] See Lovejoy, 'Plantations in the Economy'; *Slavery, Commerce and Production.*

[5] On this last point see James Richardson's description of Zinder, which was dependent upon slave raiding for trading goods across the Sahara, in James Richardson, *Narrative of a Mission to Central Africa, Performed in the Years 1850–51* (London, 1853), pp. 204–18; 263–72.

[6] Max Weber, 'The Three Types of Legitimate Rule', trans. Gerth, *Berkeley Publications in Society and Institutions*, 4:1 (1958), 1–11, at p. 8.

[7] Clapperton's interaction with Bello is recognised as a significant early encounter between a West African ruler and the agent of a Western power. See Jamie Bruce Lockhart and Paul E. Lovejoy, *Hugh Clapperton into the Interior of Africa: Records of the Second Expedition, 1825–1827* (Leiden, 2005); Lovejoy, *Jihād in West Africa.*

[8] See Nasiru I. Dantiye, 'A Study of the Origins, Status and Defensive Role of Four Kano Frontier Strongholds (Ribats) in the Emirate Period (1809–1903)' (Unpublished PhD dissertation, Indiana University, 1985); Mohammed B. Salau, 'Ribats and the Development of Plantations in the Sokoto Caliphate: A Case Study of Fanisau', *African Economic History*, 34 (2006), 23–43; John E. Philips, *Black Africa's Largest Islamic Kingdom before Colonialism: Royal Ribats of Kano and Sokoto* (Porter Ranch, 2016).

society first originated in the Arabic texts that Bello authored during his rule. In these writings, Bello decided upon the groups suitable for reform and incorporation into Sokoto's collective identity, such as the nomadic Fulani, those to be expelled from it, such as the Tuareg, and those fated to serve it with their unfree labour and that of their descendants.[9] Indeed, by setting the standards by which a person could be legally enslaved and linking enslavability with precise geographical locations, Bello established the rules by which the plantation economy and the continued expansion of jihad functioned in tandem.

Bello's writings during this period presuppose the existence of Sokoto as a territorial entity with geographical limits, containing subjects that could be classified and controlled on his word. Such can be understood from his work *Qadḥ al-zinād fī amr hāthā-l-jihād* [Striking the flint in the matter of this jihad], which from internal references he wrote some time after the Tawaye Rebellions. The document is, at first appearance, a collection of various chapters of *Infāq al-maysūr*, which Bello wrote back in 1812. However, he updated the text of the *Infāq* to reflect the new circumstances of his rule, including changing the third person pronouns he had used to refer to his father, Usman, to refer to himself in the first:

> As for today [Hausaland] has become a house of Islam, for God has removed its blemishes and maintained its purity due to the blessing of this Shaykh [Usman]. His appearance was a gift from God, who made his hands manifest miracles and dazzling lights [...] God has subjugated this land for me [...] I uphold the prayer and I distribute zakat and I carry out holy war.[10]

This new positionality – which is also understood from his exchange with Ahmad Lobbo and confirmed by his subsequent consolidation of power after 1821 – had a demonstrable effect on discourse and the discursive form of written texts. Bello was no longer compelled to frame his thoughts and arguments within the legitimising language of the wider Sahelian *fiqh* tradition. In fact, he ceased to make 'arguments' at all and instead enacted policies that – emanating from the *Amīr al-muʾminīn* – carried inherent authority in and of themselves. With Bello's own word

[9] One is reminded of Renan's dictum on both the exclusivity and selective memory of a state: 'the essence of a nation is that all of its individuals have many things in common, and also that they have forgotten plenty'. Ernest Renan, *Œuvres complètes d'Ernest Renan* (8 vols, Paris, 1952), vol. 1, p. 892.

[10] Bello, *Qadḥ al-zinād*, f. 13a. My emphasis. Compare with Shādhilī, *Infāq al-maysūr*, pp. 299–300.

so faithfully obeyed, the authority conveyed by the quoted word became far less important. With Bello actively shaping his own local context of Sokoto, examples from the wider Muslim tradition were less relevant.

This chapter attempts to show how the familiar image of a Sokoto Caliphate had its genesis in the Arabic texts Bello composed during his rule. It also explores what we know of Abdullahi's rule of Gwandu Emirate. Few documents survive from Abdullahi's tenure as Emir between his apparent rapprochement with Bello in 1821 and his death in 1828.[11] But what we know of Gwandu's later history suggests that Abdullahi had initiated a very different kind of Muslim statecraft to Bello's Sokoto; one more in keeping with his own concepts of rightful authority in Islam.

Policies of Integration: The Hausa

As we recall, one cause for the Tawaye Rebellions was the perceived discrimination of non-Fulani by the Sokoto elite. Bello's plan for Sokoto was, in the words of John E. Philips, a 'new, urban Islamic society in which Hausa became the lingua franca but which was multi-ethnic in orientation'.[12] Of course, describing Bello's empire as 'multi-ethnic' does not suggest that he regarded all of these ethnicities equally. But it was under the term 'Hausa' that Bello sought to integrate the majority of his subjects, greatly expanding the definition of that term since the time of the Hausa *sarakai*.[13] Thus began a 'Hausafication' that continued well into the colonial period.[14] This multi-faceted process involved the reinstatement of some of the symbolism and court ritual of the old Hausa *sarauta*, as well as cultural practices from the wider Hausa world. But on the other hand, it also involved a rapprochement of the Fodiawa's own genealogical claims to Arab origin with the West African setting. Some of these processes and changes are captured in Arabic texts, while others can be surmised by

[11] Texts from Gwandu are conspicuously absent from Nigeria's national archives, although Zahradeen, *'Abd Allāh ibn Fodio's Contributions*, noted that some private manuscript collections remain in Gwandu.

[12] John E. Philips, 'Ribats in the Sokoto Caliphate: Selected Studies, 1804–1903' (Unpublished PhD dissertation, University of California, Los Angeles, 1992), p. 232.

[13] Lovejoy, *Slavery, Commerce and Production*, pp. 22–3.

[14] Moses Ochonu, 'Colonialism within Colonialism: The Hausa-Caliphate Imaginary and the British Colonial Administration of the Nigerian Middle Belt', *African Studies Quarterly*, 10:2–3 (2008), 95–127.

the observations of Hugh Clapperton and other Europeans who travelled through Sokoto during the nineteenth century.

The Fodiawa's jihad movement had the explicit aim of removing the Hausa *sarakai* from power but it also targeted Hausa cultural practices that were not expressly forbidden in Islam.[15] Such can be understood from one of Bello's earliest works, *Rafʿ al-shubha fī-l-tashabbuh bi-l-kafara wa-l-ẓalama wa-l-jahala* [Removing vagueness concerning imitating the infidels, the iniquitous and the ignorant], which supposedly records the practices of the Hausa ruling classes before the jihad. It dates to 1801, when Bello was barely 20 years old, and reflects the *jamāʿa*'s growing militancy against the Hausa *sarakai*.

When we compare the information in this document with the observations made by Hugh Clapperton during his two visits to Sokoto over twenty years later, it is remarkable how many of these practices – which the young Bello had labelled *kufr* – survived or were perhaps even revived during Bello's tenure as *Amīr al-muʾminīn*. Among Bello's list of the 'deeds of the iniquitous' is 'wearing excessively ornamented clothing and other contemptible adornments'. On his first visit to Sokoto, in 1824, Clapperton described Bello's dress without comment.[16] But upon meeting him again two years later he remarked that Bello now 'dresses better' and on that day was wearing 'the finest tobes that the country produces'.[17] Another point that Bello listed in his 1801 treatise was that the Hausa 'take a *muqaddam*', which the copyist described as 'a slave boy that precedes his mount'.[18] Clapperton remarked during his second visit that each regional emir had 'a crying man' who preceded his horse, matching this description.[19] In

[15] Stanisław Piłaszewicz, 'Legitimacy of the Holy War and of the Sokoto Caliphate in Some Fulani Writings, Oral Traditions and Court Practices', *Africana Bulletin,* 37 (1991), 35–47, at p. 36.

[16] Denham and Clapperton, *Narrative of Travels and Discoveries*, p. 83: 'He was dressed in a light blue cotton tobe, with a white muslin turban, the shawl of which he wore over the nose and mouth in the Tuarick fashion'.

[17] Lockhart and Lovejoy, *Hugh Clapperton into the Interior of Africa*, p. 28.

[18] Bello, *Rafʿ al-shubha fī-l-tashabbuh bi-l-kafara wa-l-ẓalama wa-l-jahala,* Niamey (MARA) 283. I deduce that this explanation comes from the copyist since two other examples (NU/Wilks 116 and NU/Hunwick 8) do not include a definition for *muqaddam*. The Hunwick copy, which is a market edition, also differs in its wording. The *muqaddam* is probably a reference to the *zegui*, a male of slave descent cultivated to be fervently loyal to the *Sarki*. His job was to walk before the *Sarki*'s horse and frighten enemies away with his shouts. See Rossi, *From Slavery to Aid*, p.157.

[19] Lockhart and Lovejoy, *Hugh Clapperton into the Interior of Africa*, p. 279.

1801, Bello listed playing musical instruments among the 'actions of the *jāhiliyya*', yet in 1824 Clapperton was welcomed by the 'drums and trumpets' of Bello's escort.[20] Further documents describing Bello's court show how its multitude of positions resembled the Hausa *sarauta* system, including large numbers of stable masters, court eunuchs and concubines.[21] Meanwhile, those positions that *were* Islamically sanctioned – such as *Amīr al-jaysh* [Commander of the army] – soon became known by their Hausa equivalents.[22]

We should not view the disparity between Bello's views as hypocritical. Aside from illustrating the contrast between the idealism of youth versus the pragmatism of later years, Bello was simply following his father's appeal to take into account time and circumstance, which as we saw in the preceding chapter he had advanced to advocate abandoning the literal meaning of the law in favour of *legal principles* whose applications changed according to the needs of the state. Now, as ruler of a vast empire, it made sense for Bello – as it did also for the Abbasid and Ottoman Caliphs whom he held in such high esteem – to maintain an elaborate court structure and conspicuous consumption for the purposes of patronage. More positions meant that competing groups could all be satisfied, and their loyalty bought, reducing the chance of another coordinated rebellion against him.[23]

The modified Hausa culture that Bello introduced into the elite, male-dominated and urban world of Sokoto's garrison cities cemented his rule there. However, it had little effect in the Hausa countryside, where various localised cultural practices competed with the new state ideology. One of

20 Denham and Clapperton, *Narrative of Travels and Discoveries*, p. 77.

21 See for example *Majmūʿ aṣḥāb al-sayyid amīr al-muʾminīn Muḥammad Bello* [Companions of Amīr al-muʾminīn Muhammad Bello], written by Gidado dan Layma. See also *Fihirist bi-asamāʾ wa-aṣḥāb wa-wuzarāʾ Amīr Muḥammad Bello* [Catalogue of the names, companions and ministers of Muhammad Bello]. The names of these individuals suggest a wide range of ethnicities and backgrounds.

22 Piłaszewicz, 'Legitimacy of the Holy War and of the Sokoto Caliphate', pp. 45–6.

23 For more on empire and ethnicity see Frederick Cooper, *Citizenship between Empire and Nation* (Princeton, 2014). A more immediate reason for the spread of Hausa language and culture in Sokoto society was the fact that the Fulani elite routinely married among the Hausa. Waziri Junaidu, born in 1906, was obliged to teach himself Fulfulde – and produced a handbook for others to do so – because it was no longer commonly spoken. See Hunwick and O'Fahey, *ALA 2*, p. 200.

these was *Bori*, a spirit possession ritual that remained popular in rural areas as well as in the irredentist Hausa states centred around Maradi and Tsibiri. The Fodiawa criticised *Bori* explicitly in their writings but were unable to suppress its popular appeal.[24] This was partly because *Bori* rituals were often presided over by women, typically excluded from the circles where such Arabic texts were disseminated and discussed. After the jihad, the *Inna* of Gobir (*Sarkin Gobir*'s sister) played a leading role in *Bori* ritual in Tsibiri, undoubtedly cultivating ideological resistance to Sokoto's hegemony in the region. In a striking parallel it was Bello's sister, Nana Asmau, who subverted the influence of the *Inna* by incorporating some of her rituals into the *Yan Taru*, the organisation she founded to educate rural women in basic Islamic practice. Even the distinctive *malfa* hat conferred upon *jajis* [leaders] of the *Yan Taru* resembled the ceremonial dress of the *Inna*, thus neutralising a symbol of resistance and placing it in the service of the Sokoto state.[25]

Among the Muslim Hausa, the *mallamai* (a class of itinerant religious savants who made their livelihoods producing *fāʾidas*, telling fortunes and performing other thaumaturgical practices) remained popular, again despite the Fodiawa's criticism.[26] In *Rafʿ al-shubha*, Bello specifically mentioned some of these practices as 'actions of the infidels'.[27] But Nana Asmau's book on Qur'anic medicine, *Tabshīr al-ikhwān* [Bringing good news to the brothers], prescribes very similar remedies to those of the *mallamai* and undoubtedly supplanted them in the regions where *Yan Taru* was most active.[28]

Aside from incorporating Hausa symbols into Sokoto state identity, Bello also sought to make his own genealogy closer to that of the subjects he governed. As we recall, Abdullahi claimed an Arab *nasab* for the Torobbe, stating that they descended from a union between a Byzantine princess

[24] See Usman, *Ajwiba muḥarrara*, who mentions the practice.

[25] Jean Boyd, 'An Interim Report on the Yan-Taru Movement in the 20th Century, with an Account of its Origins', delivered at Popular Islam in the Twentieth Century, University of Illinois, 2–3 April 1984 and Jean Boyd, *Asma'u Fodio's use of Power* (Unpublished notes, 1990) in Jean Boyd Papers, SOAS special collections.

[26] See Usman, *Kitāb al-farq*. For more on the practices of the *mallamai* see Brenner, *Réflexions*.

[27] As discussed in Chapter 1, p. 42 n. 36, the Fodiawa's views on these topics were more nuanced than the literature would suggest.

[28] The work was composed in 1839. An MS copy exists in Jean Boyd Papers, SOAS Special Collections.

and a prestigious Arab warrior during the early Muslim conquests. What is more, according to this theory the Torobbe were the originators of the Fulani and of the Fulfulde language. In *Infāq al-maysūr*, Bello discussed Torobbe origin at length and quoted his uncle's theories uncritically, while also suggesting a servile origin for the Hausa *sarakai*.[29] However, in his response to Abdullahi's bibliographical work, *Īdāʿ al-nusūkh* (which presumably he wrote some time after his earlier statements) Bello firmly rejected them:

> As for what he [Abdullahi] mentioned about the language of the Torobbe being Fulfulde, this runs contrary to what is well known by historians, who say that the language of the Torobbe before the Fulanis was *Wakore* [Wangara], a language of the *Banbara* [Bambara].
>
> What he said about the origins of the Torobbe being from the Christians is not at all reliable. Al-Ḥasan al-Bilbālī[30] has informed me that what is upheld among them in Futa [Toro] is that the origin of the Torobbe is the Bambara, a black African people.[31]

Bello's replacement of an Arabic ancestor trope with a local origin for the Torobbe can be interpreted as another attempt to integrate the ruling Fulani elite with local populations and make non-Fulani more invested in the Sokoto state. The Fodiawa, surely seen as 'foreign' usurpers by many, would have greater acceptance among those whom they termed *Ahl al-Sūdān* such as the Hausa, Bā Arewa and other non-Fulani if they could emphasise their own ancestral connection to the region.

Policies of Enslavement

As Paul Lovejoy has forcefully argued, Sokoto's was 'a political order based on systematic enslavement' in which unfree labour was used in 'virtually all sections' of the economy.[32] The majority of the enslaved who remained within Sokoto's borders laboured on the *gandu*, producing cash crops such as cotton for the regional economy. However, it bears remembering that slavery and slave raiding was already well established

[29] Shādhilī, *Infāq al-maysūr*, pp. 329–36.
[30] See Chapter 2, p. 61 n. 55.
[31] Ar. بَنْبَرٌ من أهل السودان [Banbara min Ahl al-Sūdān]. Bello, *Ḥāshiya ʿalā muqaddimat Īdāʿ al-nusūkh*, ff. 298b–299a.
[32] Lovejoy, *Slavery, Commerce and Production*, p. 14.

in Hausaland before the jihad, given the region's location at the crossroads between the Atlantic coast and Trans-Saharan slave routes.

There is a long and fraught debate within African studies as to why slavery and slave systems were so prevalent in pre-modern West Africa. Some scholars point to the relative abundance of land to people throughout most of the African continent in comparison to the Western world, and to Europe in particular.[33] In such a context, political power was less about the control of territory and more the control of people, whether through the propagation of strong ideologies of loyalty to the ruler or through physical capture and exploitation of outsiders. The borders of a state therefore reached only as far as the ruler's influence. Those outlying areas too costly to control became sites of 'institutionalised raiding or undisguised pillage'.[34] Jeffrey Herbst even notes that the exploitation of outsiders and enslavement systems were 'part of the process by which African states grew'.[35]

Sahelian jurisprudential elites never attempted to end the practice of slavery. However, in spite or perhaps because of such demographic pressures, they had long sought to create strict paradigms for enslavability. The most well-known contribution was that of Ahmad Baba, who established in his 1614 fatwa that non-belief in Islam rather than skin colour was the definitive factor when deciding whether captives could be legally enslaved. Based on his knowledge of the Sahel, Baba provided a list of Muslim and non-Muslim regions (or rather, of peoples whose locations were presumed fixed to specific geographical spaces). Captives who were found to come from Muslim regions must be released, while captives from non-Muslim areas could be legally enslaved (Map 2). Although it is difficult to assess how influential Baba's fatwa was during the intervening centuries, the Fodiawa certainly used it as a source of authority when discussing the belief status of Hausaland before the jihad.[36]

As discussed in Chapter 2, Usman vacillated between Baba's judgement that most of Hausaland was Muslim before the jihad and that of al-Mukhtār ibn Aḥmad al-Kuntī, who more than a century later declared

[33] Suzanne Miers and Igor Kopytoff, *Slavery in Africa: Historical and Anthropological Perspectives* (Madison, 1977); Jeffrey Herbst, *State and Power in Africa: Comparative Lessons in Authority and Control* (Princeton, 2000), pp. 1–35. For a summary of this literature see Salau, *Plantation Slavery in the Sokoto Caliphate*, pp. 8–11.

[34] Miers and Kopytoff, *Slavery in Africa*, pp. 43–4.

[35] Herbst, *State and Power in Africa*, p. 21.

[36] See Chapter 2, pp. 64–5.

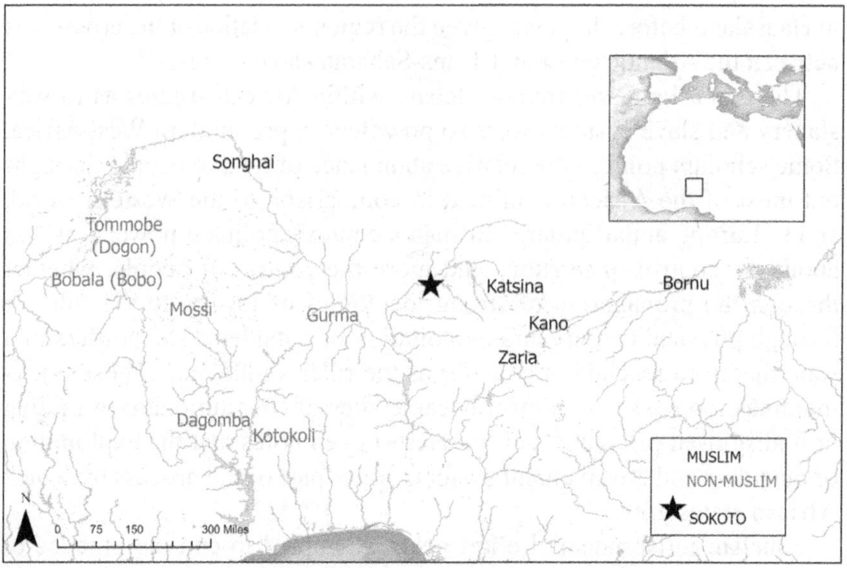

Map 2 Enslavable and unenslavable regions in Usman's *Ajwiba muḥarrara*, quoting *al-Kashf wa-l-bayān* of Ahmad Baba (1614)[37]

the whole of the *Bilād al-Sūdān* non-Muslim. At no point did Usman (or Abdullahi) comment on the inherent discrepancy between the two judgements.[38] Similarly, there was no acknowledgement that most of the regions Baba had mentioned were far to the west of Hausaland, and thus of limited relevance to the question at hand. The judgements of Ahmad Baba and al-Mukhtār were simply two legal opinions that carried authority.

Even before he became *Amīr al-mu'minīn*, Muhammad Bello had a more practical approach to matters of belief (and thus enslavability). In *Infāq al-maysūr*, Bello provided a very detailed account of the Hausa region and which of its inhabitants were Muslim and non-Muslim (Map 3). While many of the places Bello listed in this text as being 'lands of Islam' are much the same as Baba's ruling, there is no mention of Ahmad

[37] I am grateful to Ali Diakite for his help with Map 2. I was unable to identify a non-Muslim group Usman called غَصبِي, غصى or غَضبِي.

[38] In the final chapter of his voluminous legal compendium, *Ḍiyā' al-siyāsāt*, Abdullahi included Ahmad Baba among other legal commentators on enslavement policy but exhibited no preference among them. See Kani, *Ḍiyā' al-siyāsāt*, p. 164.

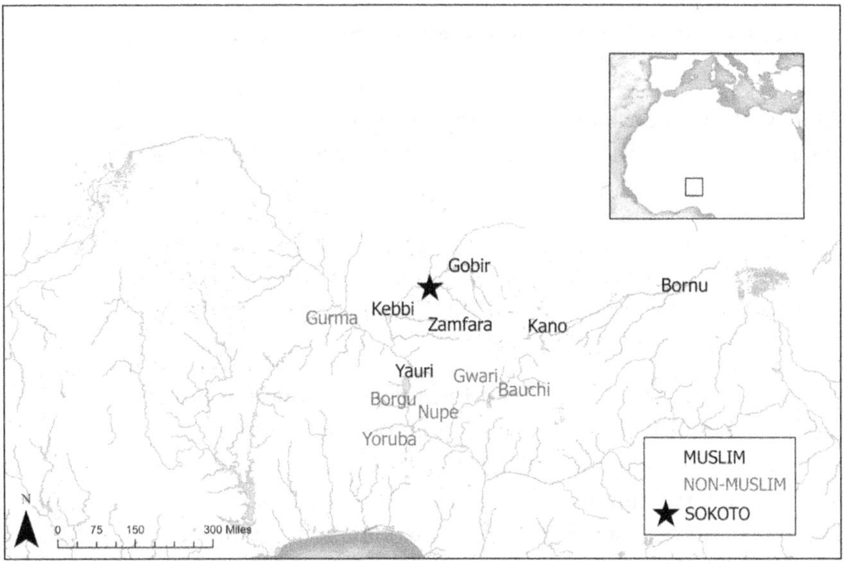

Map 3 Muslim and non-Muslim regions in Muhammad Bello's *Infāq al-maysūr* (1812)

Baba or his *Kashf al-bayān* in any surviving copies of the *Infāq*. Further, Bello did not include any of the regions Ahmad Baba mentioned that were outside of Hausaland or Bornu. He also added regions such Kebbi and Zamfara (Muslim) and Nupe and Yauri (non-Muslim) that seem to have accurately reflected the extent of the jihad campaigns at the time Bello was writing.

Unlike Usman and Abdullahi, Bello also went on to point out the contradiction between the rulings of Baba and al-Kuntī on the status of Hausaland and sought to resolve this discrepancy through reasoned analysis:

> As for the words of Ahmad Baba who answered that these lands of Bornu, Katsina, some of Zakzak [Zaria] and [those lands] nearby are lands of Islam, it could have been (1) because they became Islamised in the times preceding Ahmad Baba and then apostasised afterwards; (2) due to his lack of inspection of them and knowledge of the truth, he ruled by what appeared to him and spread in the news; or (3) he was referring to the spread of Islam among them with the exception of their rulers [...] And the second possibility is more apparent, because if they had Islamised and then abandoned their religion, we would have heard. However, it has not reached us that they have abandoned the ways of their pagan

> ancestors up to the present day, even if they exhibited good [behaviour] and Islam outwardly.[39]

And while Usman had found ways to get around the inconvenience of Baba's statement that Hausaland had been Muslim before the jihad, Bello simply overruled it through his own observations:

> What we have mentioned is closer to the truth and worthier and more deserving of acceptance because we have lived in their company and mixed with them and know their ways. It is the homeowner who knows best what is inside his home.[40]

After he became ruler, Bello formulated a coherent policy of enslavement for Sokoto's territories and hinterlands. Comparing the text of the *Infāq* to *Qadḥ al-zinād*, written after 1821, Bello inserted some additional text after the passage in which he dismissed Baba's fatwa. Here he noted, in the manner of Ahmad Baba, those populations living in or near Sokoto who could be legally enslaved:

> If the acquired person is not from our country, namely those acquired from the lands of Bade, Ghijiwi, Karekare, Bauchin Kano, Bauchin Zakzak, Gwari and similar places,[41] then there is no harm in enslaving him without any investigation or hesitation. Since Islam had not spread to them until this jihad [of 1804] took place, the Muslims fought them and filled their hands with their captives.[42]

This information provided, no doubt, a rubric for the local representatives in the outlying provinces of Sokoto to whom this work was addressed who had to make such decisions on the ground. While the geographical regions cited by Bello will no doubt inform our understanding of enslavement patterns in the early history of Sokoto, my focus here is

[39] Shādhilī, *Infāq al-maysūr*, pp. 298–9.

[40] *Ibid.*, p. 299.

[41] According to Murray Last, 'Bauchi' was a standard term for any pagan area, in this case pagan areas of Kano and Zaria. See Murray Last, 'Ancient Labels and Categories: Exploring the "Onomastics" of Kano', in Anne Haour and B. Rossi (eds), *Being and Becoming Hausa: Interdisciplinary Perspectives* (Leiden, 2010), pp. 59–84. I am grateful to Dr Last for his help in deciphering these ethnonyms.

[42] Bello, *Qadḥ al-zinād*, f. 15a. Bello also noted that it was legal to enslave *Maguzawa* wherever they lived as well as the former rulers of Hausaland and Bornu. I was unable to trace the identities of Ghijiwi: غجو (seen here in the list of enslaveable groups) and سنوى (in the list of non-enslaveable groups).

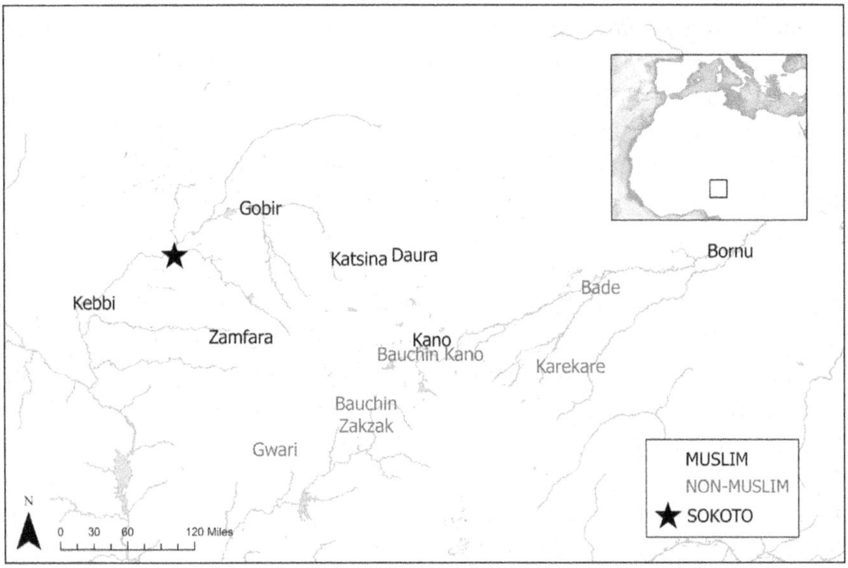

Map 4 Enslavable and unenslavable regions in Muhammad Bello's *Qadḥ al-zinād fī amr hāthā-l-jihād* (after 1821)

on Bello's positionality. He did not opine on matters of enslavability by invoking the authority of Ahmad Baba. Rather, Bello saw himself as the Ahmad Baba of his time, assuming the right to divide his subjects into Muslim and non-Muslim for reasons that were no doubt both practical and political, and informed by his 'real-time' knowledge of the region.

Policies of Exclusion: The Tuareg

The Fodiawa's relations with the various Tuareg groups who lived in Sokoto's northern regions were changeable and complex. The Fodiawa had longstanding links to scholars of the region such as Jibril ibn ʿUmar, from whom Usman and Abdullahi received some of their early education. During the jihad of 1804, Tuareg cavalry frequently switched sides, playing a decisive role in both the wins and losses of the jihadists.[43] Some Tuareg, such as Aghali of the Kel Gress, had been important supporters of Usman in the early days of the jihad, and Aghali gave one of his daughters in marriage to Bello. Bello's Wazir, Gidado dan Layma, listed

[43] See Minna, 'Intellectual Contribution', p. 96.

seven Tuareg *ṭubūl* [war leaders] as supporters of Sokoto.[44] However, many *imajeghen* Tuareg sided with the Hausa against the jihadists. In the first years of Bello's reign, some Tuareg also joined the Tawaye and fought with them against him.

Before he became ruler, Bello had attempted to reform the Tuareg from the inside by supporting the movement of Muhammad al-Jaylānī, an *aneslem,* and advised him on how to sedentarise his nomadic supporters from the Tuareg.[45] However, in 1816 al-Jaylānī was defeated by a confederation headed by Ibra of the Temezgidda (himself also an *aneslem*). Enthusiasm for his movement collapsed and he abandoned the urban outpost he had established near Tahoua to seek sanctuary with Bello in Sokoto. As his authority and territory increased, Bello was able to gain more leverage over Tuareg groups. The Kel Gress and Itesen needed to be on good terms with Sokoto to guarantee access to its markets, and to grazing land that now lay within Sokoto's northern territories.[46] Similarly, the Sultan of Agadez had an interest in keeping cordial relations with Sokoto due to the desert salt trade and other commercial ties. That said, Tuareg caste and social structure allowed for a fragmented authority and did not impose serious punishment for divided loyalties. While the Sultan of Agadez gave his allegiance to Bello, many of his tributaries made regular raids on Sokoto territory.[47]

By 1821, Bello clearly felt that the nomadic Tuareg were not compatible with the urban Muslim society he was building in Sokoto and formulated a policy to systematically stigmatise and exclude them from the Sokoto project.[48] *Miftāḥ al-sadād fī aqsām hāthihi al-bilād* [The appropriate key to the classifications of these lands], is in effect a history of defining belief and non-belief in the Sahel region, which Bello wrote during his rule of

44 Last, *Sokoto Caliphate*, p. 19.

45 Bello, *Jawāb shāfin wa-khiṭāb minnā kāfin ilā Muḥammad al-Jaylānī* in Norris, *The Tuaregs*, p. 152. See analysis of this document in Zehnle, *A Geography of Jihad*, pp. 293–8.

46 See Heinrich Barth, *Travels and Discoveries in North and Central Africa: Being a Journal of an Expedition Undertaken under the Auspices of H.B.M.'s Government, in the Years 1849–1855* (New York, 1857), who mentions the important role such groups played in Trans-Saharan trade.

47 Ibra remained an implacable enemy of Bello, harassing the northern territories until his final defeat in 1836.

48 To my knowledge, the only extensive examination of Bello's relations with the Tuareg is in Minna, 'Intellectual Contribution', pp. 94–9. It does not mention either of the texts discussed below.

Sokoto. While much of its content is reminiscent of earlier writings by Usman and Abdullahi, Bello includes a lengthy section on the beliefs of the Tuareg, whom neither mentioned. As with the other groups Bello discusses in this text, he compared the beliefs of the Tuareg before and after the jihad:

> The Tuareg in the country before this jihad were of three types: a part of them were thieves and brigands (*muḥāribūn*) who claimed that they were Muslim but had little care for religion and rather more for bloodshed, stealing of property and maintaining many customs from the time before Islam, and this type is of the majority in this country.
>
> The Tuareg in our country today are apostates of God and infidels for making friends with the infidels (*muwālāt*), taking sides with them and aiding them [against the Muslims].[49]

While the immediate impetus for Bello's judgement was Tuareg support of the Tawaye Rebellions, it also drew on the historical attempts of Sahelian *fiqh* scholars to place nomadic groups within a recognisable category of legal classification. Bello took the term *muḥāribūn* directly from *al-Jurʿa al-ṣāfiya* of al-Mukhtār ibn Aḥmad al-Kuntī, who concluded that the Tuareg had the legal status of *mustaghraq al-dhimma* (also known as *ḥarbī* or *muḥāribūn*) because they were thought to gain their possessions through raiding and theft. As such, they had no legal right to what they owned and consequently their possessions could be counted as *fayʾ* [war booty] if captured in raids. As Bruce Hall explains, the judgement of *mustaghraq al-dhimma* was 'a way to exclude warrior lineages from wider Muslim society, legitimise the confiscation of their possessions and forc[e] them to live under the authority of the scholarly class'.[50] That Bello regarded the possessions of the Tuareg as belonging to him is clear from an exchange of letters between Bello and al-Jaylānī. Bello had criticised al-Jaylānī for plundering caravans belonging to his Tuareg allies. According to Norris, al-Jaylānī replied that Bello had told him that 'the property of the Tuareg are forms of legal booty' and had watched Bello himself presiding over the theft of Tuareg property with regularity.[51]

49 Bello, *Miftāḥ al-sadād fī aqsām hāthihi al-bilād*, Kaduna (NA), f. 9a.

50 Hall, *History of Race*, p. 74.

51 Al-Jaylānī's reply to Bello in Norris, *The Tuaregs*, pp. 156–7. Norris gives no title or source for this reply.

Bello's judgement on the Tuareg, made irrespective of grouping or caste, could also have been a way to seek revenge for the regular Tuareg raids that threatened the security and prosperity of Sokoto, and curtailed his ability to communicate with other regions. Bello understood Tuareg social structure and no doubt knew that trading and raiding groups were linked by clan ties. Perhaps he saw that the only way to stamp out these threats for good was by allowing raids on all Tuareg groups regardless of caste status, thus bleeding the resources of the warrior groups. Such can be assumed by Al-Jaylānī's retort that Bello had been raiding the caravans of Tuareg traders 'before they waged war against Muslims and before their apostasy'[52] to avenge himself of the warrior groups to whom they were tied. Similarly, after a raid by the Kel Gress inside Sokoto territory, Clapperton witnessed Bello sending a proclamation that 'all the Tuaricks belonging to that tribe should depart from Bello's dominions in three days, under the penalty of death'.[53]

While Bello's judgement on the Tuareg was highly pragmatic, it relied on the link between *muwālāt* with non-believers and apostasy from Islam developed by Usman during the discourse of dissent, as well as Sahelian jurisprudential norms. However, when we turn to Bello's second work concerning the Tuareg, *al-Nuqūl al-nawāṭiq fī sha'n al-Barbar wa-l-Tawāriq* [Pronouncements regarding the Berbers and the Tuareg], we sense a more assertive position grounded less on the authority of legal texts and more on Bello's will as *Amīr al-mu'minīn.* From its outset, *al-Nuqūl* is not a reasoned argument, but a policy directive written 'to advise the Umma not to trust the Tuareg'.[54]

As I have made clear elsewhere, Muhammad Bello keenly sensed the relative temporality between the authorities from which he quoted, and he was not afraid to go against established norms if he could find local evidence that they were unfounded. However, in this second work Bello deliberately conflated different historical periods and peoples to portray the Tuareg as atavistically treacherous and, because of their nomadism, inherently immoral. Throughout the work, Bello conflates 'Tuareg', 'Berber' and 'Bedouin', drawing on stories of the treachery of the Arab *qabā'il* who rebelled against Caliph Abu Bakr, the *Amazigh* [Berbers] who repelled the early Muslim conquests of North Africa and even the

[52] *Ibid.*, pp. 156–7.

[53] Denham and Clapperton, *Narrative of Travels and Discoveries*, p. 108.

[54] Bello, *al-Nuqūl al-nawāṭiq*, Niamey (MARA) 273. I could only access this manuscript for a short time and did not note down the folio numbers for this and subsequent references.

Jews of Yathrib, stock figures of treachery in Islamic thought.[55] Rather than sticking to established legal texts, Bello seized upon any derogatory statements he could find about these groups, regardless of their merit or authenticity, as well as a clearly apocryphal hadith about the Tuareg themselves.[56] He even turned to the Tamashek language for further evidence of the Tuareg's infidelity:

> And there is the appearance of heathenism in the languages and utterances of some of the Tuareg, some of which can be explained and some of which cannot, such as some of them calling God '*Bāba*' [Father] or referring to him as 'uncle'.[57]

When Bello was writing his treatise on the sedentarisation of the Tuareg addressed to Muhammad al-Jaylānī, he evidently believed that it was possible to make certain Tuareg groups amenable citizens of a largely urban Islamic society. However, with the failure of al-Jaylānī's movement and continued manoeuvres against him from various Tuareg clans, in his later works on the Tuareg Bello relied on crude stereotypes to conclude that they were a treacherous, uneducated and inherently 'foreign' people who could only be made to submit to authority with violence and intimidation rather than dialogue and reason.[58] These comments are not because Bello was ignorant of Tuareg society. As we have seen, he was no stranger to the Tuareg. Bello had a Tuareg wife, and he had some knowledge of the Tamashek language. However, Bello considered the Tuareg – as nomadic pastoralists – an existential threat to the sedentary and centrally educated society he had in mind for Sokoto.

[55] Yathrib, the former name of Medina. According to Islamic history, the Banū Qurayza, a Jewish *qabīla* who also lived in the oasis town, made a pact with Muhammad but later broke it and betrayed the Muslims, leading Muhammad to order their massacre.

[56] Bello, *al-Nuqūl al-nawāṭiq*: 'You will find trust and faith and carrying out promises and righteousness scarce among the Tuareg and lies and deceit and treachery widespread'.

[57] Bello, *al-Nuqūl al-nawāṭiq*.

[58] Bello ended *al-Nuqūl* with a quatrain from the Abbasid poet al-Mutanabbī, proverbial in Arabic-speaking countries, which nicely summarises his attitude towards the Tuareg: 'A courtesy lent to a courteous person wins you his favour / While courtesy to a lowly person only results in arrogance / In this case putting dialogue in place of the sword / Is more harmful than putting the sword in place of dialogue'.

Policies of Sedentarisation: The Fulani

Two distinct branches of the Fulani existed in Hausaland. The first were scholarly communities who identified as Torobbe, such as the Fodiawa.[59] While often living in remote rural encampments like Usman's birthplace of Degel, Torobbe-Fulani were not truly nomadic and generated income from their services as teachers, advisers and other literate professions rather than exclusively from animal husbandry.[60] The second branch consisted of various pastoralist groups who moved with their herds and consequently, like the Tuareg, had no fixed location.[61] While some of these Fulani pastoralist groups were Muslim, many were not, or at least did not connect their cultural identity exclusively with the performance of Islam as the Torobbe did.[62]

Bello's views on this pastoralist branch of the Fulani were far less accommodating than either Usman or Abdullahi.[63] Unlike his views on the Tuareg, which changed depending on the geopolitical circumstances he faced, Bello's attitude towards the pastoralist Fulani was remarkably consistent. Before the jihad, he had linked the future success of the *jamāʿa* to the sedentarisation of the Fulani, relating a prophecy that Usman's Fulani supporters 'will not herd cattle, as is the custom of the Fulani'.[64] During the jihad campaigns, Bello expressed frustration that the Fulani clans were too pre-occupied with their herds to participate in the fighting, writing to complain to Yaʿqūb of Bauchi that the 'owners of cattle' were lagging behind the troops.[65] In his treatise on the sedentarisation of the Tuareg, which Bello wrote for Muhammad al-Jaylānī around 1815, he also mentioned that 'this *qabīla* of ours [the Fulani] has

[59] For a discussion of the origins of the Torobbe, see Chapter 1, p. 46.

[60] Usman himself acted as a teacher and adviser to *Sarkin Gobir* Yunfa before the jihad. See Last, *Sokoto Caliphate*, pp. 12–13.

[61] *Ibid.*, p. lxxii, describes these groups as 'cattle Fulani' (Fulfulde: *Fulɓe na'i*).

[62] C. Edward Hopen, *The Pastoral Fulbe Family in Gwandu* (Oxford, 1958), stated that Muslim *Fulɓe na'i* referred to non-Muslim Fulani as *Bororo'en.*

[63] As discussed above, although he glorified the Torobbe in particular, Abdullahi believed that all the Fulani descended from the Arab Islamisers of the Bilād al-Sūdān. Meanwhile, Usman ruled that, since most of the Fulani were Muslim, no Fulani captive could be legally enslaved. He also persuaded pastoralist Fulani to join the jihad by upholding their grievances against the Hausa *sarakai*, later excusing the excesses they committed in the jihadist army.

[64] Bello, *Infāq*. Translation in Shareef, *Easy Expenditure*, Chapter 10, p. 1.

[65] Bello *[Letter to Emir Yaʿqūb].*

become infatuated with the love of cows and cattle, despite the fact that the Prophet did not own them'.[66] At the start of his reign he warned his own emirs, who were for the most part Fulani: 'When you become overly concerned with earning questionable profit and following the tails of cows, and become content with farming and you leave the struggle; Allah will subjugate you with humiliation'.[67]

Later, in 1820, Bello composed a short treatise in which he discussed the best ways of earning a living in an Islamic society. Jihad was at the top of the list, 'because it is universally beneficial for what is in it of keeping the Islamic social order from being destroyed',[68] while herding was at the bottom. At around the same time he wrote *Kifāyat al-muhtadīn fī aḥkām al-mukhallifīn min al-mujāhidīn* [Sufficient information for the rightly guided regarding the judgements upon those warriors who stay behind], berating young men who preferred to remain in commercial and agricultural occupations rather than join the jihad in Sokoto's outlying provinces.

As he had done with the Tuareg, Bello discussed the beliefs of the pastoralist Fulani in a chapter of *Miftāḥ al-sadād*. While he described some Fulani clans as 'infidels, who do not call themselves Muslims, deny resurrection and practice sorcery', Bello concluded that the majority of the Fulani were Muslims: 'Their description is close to that of the Tuareg except that they do not preserve pre-Islamic customs, nor do they help the infidels against the Muslims'.[69] While he decided that pastoralist Fulani could be integrated into the Sokoto project, like the nomadic Tuareg their present way of life was incompatible with an urban Muslim society. Bello sought to subject the pastoralist element of the Fulani to the same programme of sedentarisation and re-education that he had proposed for al-Jaylānī's erstwhile Tuareg followers.

Such views on nomadism versus sedentary living were not controversial or unusual for a Sahelian scholar. Prophet Muhammad encouraged living in towns, and Islamic jurists agreed that an abandoned child found

[66] Bello, *Jawāb shāfin wa-khiṭāb minnā kāfin*. Translation in Norris, *The Tuaregs*, p. 152.

[67] Bello, *Risāla li-l-amrāḍ shāfiya* in Shareef, *A Letter of Healing*, p. 110. Zehnle, *A Geography of Jihad*, p. 298 reports that Bello encouraged Muhammad al-Jaylānī to breed camels and horses for use in the jihad instead of herds of cattle.

[68] Bello, *Tanbīh al-ṣāḥib ʿalā aḥkām al-makāsib*. Translation in Muhammad Shareef, 'Advice to the Friend' (1990) http://siiasi.org/wp-content/uploads/2014/12/Tanbeeh-as-Saahib.pdf [accessed 9 September 2020], p. 27.

[69] Bello, *al-Nuqūl al-nawāṭiq*.

in the countryside could be taken to the city but not vice versa, setting a legal precedent.[70] In wider Sahelian culture, deserts and other wild places were thought to contain evil forces that could corrupt good Muslims should they live there long enough. Breeding cattle and other livestock was especially denigrated, since it was associated in the popular imagination with lustful actions.[71] As al-Jaylānī stated to Bello, 'the desert is the ruin of religion, the feebleness of Islam and its negation'.[72] But at the same time, the jihadist movement had gained support predominantly in the countryside. Bello's father, Usman, and those before him had lived in small rural settlements precisely to avoid the 'corruption' of the cities.[73] In the epic poems of Abdullahi, discussed above, he frequently described rural and desert areas as a welcome sanctuary from iniquity, or at least a place to gain closeness to God through solitude and hardship.[74] Such contrary associations run deep in Islamic discursive tradition and can perhaps be traced to Ibn Khaldun's statement that 'sedentary life constitutes the last stage of civilisation and the point where it begins to decay'.[75]

But in this case, Bello's preference for urban living was more pragmatic than ideological. As Ibn Khaldun also observed, urban settlements were far easier to defend and control than rural outposts.[76] Bello's ribat system was inspired by major urban centres of the Muslim world such as Basra, Kufa and al-Fusṭāṭ, all of which began as fortress towns placed at the outward limit of the Muslim conquests, which Stephanie Zehnle has termed 'jihadist frontier urbanisation'.[77] The construction of ribats and the sedentarisation of pastoralist Fulani thus went hand in hand. As Philips states, 'by settling the Fulani and stationing former herders away from areas controlled by clan leaders he [Bello] strengthened the authority of

[70] Hakim and Ahmed, 'Rules for the Built Environment', pp. 2–3.

[71] See Abdullahi, *Risālat al-naṣā'iḥ*. Transation in Hiskett, *Tazyīn al-Waraqāt*, p. 100. Abdullahi appeals to the Torobbe to: 'tur[n] away from the abyss of lust. It is in the pastures of lust that you tend flocks; and verily you set a bad example'. Zehnle, *A Geography of Jihad*, pp. 295–8 makes a thorough analysis of these concepts.

[72] Bello, *Jawāb shāfin wa-khiṭāb minnā kāfin* in Norris, *The Tuaregs*, p. 149.

[73] Last, *Sokoto Caliphate*, pp. lxx–lxxiv.

[74] Hiskett, *Tazyīn al-Waraqāt*, pp. 122–3, among other references.

[75] Ibn Khaldūn, *Muqaddima* in Rosenthal, *The Muqaddimah: An Introduction to History*, vol. 1, p. 255.

[76] *Ibid.*, vol. 2, pp. 235–40.

[77] Zehnle, *A Geography of Jihad*, pp. 295–8.

himself and the scholars whom he thought ought to be ruling society'.[78] While the ribats founded by Bello quickly became multi-ethnic urban centres of commerce and learning, they also remained under the control of Bello, members of his immediate family or governors handpicked by Bello himself.[79]

Bello's works on the Fulani and sedentarisation offer another opportunity to see how much he felt able to dictate correct behaviour for his subjects, communicated via Arabic texts. While Bello integrated Hausa culture and language, he reserved 'othering' discourse for those who did not fit into his vision of urban society, and that included those pastoralist Fulani who did not change their ways. For Bello, no amount of Arabic genealogy would give the Fulani the status of a natural 'ruling race'. Only through abandoning a nomadic lifestyle could they play a part in his multi-ethnic empire.

Meanwhile, in Gwandu...

When Abdullahi and Bello renewed their communication after Kalambayna, Bello was in his political and literary prime while Abdullahi, at 55 years old, had largely retired from matters of government.[80] Since 1812, he had left the running of Gwandu in the hands of his sons, Muhammad Wani and Khalilu, and later put a nephew, Muḥammad al-Bukhārī, in charge of Nupe. While Abdullahi continued to write, the only documents surviving from this period show him a mature scholar with a concern for his soul, rather than an administrator concerned with the government of his territories.[81]

[78] Philips, 'Ribats in the Sokoto Caliphate', p. 231.

[79] For a comprehensive list of ribats in Sokoto and their commanders see *ibid.*, pp. 236–7.

[80] There is a story (Muhammad Shareef, personal correspondence) that before his death Usman had written to Abdullahi explaining the reasons that he had retired from active rule and encouraged him to do the same. However, the letter was not delivered until after Kalambayna. The text is known as *Waṣiyya* and although a market edition exists (Zaria, Gaskiya Corporation) I have not been able to consult it.

[81] *Dawāʾ al-waswās* (1826) is a manual for the correct performance of prayer; *Tahdhīb al-insān* (1827) concerns the education of young children; *Ḍiyāʾ al-qawāʿid* (1828) encourages men of religion to live in seclusion and focus on the redemption of their souls rather than seeking to correct others' behaviour.

There may be other reasons that documentation from the early history of Gwandu Emirate does not survive. Perhaps Gwandu's literary output was not considered politically expedient to preserve. Alternatively, its records may have been misplaced or destroyed due to the frequent attacks on Gwandu by the Kebbawa rebels, or the complicated nature of Gwandu's apportionment among France, Germany and Britain at the turn of the twentieth century.[82] Whatever the case, there is some evidence to suggest that even if Abdullahi had ceased writing political treatises, his earlier ideas about correct Muslim statecraft did influence the running of Gwandu in a significant way.

According to his companion, Saʿd ibn ʿAbd al-Raḥmān, Abdullahi journeyed to Gwandu with 750 scholars.[83] There, unlike Bello, he undoubtedly intended to keep authority among a circle of legal specialists instead of concentrating power in the hands of an *Amīr al-muʾminīn* and his court. S. A. Balogun reports that Gwandu had few titled officials, with administrative decisions made by a 'council of elders',[84] while Murray Last suggests that Gwandu under Abdullahi would have resembled an 'old-style *Tsangaya* community'.[85] There are perhaps also certain parallels with the *Batu mawdo* [great council] of Ahmad Lobbo in Hamdallahi, predominantly composed of legal scholars and Fulani clan leaders. Daily discussions of state, as well as state appointments, took place in a secluded inner council.[86] This arrangement would certainly match Barth's description of Gwandu's court under Abdullahi's successor Khalilu, to which he was not allowed admittance and from which Khalilu and his officials rarely emerged.[87]

[82] For the remainder of Abdullahi's life, Gwandu was involved in a protracted defensive struggle with the Kebbawa, which continued largely unabated until the annexation of Gwandu by the British in 1903. For more on this topic, see Sidney J. Hogben, *An Introduction to the History of the Islamic States of Northern Nigeria* (Ibadan, 1967); Johnston, *Fulani Empire*; Balogun, 'Succession Tradition'; 'The Place of Argungu'; Gwandu, 'Abdullahi B. Fodio as a Muslim Jurist'.

[83] Saʿd b. ʿAbd al-Raḥmān, *Tartīb al-aṣḥāb* in 'Abdullahi B. Fodio as a Muslim Jurist', who lists 240 of them by name.

[84] Balogun, 'Succession Tradition', pp. 22–3.

[85] Last, 'From Dissent to Dissidence', p. 10, referring to Nigeria's traditional Qur'anic school system.

[86] Loimeier, *Muslim Societies in Africa*, p. 122. See also Mohamed Diagayete, 'The Contributions of Fulani Scholars to the Development of Islamic Scholarship in Mali, 18th–19th Centuries', delivered at Wednesdays@PAS, Program of African Studies, Northwestern University, 28 September 2017.

[87] See Barth, *Travels and Discoveries*, pp. 196–7.

In Gwandu, age and seniority seemed to outweigh any other leadership qualities. It soon became accepted that Abdullahi's eldest surviving son would become *Dan Galadima*, effectively a prince regent succeeding the Emir upon his death.[88] While this seems incongruous with Abdullahi's horror of hereditary rule, giving preference to age followed precisely the arguments that he had put forward during his debate with Bello over the succession. However, it was also likely that a stable succession tradition was meant to prevent Sokoto's interference in Gwandu affairs. Power in Gwandu therefore rested in the hands of a few elite families of Torobbe scholars who had little to do with the Hausa majority, and Fulfulde remained the language of government.[89] Such an arrangement concurs with Abdullahi's views of Torobbe origin and the Fulfulde language, ideas Bello had since found to be a hindrance as he attempted to integrate the Hausa majority into the running of the state.

The small number of titled positions, a rigid succession tradition and the preferential status enjoyed by Torobbe-Fulani were all to have an adverse effect on Gwandu's development. Without the patronage tools of administrative positions, marriage alliances or the promise of integration into the political elite, the Emirs of Gwandu had trouble maintaining loyalty (and thus a flow of tribute) from their emirates and sub-emirates.[90] Sokoto used its two major centres of production, Kano and Zaria, to establish a strong regional economy of leather, textiles and agricultural products. But even with a greater quantity of productive land, Gwandu never exerted the necessary control over its production centres of Jega and Nupe to do the same.[91]

88 See Balogun, 'Succession Tradition'.

89 See Gwandu, 'Abdullahi B. Fodio as a Muslim Jurist', p. 56; Willis, 'Torodbe Clerisy', p. 208. Sambo Kulwa, author of *Kanz al-awlād*, and his son, Bayero, clearly considered themselves a part of this Gwandu-centric Torobbe elite. Much of the text concerns the tracing of their *nasab* and encouraging the use and study of the Fulfulde language.

90 Elderly residents interviewed by Hopen, *The Pastoral Fulbe Family in Gwandu*, p. 45, reported that before the British annexation of Gwandu Emirate they had paid the annual tribute to Gwandu only every two to three years, if at all, without facing any penalty. Tribute from sub-emirates was particularly important for Gwandu, since the only tax paid in Gwandu proper was zakat. See Ibrahim M. Jumare, 'Land Tenure in the Sokoto Sultanate of Nigeria' (Unpublished PhD dissertation, York University, 1995).

91 Charles Stewart's unpublished work, 'A Condensed Summary of Historians and History Writing in Nigeria', mentioned above, also discusses this period of Gwandu's history in some detail.

In modern times, those in Sokoto often refer to Gwandu as the 'little brother', an appellation that recalls both their shared kinship and their intense rivalry for seniority.[92] While the literature often refers to Sokoto and Gwandu as 'twin capitals', Heinrich Barth discovered the extent of Sokoto-Gwandu rivalry during his travels through the Emirate. Before his departure, it was discovered that his gift to Emir Gwandu Khalilu was inferior in value to that which he gave to *Amīr al-muʾminīn* Atiku in Sokoto. Barth was forced to make up the value of his gift before Khalilu would allow him to leave.[93] The roots of this rivalry stem from a historic event: the succession of Muhammad Bello and the chagrin of his uncle, Abdullahi. However, what is of interest to our study is that the differing concepts of government in Sokoto and Gwandu seem to have been the direct result of the transfer of ideas through written texts. Murray Last framed the conflict between Abdullahi and Usman as a choice between government through a 'circle of scholars' or 'a more positive political leadership'.[94] While Abdullahi saw the *ulama* as the primary interpreters of the law, Usman envisioned that the judgements of the ruler and his administration would supersede them. Although it is difficult say exactly how Gwandu was governed while Abdullahi was alive, we understand that it was, in part, influenced by the concept of correct Islamic governance he had espoused repeatedly in his writings.

Conclusion

Returning to the observation of Hugh Clapperton that began this final chapter, Sokoto's inhabitants obeyed Muhammad Bello not because his orders were buttressed by lengthy demonstrations of their compatability with Maliki legal norms, nor because they were carefully justified by precedents from the Islamic past. They obeyed him because historical events – from the jihad of 1804, to Bello's succession, to his repression of the Tawaye and his other enemies –made it abundantly clear that God had bestowed Muhammad Bello with leadership of the Muslim community. His will was God's will.

What was more, released from the necessity of speaking through the quoted word, in which many of his earlier disputes with Abdullahi, Ahmad Lobbo and others had taken place, Bello could issue direct orders and

[92] In West Africa the term suggests one with less power.

[93] Barth, *Travels and Discoveries*, p. 198–9.

[94] Murray Last, 'An Aspect of Caliph Muhammad Bello's Social Policy', *Kano Studies*, 2 (1966), 56–105.

policies that would lead to increased prosperity for many of his subjects. The patronage networks created by the proliferation of land grants and royal titles, the immense wealth generated by the plantation system and the markets of the new cities and garrison towns increased the number of people invested in the tenure of Muhammad Bello, and the Sokoto project.

After his death in 1837, Bello was succeeded by his brother, Abū Bakr ʿAtīq, known as Atiku. According to Al-Ḥājj Saʿīd, Atiku 'changed many of the reprehensible practices which came about through Bello's policies'. His first act as *Amīr al-muʾminīn* was supposedly to order the killing of the royal drummers Clapperton had remarked upon during his visit to Sokoto.[95] Still, Muhammad Bello had set a lasting precedent that would give Sokoto many of its distinctive characteristics. Atiku, for his part, came to rely more on the selective revelation of hidden spiritual knowledge that his father, Usman, had supposedly bestowed upon him, rather than any return to a government of scholars.[96] Bello's pragmatic governance model allowed Sokoto to outlast its neighbouring states and maintain a stong cultural presence in the region, while Abdullahi's alternative to it in Gwandu largely faded into obscurity.

[95] Al-Ḥājj Saʿīd, *Taqāyīd mimmā waṣala ilaynā*, Arabe 5422, f. 7a.

[96] See *Kitāb al-asrār*, attribruted to Atiku and discussed in Last, *Sokoto Caliphate*, pp. 65; 81.

Conclusion

> Abdulkadiri dan Tafa … read *Ḍiyāʾ al-sulṭān* to the people saying: 'the Sultan must have such and such characteristics', challenging [*Amīr al-muʾminīn* Atiku] and pointing at him.
>
> – Al-Ḥājj Saʿīd, *Taqāyīd mimmā waṣala ilaynā*, Paris (BnF) Arabe 5422, f. 8b.

Between 1804 and 1837 the Fodiawa rose from rebels fighting to overturn the political order to rulers seeking to enforce obedience across a vast territorial empire. Throughout this period, they engaged with Islam's fluid set of discursive traditions to justify and excuse their evolving ideas on authority and legitimacy in a steady stream of Arabic texts. But far from being a united 'triumvirate', the Fodiawa soon came to disagree about what the aims of the jihadist movement should be, and about where authority in a Muslim society should ultimately lie. This book has followed numerous 'questions and disagreements' between the Fodiawa themselves as well as their contemporaries from the Sahelian knowledge elite. In so doing, it offers a deeper understanding of how the new Muslim states of the nineteenth-century Sahel gained legitimacy, and the key role Arabic texts played in the process. In this concluding section, it would be apposite to briefly follow these discourses of (de)legitimation onwards in time and reflect on the changing function of Arabic texts – specifically, why the death of Muhammad Bello in 1837 marked an abrupt bust to a thirty-year literary boom.

Usman dan Fodio, Abdullahi and Muhammad Bello were some of the most prolific writers in a century during which West African rulers and scholars expressed their views on statecraft in an unprecedented wealth of Arabic texts. In comparison, *Amīr al-muʾminīn* Atiku and Khalilu, Emir of Gwandu (the successors of Bello and Abdullahi, respectively) left behind only a handful of writings. Gidado dan Layma and his descendants, the hereditary wazirs of Sokoto, concentrated most of their literary efforts on retelling the lives of the Fodiawa and continuing to refine the official narrative of Sokoto's early history. Dan Layma's wife, Nana Asmau, daughter of Usman and a prolific poet, was a notable exception to this trend towards purely derivative works.

Al-Ḥājj Saʿīd's anecdote in the epigraph of this concluding chapter demonstrates an important point. It was not that successive generations of Sokoto's rulers no longer considered Arabic texts as vehicles for political legitimation. On the contrary, it was simply that the legitimacy gained by preserving, copying and quoting from the Fodiawa's extant writings surpassed the legitimacy gained by the creation of new texts. As the political power and geopolitical reach of Sokoto continued to expand after Bello's death, elites gradually curated and aggrandised Sokoto's early history to project unity where there had been deep divisions, in parallel to raising Usman and Bello – but not Abdullahi – to the status of saints.[1] This narrative of Sokoto's early history formed a sufficient foundation for the performative power of the state.

David Robinson once stated that Al-Ḥajj ʿUmar's 'Toucouleur Empire' was neither of the Toucouleur, nor was it an empire.[2] Similarly, this book argues that for most of the period 1804–1837, the 'Sokoto Caliphate' was neither considered a caliphate, nor was its identity intimately connected to a town named Sokoto. The narrative of the jihad and of the early history of Sokoto told to British colonists in 1903 was already the product of decades of evolution. Although it is unclear exactly when the idea of a 'Sokoto Caliphate' was born, as with the idea of a 'Toucouleur Empire' promulgated in French West Africa, it appealed as much to the administrators of British indirect rule in Nigeria as it later did to the architects of Northern Nigerian nationalism.

That said, the later nineteenth century also witnessed several countertrends to Sokoto's hegemony. These events demonstrate that the discursive cycles of legitimacy making and breaking which have been this book's purview remained very much active. Even though the arguments employed in the discourse of dissent were no longer necessary or relevant for Sokoto's rulers, these early Fodiawa texts continued to be copied, studied and discussed across the Sahelian scholarly world. As the century

[1] See Gidado dan Layma, *Rawḍ al-jinān fī dhikr baʿḍ manāqib al-shaykh ʿUthmān* (1816–17); *al-Kashf wa-l-bayān ʿan baʿḍ aḥwāl al-sayyid Muḥammad Bello b. al-shaykh ʿUthmān* (1838). These texts have much in common with the genre of Sufi hagiographies known as *karāmāt al-awliyāʾ*, or *karāmāt* literature.

[2] Loimeier, *Muslim Societies in Africa*, p. 110, citing David Robinson, 'D'empire en empire: l'empire toucouleur dans la stratégie et la mémoire de l'empire français', *Islam et sociétés au Sud du Sahara*, 16 (2002), 107–17.

progressed, the kind of authority claimed by the rulers of West Africa's Muslim states became ever more removed from the idealistic vision of an Islamic golden age that had catapulted many of them to power. It therefore became ever more likely that the discourse of dissent, which had toppled the Hausa *sarakai* and so many others, could threaten them as well. Thus it was that in 1862, Umar Tal sacked Hamdallahi and executed its ruler, Ahmad III (Ahmad Lobbo's grandson) because of his '*muwālāt*' with non-Muslim powers, citing Usman's equation of *muwālāt* with apostasy.[3] Tal claimed that Muhammad Bello had secretly been initiated into the rival Tijani tariqa, an allegation that threatened the spiritual authority of Sokoto's rulers.[4]

Meanwhile, a resurgence of Mahdist movements – and eventually the emergence of a Mahdist state in the Sudan – shattered the illusion that the Sokoto elite had privileged insight into millenarian knowledge or could control its destructive forces. During Atiku's reign there were a series of mass eastward migrations out of Sokoto's territories in expectation of the Mahdi's coming, which Bello himself had predicted.[5] Muhammad Ahmad, the Mahdi of the Sudan, appointed Hayatu, a grandson of Usman dan Fodio, to be his representative in Sokoto where he fomented dissent against the Sokoto elite. Similarly, Sokoto's '*muwālāt*' with the British colonial occupation in 1903 caused a schism in the *jamāʿa*. Those loyal to the deposed ruler, Muhammadu Attahiru I, made their own Usmanesque hijra to the margins where they founded the town of Maiurno, on the Blue Nile. Descendants of these migrants continue to claim the rightful leadership of the Sokoto project and maintain their own unique tradition of Muslim governance.[6]

3 See Sidi Mohamed Mahibou and Jean-Louis Triaud, *Voilà ce qui est arrivé. Bayân mâ waqa'a d'al-Hâjj 'Umar al-Fûtî. Plaidoyer pour une guerre sainte, en Afrique de l'Ouest au XIXe siècle* (Paris, 1983).

4 See Al-Ḥājj ʿUmar Tāl, *Bayān mā waqaʿa baynanā wa-bayn Amīr Māsina Aḥmad b. Aḥmad b. al-Shaykh Aḥmad b. Muḥammad Lubbu.* Several Tijaniyya texts exist that are attributed to Muhammad Bello including *Shamsiyyat al-ikhwān* (MS NU/Falke 1686; 1885; 1935; MX NU/Wilks 72) and *Taḥqīq al-murībīn wa-l-mushakkikīn wa-l-munkirīn* (MS Kaduna (NA), digitised as BL (EAP) 535 1/3/4/3). Gidado dan Layma wrote a defence of Bello entitled *Kashf al-ḥijāb wa-rafʿ al-niqāb.* For more on the Tijaniyya controversy see Minna, 'Intellectual Contribution', pp. 363–89.

5 See Atiku, *al-Intiqāl min balad Hawsa ilā-l-Ḥijāz*, MX Niamey (MARA) 1407.

6 See Mark R. Duffield, 'Hausa and Fulani Settlement and the Development

In more modern times, various groups borrow selectively from Sokoto's legacy to bolster their own strategies of legitimation, demonstrating the flexibility that this narrative still has. Anti-Sufi movements such as *Sunnance* and *Izala* draw on the Fodiawa's religious reformism, while ignoring the vital role of the Qadiriyya in Usman's movement.[7] Likewise, Boko Haram, whose ideology is shaped more by global jihadi-salafi thought than any West African discursive tradition, make parallels between their war on the 'infidel' government of Nigeria and the 1804 jihad.[8]

Conversely, we also see some of the same patterns from Sokoto's early history repeated in a different historical context. Many of Usman's followers believed that his spiritual meeting with ʿAbd al-Qādir al-Jīlānī had allowed him to 'jump the chain', bypassing the Qadiriyya Mukhtariyya. The rapid spread of the Tijaniyya in Hausaland from the late nineteenth century onwards similarly allowed for the establishment of an alternative politico-spiritual hierarchy in the region. This Tijani hierarchy was, in turn, displaced in many parts of West Africa by the *Fayda* movement of Ibrahim Niasse, who announced that Aḥmad al-Tijānī had appeared to him in a vision and appointed him *muqaddam* in place of the existing head of the Tijani order in the region.[9] Today it is Salafism, which rejects Sufism and local knowledge traditions in general, that is subverting local hierarchies and offering outsiders a new avenue to political power. Looking outside of West Africa, some Muslim groups in the Americas reconceptualise the

---

of Capitalism in Sudan: With Special Reference to Maiurno, Blue Nile Province' (Unpublished PhD dissertation, University of Birmingham, 1978). Muhammad Shareef and his colleagues have conducted extensive research and digitisation of Maiurno's collection of Arabic MSS.

7 For a general summary, see Roman Loimeier, *Islamic Reform in Twentieth-Century Africa* (Edinburgh, 2016). For the Izala, see Ousmane Kane, *Muslim Modernity in Postcolonial Nigeria: A Study of the Society for the Removal of Innovation and Reinstatement of Tradition* (Boston, 2003); Abdoulaye Sounaye, 'Izala au Niger: une alternative de communauté religieuse', in L. Fourchard, O. Goerg and M. Gomez-Perez (eds), *Lieux de sociabilité urbaine en Afrique* (Paris, 2009), pp. 481–500. For the Sunnance, see Sounaye, 'Salafi Aesthetics: Preaching among the Sunnance in Niamey, Niger', *Journal of Religion in Africa,* 47:1 (2017), 9–41. For the clash between Sufism and Salafism in contemporary Nigeria, see Muhammad Sani Umar, 'Changing Islamic Identity in Nigeria from the 1960s to the 1980s: From Sufism to Anti-Sufism', in L. Brenner (ed.), *Muslim Identity and Social Change in Sub-Saharan Africa* (London, 1993), pp. 154–78.

8 See Kassim, 'Defining and Understanding'.

9 See Seesemann, *The Divine Flood.*

jihad of Usman dan Fodio in the context of black empowerment, seeking to reconnect to an African-Islamic past.[10] Meanwhile in Europe, identification with Islamic traditions from West Africa is sometimes a way for new converts to create their own religious identity, distinct from that of more established Muslim groups.[11]

What I am trying to say is that the theoretical contribution of this book should be of relevance and interest outside of the narrow field of Sokoto studies, and outside of African studies more generally. Indeed, while I have shown that we can make sense of the Arabic writings of the Fodiawa only by placing them in their precise societal context, I hope I have also made clear that the ideas within these texts are not confined to a society, culture or historical period. The shifting discursive strategies to which I make reference, and the various sources of authority and legitimacy invoked by the Fodiawa, should be familiar to many specialists of different areas and eras throughout the Muslim world, whether in the disciplines of history, sociology, political science or anthropology. In the regrettably large number of conflicts shaking these regions today, the same discursive cycles are turning as new generations of rebel-rulers seek to assert their authority, using a similar set of textual tools from Islam's rich discursive traditions.

[10] I am thinking specifically of the work of the Masjid Nur-az-Zamaan in Pittsburgh, Pennsylvania, and the Sankore Institute of Islamic-African Studies International.

[11] In 2008, the National Organisation of Russian Muslims shifted to the *'Maliki-Ashʿarī'* tradition and formed links in Cape Town as well as West Africa, seemingly to avoid being associated with Muslims from the Caucasus region.

Appendix: Sokoto Chronology

In the following tables the phrase **Dated** refers to those texts which this book assigns a specific date of composition, to a high degree of confidence. **Non-Dated** refers to those texts that could not be assigned a date of composition but likely were composed during a particular period. The **Source** column indicates the source or reasoning for the assigned dates or periods, with the **Dispute?** column indicating any instances where alternative dates or periods were proposed in other sources. Titles are abbreviated for ease of presentation. Full titles and translations can be found in the first section of the bibliography.

Writings of Usman dan Fodio

PRE-JIHAD PERIOD (1774–1804)

	Text	Source	Dispute?
Dated			
1784–1785	*Miʿrāj al-ʿawām*	Al-Hajj (1977); Hunwick and O'Fahey (1995)	
1793	*Iḥyāʾ al-Sunna*	Balogun (1967)	
11 Aug 1794	*Tabshīr al-umma*	Hunwick and O'Fahey	
1794?	*[Lamma balaghtu]*	Contextual reference	Doubts over authorship in Last (2008)
8 Mar 1803	*Masāʾil muhimma*	Hunwick and O'Fahey	Al-Hajj: 1802
Non-Dated			
c.1774–1804	*Ḥiṣn al-afhām*	Al-Hajj	
c.1774–1804	*Ḥukm juhhāl bilād al-Ḥawsa*	Al-Hajj	
c.1774–1804	*Ifhām al-munkirīn*	Al-Hajj	

c.1774–1804	*Kifāyat al-muhtadīn*	Al-Hajj	
c.1774–1804	*Mir'āt al-ṭullāb*	Al-Hajj	
c.1774–1804	*Naṣā'iḥ al-umma*	Al-Hajj	
c.1774–1804	*Shifā' al-ghalīl fī-mā ashkala min kalām shaykh shuyūkhinā Jibrīl*	Al-Hajj	
c.1774–1804	*Tamyīz al-muslimīn*	Al-Hajj	
c.1804	*[Letter to a Hausa leader]*	Contextual reference	

JIHAD PERIOD (1804–1810)

	Text	Source	Dispute?
Dated			
17 Apr 1805	*al-Amr bi-muwālāt*	Date in MS	Hunwick and O'Fahey: 22 January 1812 or 1 February 1811
1806	*Bayān wujūb al-hijra*	El-Masri (1978)	Hunwick and O'Fahey: 1809, which does not correspond to the Hijri date they provide
20 Nov 1808	*Miṣbāḥ li-ahl hadhā-l-zamān*	Hunwick and O'Fahey	
8 Oct 1808	*Tanbīh al-fāhim 'alā ḥukm muddat al-dunyā wa-khalq al-'ālam*	Date in MS	
23 Jul 1809	*Amr al-sā'a wa-ashrāṭihā*	Date in MS	Hunwick and O'Fahey: 1803–1804
Non-Dated			
after 1806	*Kitāb al-farq*	Last and Al-Hajj (1965)	
before 1809	*Muddat al-dunyā*	Contextual reference	
before 1809	*Tanbīh al-umma 'alā qurb hujūm ashrāṭ al-sā'a*	Contextual reference	
c.1804–1810	*al-Maḥdhūrāt min 'alāmāt khurūj al-mahdī*	Al-Hajj	
c.1804–1810	*Wathīqa ilā jamī' Ahl al-Sūdān*	Al-Hajj	

MODERATION (c.1810–1812)

	Text	**Souce**	**Dispute?**
Dated			
1811	*al-Khabar al-hādī*	Al-Hajj (1973)	
1811	*Naṣīḥat ahl al-zamān*	Hunwick and O'Fahey citing Kani (1988)	
4 Sep 1811	*Sirāj al-ikhwān*	Hunwick and O'Fahey	
11 Nov 1811	*Tanbīh al-ikhwān*	Date in MS	

INTELLECTUAL CONFLICT (c.1812–1817)

	Text	**Source**	**Dispute?**
Dated			
6 Dec 1812 – 3 Jan 1813	*Najm al-ikhwān*	Hunwick and O'Fahey	
20 May 1813	*Shams al-ikhwān*	Hunwick and O'Fahey	
19 Jun 1813	*Tawqīf al-Muslimīn*	Date in MS	Hunwick and O'Fahey: 9 June
7 Dec 1813	*Ta'līm al-ikhwān*	Martin (1967)	
15 Nov 1814	*Taḥdhīr al-ikhwān*	Hunwick and O'Fahey	

DATE NOT ASSIGNED

	Text	**Source**	**Dispute?**
	Ajwiba muḥarrara		Al-Hajj estimates c.1774–1804
	Nūr al-albāb		Al-Hajj estimates c.1810–1817
	Wathīqa ilā al-rajul		

Writings of Abdullahi dan Fodio

PRE-JIHAD PERIOD (1774–1804)

	Text	Source	Dispute?
Dated			
26 Mar 1800	*Kifāyat al-ʿawām fī-l-buyūʿ*	Hunwick and O'Fahey (1995)	

JIHAD PERIOD (1804–1810)

	Text	Source	Dispute?
Dated			
Dec 1805 – Jan 1806	*Kashf al-liʾm*	Date in MS	
1807–1808	*Ḍiyāʾ al-ḥukkām*	Contextual reference	Hunwick and O'Fahey: c.1806–1807
28 Dec 1810	*Ḍiyāʾ ūlī [walīy?]-l-amr*	Date in MS	Hunwick and O'Fahey: 8 February 1810
Non-Dated			
before 1807?	*Ḍiyāʾ al-muqtadīn*	Contextual reference	

MODERATION (c.1810–1812)

	Text	Source	Dispute?
Dated			
10 Aug 1811	*Ḍiyāʾ al-mujāhidīn*	Hunwick and O'Fahey	
1811–1812	*Ḍiyāʾ al-umma fī adillat al-aʾimma*	Hunwick and O'Fahey	

INTELLECTUAL CONFLICT (c.1812–1817)

	Text	Source	Dispute?
Dated			
19 Jan 1812	*Ḍiyāʾ al-sulṭān*	Hunwick and O'Fahey	
7 Oct 1812	*Īdāʿ al-nusūkh*	Hunwick and O'Fahey	
30 Jun 1813	*Ḍiyāʾ al-umarāʾ*	Alkali (2004)	

14 Oct 1813	*Tazyīn al-waraqāt*	Hunwick and O'Fahey	
30 Oct 1815	*Ḍiyā' al-wilāyāt*	Hunwick and O'Fahey	
Non-Dated			
1815–1816	*[al-Ajwiba li-'Abd Allāh ibn Fūdī 'alā as'ilat Aḥmad Lubbu]*	Contextual reference	

SUCCESSION CRISIS (1817–1821)

	Text	Source	Dispute?
Dated			
18 May 1817	*Sabīl al-salāma*	Date in MS	Hunwick and O'Fahey are a month out on their Hijri date
29 Mar 1820	*Ḍiyā' al-siyāsāt*	Kani (1988); Hunwick and O'Fahey	
Non-Dated			
after 1817	*Kitāb al-nasab*	Hunwick and O'Fahey	

RULE OF GWANDU (1821–1828)

	Text	Source	Dispute?
Dated			
17 Aug 1826	*Dawā' al-waswās*	Hunwick and O'Fahey	Shareef (1994): 1807–1808
1827	*Tahdhīb al-insān*	Shareef (2003)	Hunwick and O'Fahey: 1828–1829
24 Feb 1828	*Ḍiyā' al-qawā'id*	Hunwick and O'Fahey	

DATE NOT ASSIGNED

	Text	Source	Dispute?
	Aṣl al-Fulātiyyīn		

Writings of Muhammad Bello

PRE-JIHAD PERIOD (1774–1804)

	Text	Source	Dispute?
Dated			
1801	*Rafʿ al-shubha*	Date in MS	

JIHAD PERIOD (1804–1810)

	Text	Source	Dispute?
Non-Dated			
1805–1806	*Miftāḥ al-baṣāʾir*	Referring to the same event as *Kashf al-liʾm*	
c.1810	Replies to *al-Kānamī* (in *Infāq al-maysūr*)	Minna (1983); Brenner (1992)	

MODERATION (c.1810–1812)

	Text	Source	Dispute?
Dated			
10 Nov 1812	*Infāq al-maysūr*	Hunwick and O'Fahey (1995)	
Non-Dated			
c.1812	*al-Ghayth al-shuʾbūb*	Contextual reference	

INTELLECTUAL CONFLICT (c.1812–1817)

	Text	Source	Dispute?
Non-Dated			
after 1812	*Ḥāshiya ʿalā muqad-dimat Īdāʿ al-nusūkh*	Contextual reference	
after 1815	*Jawāb shāfin wa-khiṭāb minnā kāfin*	Contextual reference	

SUCCESSION CRISIS (1817–1821)

	Text	Source	Dispute?
Dated			
22 Jul 1817	*al-Inṣāf fī dhikr mā-fī masāʾil al-khilāfa min wifāq wa-khilāf*	Date in MS	
21 Sep 1819	*Kashf al-ghiṭāʾ*	Date in MS	

27 Jul 1820	*al-Qawl al-mukhtaṣar*	Hunwick and O'Fahey	
Nov–Dec 1820	*[Risāla ilā Muḥammad al-Jaylānī]*	Date in MS	
13 Jun 1820	*Tanbīh al-ṣāḥib ʿalā aḥkām al-makāsib*	Hunwick and O'Fahey	
1820–1821	*al-Ghayth al-wabl fī sīrat al-imām al-ʿadl*	Hunwick and O'Fahey	
Non-Dated			
c.1817	*Sard al-kalām*	Contextual reference	
after 1817	*al-Ishāʿa fī ḥukm al-khārijīn min al-ṭāʿa*	Contextual reference	
after 1817	*Shifāʾ al-asqām*	Hunwick and O'Fahey	
c.1818	*Risāla li-l-amrāḍ shāfiya*	Shareef (1995)	
after 1817	*[Letter to Emir Yaʿqūb]*	Contextual reference	
c.1817–1821	*al-Taḥrīr fī qawāʿid al-tabṣīr*	Contextual reference	

RULE OF SOKOTO (1821–1837)

	Text	Source	Dispute?
Dated			
c.1825–1826	*[Letter to al-Mukhtār ibn Muḥammad ibn al-Mukhtār al-Kuntī]*	Contextual reference	
Non-Dated			
c.1821	*Jawāb shāfin li-l-murīd*	Contextual reference	
c.1821–1828	*[Maktūb fī radd masāʾil ʿan Aḥmad Lubbu]*	Contextual reference	
after 1821	*Kifāyat al-muhtadīn*	Contextual reference	
after 1821	*Miftāḥ al-sadād*	Contextual reference	
after 1821	*al-Nuqūl al-nawāṭiq*	Contextual reference	
after 1821	*Qadḥ al-zinād*	Contextual reference	

DATE NOT ASSIGNED

	Text	Source	Dispute?
	[Majmūʿ baʿḍ al-rasāʾil]		
	Wathīqa ilā jamāʿat al-muslimīn		

Chronology of key texts I

	USMAN DAN FODIO		ABDULLAHI DAN FODIO		MUHAMMAD BELLO
			PRE-JIHAD PERIOD (1774–1804)		
Dated					
1784–1785	*Mi'rāj al-'awām*	*26 Mar 1800*	*Kifāyat al-'awām fī-l-buyū'*	1801	*Raf' al-shubha*
1793	*Iḥyā' al-Sunna*				
11 Aug 1794	*Tabshīr al-umma*				
1794?	*[Lamma balaghtu]*				
8 Mar 1803	*Masā'il muhimma*				
Non-Dated					
c.1774–1804	*Ḥiṣn al-afhām*				
c.1774–1804	*Ḥukm juhhāl bilād al-Ḥawsa*				
c.1774–1804	*Ifhām al-munkirīn*				
c.1774–1804	*Kifāyat al-muhtadīn*				
c.1774–1804	*Mir'āt al-ṭullāb*				
c.1774–1804	*Naṣā'iḥ al-umma*				
c.1774–1804	*Shifā' al-ghalīl fī-mā ashkala min kalām shaykh shuyūkhinā Jibrīl*				
c.1774–1804	*Tamyīz al-muslimīn*				
c.1804	*[Letter to a Hausa leader]*				

JIHAD PERIOD (1804–1810)					
Dated					
17 Apr 1805	*al-Amr bi-muwālāt*	Dec 1805–Jan 1806	*Kashf al-liʿm*	1805–1806	*Miftāḥ al-baṣāʾir 1806*
1806	*Bayān wujūb al-hijra*	1807–1808	*Ḍiyāʾ al-ḥukkām*	c.1810	Replies to *al-Kānamī* (in *Infāq al-maysūr*)
20 Nov 1808	*Miṣbāḥ li-ahl hadhā-l-zamān*	28 Dec 1810	*Ḍiyāʾ ūlī [walīy?]-l-amr*		
8 Oct 1808	*Tanbīh al-fāhim ʿalā ḥukm muddat al-dunyā wa-khalq al-ʿālam*				
23 Jul 1809	*Amr al-sāʿa wa-ashrāṭihā*				
Non-Dated					
after 1806	*Kitāb al-farq*				
before 1809	*Muddat al-dunyā*				
before 1809	*Tanbīh al-umma ʿalā qurb hujūm ashrāṭ al-sāʿa*				
c.1804–1810	*al-Maḥdhūrāt min ʿalāmāt khurūj al-mahdī*	before 1807?	*Ḍiyāʾ al-muqtadīn*		
c.1804–1810	*Wathīqa ilā jamīʿ Ahl al-Sūdān*				
MODERATION (c. 1810–1812)					
Dated					
1811	*al-Khabar al-hādī*	10 Aug 1811	*Ḍiyāʾ al-mujāhidīn*	10 Nov 1812	*Infāq al-maysūr*

1811	*Naṣīḥat ahl al-zamān*	1811–12	*Ḍiyāʾ al-umma fī adillat al-aʾimma*		
4 Sep 1811	*Sirāj al-ikhwān*				
11 Nov 1811	*Tanbīh al-ikhwān*				
Non-Dated					
				c. 1812	*al-Ghayth al-shuʾbūb*
		INTELLECTUAL CONFLICT (c.1812–1817)			
Dated					
6 Dec 1812 – 3 Jan 1813	*Najm al-ikhwān*	19 Jan 1812	*Ḍiyāʾ al-sulṭān*		
20 May 1813	*Shams al-ikhwān*	7 Oct 1812	*Īdāʿ al-nusūkh*		
19 Jun 1813	*Tawqīf al-Muslimīn*	30 Jun 1813	*Ḍiyāʾ al-umarāʾ*		
7 Dec 1813	*Taʿlīm al-ikhwān*	14 Oct 1813	*Tazyīn al-waraqāt*		
15 Nov 1814	*Taḥdhīr al-ikhwān*	30 Oct 1815	*Ḍiyāʾ al-wilāyāt*		
Non-Dated					
		1815–1816	*[al-Ajwiba li-ʿAbd Allāh ibn Fūdī...]*	after 1812	*Ḥāshiya ʿalā muqaddimat Īdāʿ al-nusūkh*
				after 1815	*Jawāb shāfin wa-khiṭāb minnā kāfin*

Chronology of key texts II

	ABDULLAHI DAN FODIO		MUHAMMAD BELLO		SOKOTO & GWANDU ELITES		OTHERS
			SUCCESSION CRISIS (1817–1821)				
Dated							
18 May 1817	*Sabīl al-salāma*	22 Jul 1817	*al-Inṣāf fī dhikr…*	1817	*Rawḍ al-jinān* (Gidado dan Layma)	1818	*Kanz al-awlād* (Sambo Kulwa)
29 Mar 1820	*Ḍiyā᾿ al-siyāsāt*	21 Sep 1819	*Kashf al-ghiṭā᾿*				
		27 Jul 1820	*al-Qawl al-mukhtaṣar*				
		13 Jun 1820	*Tanbīh al-ṣāḥib ʿalā aḥkām al-makāsib*				
		Nov–Dec 1820	*[Risāla ilā Muḥammad al-Jaylānī]*				
		1820–1821	*al-Ghayth al-wabl fī sīrat al-imām al-ʿadl*				
Non-Dated							
after 1817	*Kitāb al-nasab*	c. 1817	*Sard al-kalām*				
		after 1817	*al-Ishāʿa fī ḥukm al-khārijīn min al-ṭāʿa*				
		after 1817	*Shifā᾿ al-asqām*				
		c.1818	*Risāla li-l-amrāḍ shāfiya*				

		after 1817	*[Letter to Emir Ya'qūb]*				
		c. 1817–1821	*al-Taḥrīr fī qawā'id al-tabṣīr*				
RULE OF GWANDU (1821–1828)				***RULE OF SOKOTO (1821–1837)***			
Dated							
17 Aug 1826	*Dawā' al-waswās*	c. 1825–1826	*[Letter to al-Mukhtār ibn Muḥammad ibn al-Mukhtār al-Kuntī]*	1823	*Rawḍāt al-afkār* (Abdulkadiri dan Tafa)	1826	*Narrative of Travels and Discoveries* (Clapperton)
1827	*Tahdhīb al-insān*					1830	*Records of Captain Clapperton's Last Expedition* (Lander)
24 Feb 1828	*Ḍiyā' al-qawā'id*						
Non-Dated							
		c. 1821	*Jawāb shāfin li-l-murīd*				
		c. 1821–1828	*[Maktūb fī radd masā'il 'an Aḥmad Lubbu]*				
		after 1821	*Kifāyat al-muhtadīn*				
		after 1821	*Miftāḥ al-sadād*				
		after 1821	*al-Nuqūl al-nawāṭiq*				
		after 1821	*Qadḥ al-zinād*				

Chronology of key texts III

	SOKOTO & GWANDU ELITES		OTHERS
	SUCCESSORS OF BELLO		
Dated			
1838	*al-Kashf wa-l-bayān* (Gidado dan Layma)	24 May 1832	*[Additions to Kanz al-awlād]* (Bayero b. Sambo Kulwa)
1840–1841	*Tartīb al-aṣḥāb* (Sa'd b. 'Abd al-Raḥmān)	c.1854	*Taqāyīd mimmā waṣala ilaynā (Al-Ḥājj Sa'īd)*
		1857	*Travels and Discoveries in North and Central Africa* (Barth)
		1861	*Bayān mā waqa'a* (Al-Ḥājj 'Umar Tāl)
Non-Dated			
c.1837–1842	*[Abū Bakr 'Atīq MS] (Amīr al-mu'minīn* Atiku)		
c.1837–1842	*al-Intiqāl min balad Hawsa (Amīr al-mu'minīn* Atiku)		
c.1837–1851	*[Kashf al-ḥijāb wa-raf' al-niqāb]* (Gidado dan Layma)		
	EARLY BRITISH COLONIAL ADMINISTRATION (1903–1920s)		
1905	*Ta'nīs al-ikhwān* (Muḥammad al-Bukhārī)	1909	*Historical Notes on Certain Emirates and Tribes* (Burdon) – informed by Muḥammad al-Bukhārī
1908	*Lubāb mā fī Tazyīn al-waraqāt wa-Infāq al-maysūr* (Aḥmad b. Sa'd)	1909	*History of Gando* (McAllister) – informed by Aḥmad b. Sa'd (?)
		1914–1915	*An Early Fulani Conception of Islam* (Palmer) – informed by Muḥammad al-Bukhārī

		1922	*The Rise of the Sokoto Fulani* (Arnett)
EARLY NIGERIAN NATIONALIST PERIOD (1950s–mid-1970s)			
1956–1966	Historical works of Sir Ahmadu Bello (*Sardauna* of Sokoto)	1967	*Islamic States of Northern Nigeria* (Hogben) – foreword by Sir Ahmadu Bello
1959–1978	Historical works of Muhammadu Junaidu (Waziri of Sokoto)	1967	*The Fulani Empire of Sokoto* (Johnston) – informed by Waziri Junaidu
		1967	*The Sokoto Caliphate* (Last) – informed by Waziri Junaidu

Bibliography

Primary Sources

Below is a list of the primary source material cited in this book, principally the Arabic texts composed by the Fodiawa and their contemporaries. The texts are sorted by their author and then alphabetically. Each entry includes the full transliterated title of the text, a translation of this title and, where possible, the definite or estimated date that the text was composed. This is followed by details about the manuscript copies that I consulted. Any published editions and translations of these texts that I have used are also noted briefly here, with full references appearing in the 'Secondary literature' section. For a chronological rendering of this material and for more on the assignment of dates, see the Appendix. Devised titles for primary source material with no formal title are shown between [square brackets]. Digitised items feature hyperlinks to the material that can be accessed in PDF or online versions of the book. Note that during my research in Niamey I discovered that at some point after the 1000 mark, the Al-Furqan catalogue for the MARA collection (*Catalogue of Islamic Manuscripts at the Institut des Recherches en Sciences Humaines (IRSH) – Niger*) introduces an error, giving an item number that is one higher than the item numbers in situ. I give the latter, wherever possible.

Usman dan Fodio

Ajwiba muḥarrara ʿan asʾila muqarrara fī wathīqat al-Shaykh Al-Ḥājj al-maʿrūf bi-laqabihi Shīṣumaṣ ibn Aḥmad (n.d.) [Liberating answers to repeated questions in a letter to Shaykh Ḥājj known as Shīṣumaṣ ibn Aḥmad' MX Kaduna (NA), digitised as BL (EAP) 535 1/4/2/18 (https://eap.bl.uk/archive-file/EAP535-1-4-2-18); Niamey (MARA) 898.

al-Amr bi-muwālāt al-muʾminīn wa-l-nahā ʿan muwālāt al-kāfirīn (17 April 1805) [Commanding friendship with the faithful and denying friendship with the infidels] MS Kaduna (NA), digitised as BL (EAP) 535 1/2/25/4 (https://eap.bl.uk/archive-file/EAP535-1-2-25-4).

Amr al-sāʿa wa-ashrāṭihā (23 July 1809) [On the hour and its signs] MS Kaduna (NA), digitised as BL (EAP) 535 1/4/2/9 (https://eap.bl.uk/archive-file/EAP535-1-4-2-9).

Bayān wujūb al-hijra ʿalā al-ʿibād wa-bayān wujūb naṣb al-imām wa-iqāmat al-jihād (1806) [Declaring the obligation of emigration upon the servants of God and the exposition of the obligation of appointing an imam and undertaking jihad] English translation in El-Masri (1978).

*al-Farq bayn wilāyāt ahl al-Islām wa-bayn wilāyāt ahl al-*kufr (after 1806) [The difference between the governments of the Muslims and the governments of the unbelievers] (known as *Kitāb al-farq*) in Hiskett (1960).

Ḥiṣn al-afhām min juyūsh al-awhām (c.1774–1804) [Stronghold of understanding from the armies of tumult] in Siddiqi (1989).

Ḥukm juhhāl bilād al-Ḥawsa (c.1774–1804) [Judgement concerning the ignorant ones of Hausaland] MS Niamey (MARA) 1669.

Ifhām al-munkirīn ʿalayya fī-mā āmur al-nās bihi wa-fī-mā anhāhum ʿanhu fī dīn Allāh (c.1774–1804) [Informing those who disavow me regarding what people are ordered to do and prevented from doing in God's religion] MX Niamey (MARA) 229; NU/Paden 268.

*Iḥyāʾ al-Sunna wa-ikhmād al-*bidʿa (1793) [Revival of the Sunna and the destruction of innovation] in Balogun (1967).

Kifāyat al-muhtadīn (c.1774–1804) [Sufficient information for the rightly guided] in Shareef (2001).

al-Khabar al-hādī ilā umūr al-imām al-Mahdī (1811) [Guiding news as to matters of the Imam Mahdi] English translation in Al-Hajj (1973).

[Lamma balaghtu] (1794?) [When I reached [the age of thirty-six]] ME (Zaria, Gaskiya Corp., n.d.), copy at NU/Hunwick 122.

[Letter to a Hausa leader] (c.1804) MS Niamey (MARA) 3996 (written with Abdullahi).

al-Maḥdhūrāt min ʿalāmāt khurūj al-mahdī (c.1804–1810) [Warnings of the Mahdi's appearance] MX Niamey, Collection of Seyni Moumouni.

Masāʾil muhimma yaḥtāju ilā maʿrifatihā Ahl al-Sūdān (8 March 1803) [Important matters that the Ahl al-Sūdān need to know] MS Paris (BnF) Arabe 5678 (https://gallica.bnf.fr/ark:/12148/btv1b9065793k), ff. 150–159 (incomplete); MX Niamey (MARA) 280.

Miʿrāj al-ʿawām ilā samāʿ ʿilm al-kalām (1784–1785) [Ladder for the common people to hear knowledge of theology] ME (Zaria, Shifa Commercial Press, n.d.), copy at NU/Hunwick 127.

Mirʾāt al-ṭullāb fī mustanad al-abwāb li-dīn Allāh al-Wahhāb (c.1774–1804) [Mirror for the students concerning the reason for the categories of the religion of God the Giver] Kaduna (NA), digitised as BL (EAP) 535 1/3/2/1 (https://eap.bl.uk/archive-file/EAP535-1-3-2-1).

Miṣbāḥ li-ahl hadhā-l-zamān min ahl Bilād al-Sūdān (20 November 1808) [A lamp for the people of this time from the Bilād al-Sūdān] in Abdullahi, *Ḍiyā' al-sulṭān*.

Muddat al-dunyā (before 1809) [The length of the world] ME (Sokoto, n.d.), copy at NU/Hunwick 143.

Najm al-ikhwān yahtadūna bihi bi-idhn Allāh fī umūr al-zamān (December 1812 – January 1813) [Star of the brothers by which they will be guided – God-willing – concerning matters of the current time] MX Niamey, Collection of Seyni Moumouni.

Naṣīḥat ahl al-zamān li-Ahl al-Sūdān [wa-li-man shā'a Allāh min al-Ikhwān] min al-'Arab wa-l-'ajam fī jamī' al-buldān (1811) [Advice for the people of this time – to the Ahl al-Sūdān and to whomever God wills from the brothers whether Arab or non-Arab in all the lands] ME (Sokoto, n.d.), copy at NU/Hunwick 159.

Naṣā'iḥ al-umma al-Muḥammadiyya li-bayān al-firāq al-shayṭāniyya allatī ẓaharat fī bilādinā al-sūdāniyya (c.1774–1804) [Pieces of advice to the umma of Muhammad, making them aware of the satanic parties who have appeared in our Bilād al-Sūdān] Niamey (MARA) 264; summary and English part translation in Hiskett (1962).

Nūr al-albāb (n.d.) [The light of hearts] in Hamet (1897).

Shams al-ikhwān yastaḍi'ūna bihā fī uṣūl al-adyān (20 May 1813) [Sun of the brothers by which they are enlightened in the fundamentals of religion] MS Paris (BnF) Arabe 5500 (https://gallica.bnf.fr/ark%3A/12148/btv1b9065544d).

Shifā' al-ghalīl fī-mā ashkala min kalām shaykh shuyūkhinā Jibrīl (c.1774–1804) [Quenching the thirst concerning what is dubious from the words of the Shaykh of our Shaykh, Jibril] MX NU/Hiskett, uncatalogued MSS, Box II.

Sirāj al-ikhwān fī ahamm yuḥtāju ilayhi fī hadhā-l-zamān (4 September 1811) [Light of the brothers concerning the most important things that are needed in this age] in Shareef (2000); summary in Hiskett (1962).

Tabshīr al-umma al-Aḥmadiyya bi-bayān ba'ḍ manāqib al-Qādiriyya (11 August 1794) [Bringing good news to the umma of Muhammad concerning some of the virtues of the Qadiriyya] Kaduna (NA), digitised as BL (EAP) 535 1/2/5/1 (https://eap.bl.uk/archive-file/EAP535-1-2-5-1).

Taḥdhīr al-ikhwān min iddi'ā' al-mahdiyya al-maw'ūda ākhir al-zamān (15 November 1814) [Warning to the brothers against claiming the mahdiyya promised at the end of time] English translation in al-Hajj (1973).

Ta'līm al-ikhwān bi-l-umūr allatī kaffarnā bihā mulūk al-Sūdān alladhīna kānū min ahl hadhihi-l-buldān wa-hum mulūk Ḥaws (7 December 1813) [Instruction to the brothers in those matters for which we anathematised the kings of [the Bilād] al-Sūdān who were from the people of these lands, namely, the kings of the Hausa] English translation in Martin (1967).

Tamyīz al-muslimīn min al-kāfirīn (c.1774–1804) [Separating the Muslims from the infidels] MX Niamey (MARA) 363.

Tanbīh al-fāhim ʿalā ḥukm muddat al-dunyā wa-khalq al-ʿālam (8 October 1808) [Informing the learned of the verdict concerning the length of the world and the creation of the earth] unpublished English translation by Hermann G. Harris, Kaduna (NA), digitised as BL (EAP) 535 1/2/1/4 (https://eap.bl.uk/archive-file/EAP535-1-2-1-4).

Tanbīh al-ikhwān ʿalā aḥwāl Arḍ al-Sūdān (11 November 1811) [Admonition to the brothers regarding the circumstances of the Arḍ al-Sūdān] English translation in Palmer (1914–1915).

Tanbīh al-umma ʿalā qurb hujūm ashrāṭ al-sāʿa (before 1809) [Informing the umma about the imminent onset of the signs of the hour] English translation in Shareef (1998).

Tawqīf al-Muslimīn ʿala ḥukm madhāhib al-mujtahidīn (19 June 1813) [Stopping the Muslims from judging the madhabs of the fighters] ME (Sokoto, n.d.), copy at NU/Hunwick 124.

Wathīqa ilā jamīʿ Ahl al-Sūdān (c.1804–1810) [Dispatch to all the Ahl al-Sūdān] in Bivar (1961).

*Wathīqa ilā al-rajul yadʿī annahu ʿālim yufassir al-Qurʾān bi-ghair itqān qawānīn al-*tafsīr (n.d.) [A letter to the man claiming that he is qualified to make an exegesis of the Qur'an without mastering the laws of exegesis] ME (Sokoto, n.d.), in the possession of Seyni Moumouni.

Abdullahi dan Fodio

[al-Ajwiba li-ʿAbd Allāh ibn Fūdī ʿalā asʾilat Aḥmad Lubbu] (1815–1816) [The answers of Abdullahi dan Fodio to the questions of Ahmad Lobbo] Niamey (MARA) 1716; MS Paris (BI) 379.

Aṣl al-Fulātiyyīn (n.d.) [The Origin of the Fulani] MX Niamey, Journal de Boubou Hama, 1968–1969.

Dawāʾ al-waswās wa-l-ghafalāt fi al-ṣalāt wa-qirāʾat al-Qurʾān wa-l-daʿawāt (1826) [The cure of satanic whispering and negligence in prayer, readings of the Qur'an and supplications] in Shareef (1994).

Ḍiyāʾ al-ḥukkām fi-mā la-hum wa-ʿalayhim min al-aḥkām (1807–1808) [Guidance for the judges regarding the legal rulings by which they judge and are judged] MS Paris (BI) 175.

Ḍiyāʾ al-mujāhidīn ḥumāt al-dīn al-rāshidīn (10 August 1811) [Guidance for the fighters, protectors of the religion of the rightly guided ones] MS Paris (BnF) Arabe 5655 (https://gallica.bnf.fr/ark:/12148/btv1b9065632j).

Ḍiyāʾ al-muqtadīn li-l-khulafāʾ al-rāshidīn (before 1807?) [Guidance for those emulating the Rightly Guided Caliphs] MS Paris (BI) 192.

Ḍiyāʾ al-qawāʿid wa-nathr al-fawāʾid li-ahl al-maqāṣid (24 February 1828) [Guidance on the tenets and the dispersal of benefits to those of firm intention] in Shareef (2009).

Ḍiyāʾ al-siyāsāt wa-fatāwī-l-nawāzil mimmā huwa fī furūʿ al-dīn min al-masāʾil (29 March 1820) [Guidance on policies and legal opinions as found in the examples from the branches of religion] in Kani (1988); MX Ibadan (UC), in the possession of Paulo Fernando de Moraes Farias.

Ḍiyāʾ al-sulṭān wa-ghayrihi min al-ikhwān fī ahamm mā yuṭlabu ʿilmuhu fī umūr al-zamān (19 January 1812) [Guidance for the ruler and others from the brothers regarding the most important of what his knowledge demands of him in matters of the current time] MS Paris (BI) 205; French part translation in Mahibou (2010).

Ḍiyāʾ ūlī [walīy?]-l-amr wa-l-mujāhidīn fī sīrat al-nabī wa-l-khulafāʾ al-rāshidīn (28 December 1810) [Guidance for the responsible, the fighters in the path of the Prophet, and the Rashidun Caliphs] MS Paris (BnF) Arabe 5364 (https://gallica.bnf.fr/ark:/12148/btv1b9065560h).

Ḍiyāʾ al-umarāʾ fī-mā la-hum wa-ʿalayhim min al-ashyāʾ (30 June 1813) [Guidance for the emirs regarding those things over which they preside and by which they are bound] in Alkali (2004).

Ḍiyāʾ al-umma fī adillat al-aʾimma (1811–1812) [Guidance for the umma regarding sources of direction for the imams] MS Kaduna (NA), digitised as BL (EAP) 535 1/1/3/6 (https://eap.bl.uk/archive-file/EAP535-1-1-3-6).

Ḍiyāʾ al-wilāyāt fī-l-umūr al-dunyawiyya wa-l-dīniyyāt (1815) [Guidance on governance in temporal and spiritual matters] MS Paris (BnF) Arabe 5697 (https://gallica.bnf.fr/ark:/12148/btv1b90658164), ff. 43a–44a.

Īdāʿ al-nusūkh man akhadhtu ʿanhu min al-shuyūkh (1812) [The repository of texts concerning those Shaykhs from whom I took knowledge] English translation in Hiskett (1957).

Kashf al-liʾm la-nā wa-li-man tabiʿnā fī amr al-sharīf ʿAbd Allāh Ḥanuna Gīwa (December 1805–January 1806) [Finding agreement for us and for those who follow us concerning the matter of Sharif ʿAbd Allāh Ḥanuna Gīwa MS Kaduna (NA), digitised as BL (EAP) 535 1/4/1/42 (https://eap.bl.uk/archive-file/EAP535-1-4-1-42).

Kifāyat al-ʿawām fī-l-buyūʿ (26 March 1800) [Sufficiency for the common people in [the laws of] sales] MS NU/Falke 117.

Kitāb al-nasab (after 1817) [Book of noble heritage] MX NU/Wilks 115.
Sabīl al-salāma fi-l-imāma (18 May 1817) [The way of safety concerning the imamate] MX NU/Paden 244; summary and English part translation in Minna (1983).
Tahdhīb al-insān min khiṣāl al-shayṭān (1827) [Reforming mankind from the traits of the devil] in Shareef (2003).
Tazyīn al-waraqāt bi-jam' ba'ḍ mā lī min al-abyāt (1813) [Adornment of papers by the collection of some of my verses] English translation in Hiskett (1963).

Muhammad Bello

al-Ghayth al-shu'būb fī tawṣiyyat al-amīr Ya'qūb (c.1812) [Abundant rain concerning advice to Emir Ya'qūb] in Ismail and Aliyu (1975).
al-Ghayth al-wabl fī sīrat al-imām al-'adl (1820–1821) [Abundant downpour concerning the conduct of the just leader] English translations in Bello (1983); Shareef (2002).
Ḥāshiya 'alā muqaddimat Īdā' al-nusūkh (after 1812) [A commentary to the preface of the repository of texts] MS Paris (BnF) Arabe 5432 (https://gallica.bnf.fr/ark:/12148/btv1b90654991), ff. 298b–299b; MS Niamey (MARA) 23.
Infāq al-maysūr fī ta'rīkh bilād al-Takrūr (10 November 1812) [Easy expenditure regarding the history of the lands of Takrur] in Shādhilī's (1996) critical edition; English translation in Shareef (2008).
al-Inṣāf fī dhikr mā-fī masā'il al-khilāfa min wifāq wa-khilāf (22 July 1817) [Fair judgement of conflicting views on questions concerning the caliphate] MS Paris (BI) 206.
al-Ishā'a fī ḥukm al-khārijīn min al-ṭā'a (after 1817) [Making known the judgement of those who become disobedient] MX Kaduna (NA), digitised as BL (EAP) 535 1/4/1/7 (https://eap.bl.uk/archive-file/EAP535-1-4-1-7).
Jawāb shāfin li-l-murīd (c.1821) [A healing answer for the desirous] MS Kaduna (NA), digitised as BL (EAP) 535 1/2/1/10 (https://eap.bl.uk/archive-file/EAP535-1-2-1-10).
Jawāb shāfin wa-khiṭāb minnā kāfin ilā Muḥammad al-Jaylānī (after 1815) [A healing answer and sufficient address from us to Muhammad al-Jaylānī] English part translation in Norris (1975).
Kashf al-ghiṭā' wa-l-sitr fī muwālāt al-kuffār (bi-ma'nā al-naṣr) (21 September 1819) [Revealing the cover and the veil concerning friendship with the infidels (meaning aiding them)] MX Kaduna (NA), digitised as BL (EAP) 535 1/4/2/50 (https://eap.bl.uk/archive-file/EAP535-1-4-2-50).

Kifāyat al-muhtadīn fī aḥkām al-mukhallifīn min al-mujāhidīn (after 1821) [Sufficient information for the rightly guided regarding the judgements upon those warriors who stay behind] MX Kaduna (NA), digitised as BL (EAP) 535 1/4/2/30 (https://eap.bl.uk/archive-file/EAP535-1-4-2-30).

[Letter to Emir Yaʿqūb] (after 1817) MS Kano (SHCB), digitised as BL (EAP) 087/1/71 (https://eap.bl.uk/archive-file/EAP087-1-71).

[Letter to al-Mukhtār ibn Muḥammad ibn al-Mukhtār al-Kuntī] (c.1825–1826) MS Paris (BnF) Arabe 5574 (https://gallica.bnf.fr/ark:/12148/btv1b9065701b/f36.item), ff. 33a–38a. Also found in [*Majmūʿ baʿḍ al-rasāʾil*], pp. 16–28.

[Majmūʿ baʿḍ al-rasāʾil] (n.d.) [Collection of letters] MX NU/Hunwick 162, from Maiduguri. Also contains letters from Bello's successors, Atiku and Aliu.

[Maktūb fī radd masāʾil ʿan Aḥmad Lubbu] (c.1821–1828) [Letter in response to some matters of Ahmad Lobbo] MX Kaduna (NA), digitised as BL (EAP) 535 1/4/1/9 (https://eap.bl.uk/archive-file/EAP535-1-4-1-9).

Miftāḥ al-baṣāʾir (1805–1806) [The key to insights] MX Kaduna (NA), digitised as BL (EAP) 535 1/4/1/43 (https://eap.bl.uk/archive-file/EAP535-1-4-1-43).

Miftāḥ al-sadād fī aqsām hāthihi al-bilād (after 1821) [The appropriate key to the classifications of these lands] MX Kaduna (NA), digitised as BL (EAP) 535 1/4/1/11 (https://eap.bl.uk/archive-file/EAP535-1-4-1-11).

al-Nuqūl al-nawāṭiq fī shaʾn al-Barbar wa-l-Tawāriq (after 1821) [Pronouncements regarding the Berbers and the Tuareg] MX Niamey (MARA) 273.

Qadḥ al-zinād fī amr hāthā-l-jihād (after 1821) [Striking the flint in the matter of this jihad] Paris (BnF) Arabe 5576 (https://gallica.bnf.fr/ark:/12148/btv1b90656707), ff. 1a–14a.

al-Qawl al-mukhtaṣar fī amr al-Imām al-Mahdī al-muntaẓar (27 July 1820) [Short discourse concerning the expected Mahdi] discussed in Albasu (1985); Minna (1982).

Rafʿ al-shubha fī-l-tashabbuh bi-l-kafara wa-l-ẓalama wa-l-jahala (1801) [Removing vagueness concerning imitating the infidels, the iniquitous and the ignorant] MX Niamey (MARA) 283; MX NU/Wilks 116; ME NU/Hunwick 8.

[Risāla ilā Muḥammad al-Jaylānī] (Nov–Dec 1820) MX Niamey (MARA) 1744. Also found in [*Majmūʿ baʿḍ al-rasāʾil*], pp. 5–11.

Risāla li-l-amrāḍ shāfiya fīhā naṣīḥa li-l-aghrāḍ kāfiya (c.1818) [A healing letter for the illnesses containing sufficient advice on matters] English translation in Shareef (1995).

Sard al-kalām fī-mā jarā baynī wa-bayn Abd al-Salam (c.1817) [The dialogue that passed between me and Abd al-Salam] MS Kaduna (NA), digitised as BL (EAP) 535 1/2/1/8 (https://eap.bl.uk/archive-file/EAP535-1-2-1-8), including unpublished English translation by Hermann G. Harris dated 1909.

Shifā' al-asqām fī dhikr madārik al-aḥkām (after 1817) [Cure for sickness by mentioning faculties of judgement] MX Niamey (MARA) uncatalogued; MS Paris (BnF) Arabe 5669 (https://gallica.bnf.fr/ark:/12148/btv1b90657354), ff. 25a–31a.

al-Taḥrīr fī qawāʿid al-tabṣīr li-l-siyāsāt (c.1817–1821) [Book of liberation in the fundamentals of clearsighted policies] ME (Zaria, Gaskiya Corp., n.d.), copy at NU/Hunwick 107.

Tanbīh al-ṣāḥib ʿalā aḥkām al-makāsib (13 June 1820) [Advice to a friend concerning the laws of earning a living] English translation in Shareef (1990).

Wathīqa ilā jamāʿat al-muslimīn (n.d.) [Dispatch to the community of Muslims] MX Niamey (MARA) uncatalogued.

Other Authors

ʿAbd al-Qādir al-Muṣṭafā (Abdulkadiri dan Tafa)

ʿAshr masāʾil fī-l-khilāf (n.d.) [Ten examples of disagreement] French translation in Mahibou (2010).

Rawḍāt al-afkār (1823) [Meadows of thoughts] in Palmer (1916).

Abū Bakr ʿAtīq b. ʿUthmān (*Amīr al-muʾminīn* Atiku)

[Abū Bakr ʿAtīq MS] (c.1837–1842) MS Dakar (IFAN), Fonds Brevié 17 in MX Kaduna (NA), digitised as BL (EAP) 535 1/2/10/3; 535 1/2/26/4 (https://eap.bl.uk/archive-file/EAP535-1-2-10-3). Summary and English part translation in Stewart (1976).

al-Intiqāl min balad Hawsa ilā-l-Ḥijāz (c.1837–1842) [The movement from Hausaland to the Hijaz] MX Niamey (MARA) 1407. Also found in [*Majmūʿ baʿḍ al-rasāʾil*], pp. 44–6.

Kitāb al-asrār (n.d.) [Book of secrets] MS NU/Falke 1150.

Aḥmad b. Saʿd b. Muḥammad al-Amīn (Chief Qadi of Gwandu)

Lubāb mā fī Tazyīn al-waraqāt wa-Infāq al-maysūr (1908) [The quintessence of Tazyīn al-waraqāt and Infāq al-maysūr] MX Niamey, uncatalogued copy of MS Sokoto (SHB) 04/59/388.

Al-Ḥājj Saʿīd

Taqāyīd mimmā waṣala ilaynā min aḥwāl umarāʾ al-muslimīn salāṭīn Ḥawsa (c.1854) [Entries from what came to us regarding the conditions of the Emirs of the Muslims, rulers of the Hausa] contained in two separate documents: (1) MS Paris (BnF) Arabe 5422 (https://gallica.bnf.fr/ark:/12148/btv1b9065549g), English translation in Whitting (n.d.) (2) MS Paris (BnF) Arabe 5484 (https://gallica.bnf.fr/ark:/12148/btv1b90654657), ff.110–112.

Gidado dan Layma (Wazir of Sokoto)

al-Kashf wa-l-bayān ʿan baʿḍ aḥwāl al-sayyid Muḥammad Bello b. al-shaykh ʿUthmān (1838) [Revealing and elucidating some qualities of Muhammad Bello, son of Shaykh Usman] unpublished English translation by Hermann G. Harris, Kaduna (NA), digitised as (EAP) 535 1/2/1/7 (https://eap.bl.uk/archive-file/EAP535-1-2-1-7).

Rawḍ al-jinān fī dhikr baʿḍ manāqib al-shaykh ʿUthmān (1817) [The meadow of paradise concerning some of the virtues of Shaykh Usman] MX Kaduna (NA), digitised as BL (EAP) 535 1/4/3/28 (https://eap.bl.uk/archive-file/EAP535-1-4-3-28).

Muḥammad al-Bukhārī (Wazir of Sokoto)

Taʾnīs al-ikhwān bi-dhikr al-khulafāʾ al-ʿuzamāʾ fī-l-Sūdān (1905) [Putting the brothers at ease by mentioning the great Caliphs in the Sūdān] discussed in Last (1967).

Muḥammad Sambo [Thanbū] b. Modibbo Aḥmad b. Mujayli (Sambo Kulwa)

Kanz al-awlād wa-l-dharārī fī taʾrīkh al-ajdād wa-l-diyār min qabāʾil al-Fullān al-aḥrār wa-dhikr ansābihim al-akhyār wa-mā yataʿallaqa bi-dhālika mimmā lā budda min dhikrihi min al-akhbār (1818) [Treasure of the children recounting the history of the forefathers and dwelling places of the Fulani clans and a mention of their noble genealogies and related noteworthy matters] MX Niamey (MARA) 1606; uncatalogued MX at Cambridge (African Studies Centre); partial copy at MX NU/Hunwick 550. Niamey and Cambridge copies include [*Additions to Kanz al-awlād*] by his son, Bayero b. Sambo Kulwa, dated 24 May 1832.

Sa'd b. 'Abd al-Raḥmān

Tartīb al-aṣḥāb wa-tajmī' al-arbāb min aṣḥāb al-shaykh 'Abd Allāh b. Muḥammad Fūdī (1840–1841) [List of companions and bringing together of venerable persons from the companions of Shaykh Abdullahi b. Muhammad Fodio] discussed in Gwandu (1977).

Anonymous Authors

Fihirist bi-asamā' wa-aṣḥāb wa-wuzarā' Amīr Muḥammad Bello (n.d.) [Catalogue of the names, companions and ministers of Muhammad Bello] MS Niamey (MARA) 383.

History of Gando (n.d.) English translation of an unknown source by Ronald McAllister, Resident Gando Division, September 1909. MX NU/Hiskett, uncatalogued MSS, Box II.

Secondary Literature, Edited and Translated Primary Sources

Abubakar, Sa'ad, 'The Emirate-Type Government in the Sokoto Caliphate', *Journal of the Historical Society of Nigeria,* 7:2 (1974), 211–29.

Adeleye, Roland A., 'Hausaland and Borno, 1600–1800', in Ajayi, J. F. Ade and Michael Crowder (eds), *History of West Africa* (2 vols, Harlow, 1971), vol. 1, pp. 577–623.

—— *Power and Diplomacy in Northern Nigeria 1804–1906: The Sokoto Caliphate and Its Enemies* (London, 1971).

Ahmed, Shahab, *What Is Islam? The Importance of Being Islamic* (Princeton, 2016).

Alkali, Hamidu, *Diya Al-'Umara: A Guide for Rulers Concerning Their Demands and Obligations* (Sokoto, 2004).

Arnett, Edward John, *The Rise of the Sokoto Fulani: Being a Paraphrase and in Some Parts a Translation of the Infaku'l Maisuri of Sultan Mohammed Bello* (Kano, 1922).

Asad, Talal, 'The Idea of an Anthropology of Islam', *Qui Parle,* 17:2, 1–30.

Ayalon, Ami, *The Arabic Print Revolution: Cultural Production and Mass Readership* (Cambridge, Mass., 2016).

Bâ, Amadou Hampaté and J. Daget, *L'empire peul du Macina* (Paris, 1962).

Balogun, S. A., 'The Place of Argungu in Gwandu History', *Journal of the Historical Society of Nigeria,* 7:3 (1974), 403–15.

—— 'Succession Tradition in Gwandu History', *Journal of the Historical Society of Nigeria,* 7:1 (1973), 17–33.

Barth, Heinrich, *Travels and Discoveries in North and Central Africa: Being a Journal of an Expedition Undertaken under the Auspices of H.B.M.'s Government, in the Years 1849–1855* (New York, 1857).

Batran, Abd al-Aziz A., 'A Contribution to the Biography of Shaikh Muḥammad ibn ʿAbd-Al-Karīm ibn Muḥammad (ʿUmar-Aʿmar) Al-Maghīlī Al-Tilimsānī', *The Journal of African History,* 14:3 (1973), 381–94.

—— 'The Kunta, Sīdī Al-Mukhtār Al-Kuntī, and the Office of Shaykh Al-Ṭarīq Al-Qādiriyya', in Willis, John Ralph (ed.), *Studies in West African Islamic History* (London, 1979), pp. 113–46.

Bello, Sir Ahmadu, *My Life: Autobiography* (Cambridge, 1962).

Benjamin, Walter, *Illuminations,* trans. Harry Zohn (New York, 2007).

Bivar, Adrian D. H., 'Arabic Documents of Northern Nigeria', *Bulletin of the School of Oriental and African Studies,* 22:1 (1959), 324–49.

—— 'The Wathīqat Ahl Al-Sūdān: A Manifesto of the Fulani Jihād', *The Journal of African History,* 2:2 (1961), 235–43.

Bloom, Jonathan M., 'Paper in Sudanic Africa', in Jeppie, Shamil and Souleymane Bachir Diagne (eds), *The Meanings of Timbuktu* (Cape Town, 2008), pp. 45–58.

Bluett, Thomas, *Some Memoirs of the Life of Job, the Son of Solomon, High Priest of Boonda in Africa* (London, 1734).

Brenner, Louis, 'The Jihad Debate between Sokoto and Borno: An Historical Analysis of Islamic Political Discourse in Nigeria', in Ajayi, J. F. Ade and J. D. Y. Peel (eds), *People and Empires in African History: Essays in Memory of Michael Crowder* (New York & London, 1992), pp. 21–43.

—— *Réflexions sur le Savoir Islamique en Afrique de l'ouest* (Talence, 1985).

—— 'Religion and Politics in Bornu: The Case of Muhammad Al-Amin Al-Kanemi', in Willis, John Ralph (ed.), *Studies in West African Islamic History* (London, 1979), pp. 160–76.

Burdon, John A., 'The Fulani Emirates of Northern Nigeria', *The Geographical Journal,* 24:6 (1904), 636–51.

—— *Northern Nigeria: Historical Notes on Certain Emirates and Tribes* (London, 1909).

Cooper, Frederick, *Citizenship between Empire and Nation* (Princeton, 2014).

Crone, Patricia and Martin Hinds, *God's Caliph: Religious Authority in the First Centuries of Islam* (Cambridge, 1986).

Delafosse, Maurice 'Traditions Musulmanes relatives à l'origine des peuls', *Revue du monde musulman,* 19 (1912), 242–67.

DeLancey, Mark D., 'Moving East, Facing West: Islam as an Intercultural Mediator in Urban Planning in the Sokoto Empire', in Falola, Toyin and Steven J. Salm (eds), *African Urban Spaces in Historical Perspective* (Rochester, 2005), pp. 3–22.

—— 'The Spread of the Sooro: Symbols of Power in the Sokoto Caliphate', *Journal of the Society of Architectural Historians,* 71:2 (2012), 168–85.

Denham, Dixon and Hugh Clapperton, *Narrative of Travels and Discoveries in Northern and Central Africa: In the Years 1822, 1823, and 1824* (Cambridge, 1826).

Dewière, Rémi, *Du lac Tchad à la Mecque: Le sultanat du Borno et son monde (XVIe–XVIIe siècle)* (Paris, 2017).

—— 'Les lettres du pouvoir au Sahel islamique. Marques, adaptations et continuités administratives Au Borno (1823–1918)', *Cahiers d'études africaines,* 236 (2020), 1047–90.

Dobronravine, Nikolai, 'Design Elements and Illuminations in Nigerian "Market Literature" in Arabic and ʿAjamī', *Islamic Africa,* 8:1–2 (2017), 43–69.

El-Masri, Fathi H., *Bayān wujūb al-hijra ʿalā al-ʿibād* (Khartoum, 1978).

—— 'The Life of Shehu Usuman Dan Fodio before the Jihād', *Journal of the Historical Society of Nigeria,* 2:4 (1963), 435–48.

Erlmann, Veit, 'Music and the Islamic Reform in the Early Sokoto Empire: Sources, Ideology, Effects', *Abhandlungen für die Kunde des Morgenlandes,* 48:1 (1986), 1–56.

Fisher, Humphrey, 'The Eastern Maghrib and the Central Sudan', in Oliver, Roland (ed), *The Cambridge History of Africa* (8 vols, Cambridge, 1977), vol. 3, pp. 232–330.

Fuglestad, Finn, 'A Reconsideration of Hausa History before the Jihad', *The Journal of African History,* 19:3 (1978), 319–39.

Gaden, Henri, *Proverbes et maximes peuls et toucouleurs, traduits, expliqués et annotés* (Paris, 1931).

Gellner, Ernest, *Saints of the Atlas* (London, 1969).

Gomez, Michael A., *Pragmatism in the Age of Jihad: The Precolonial State of Bundu* (Cambridge, 1992).

Gwandu, Abubakar Aliyu, Aminu S. Mikailu and S. W. Junaidu, *The Sokoto Caliphate: A Legacy of Scholarship and Good Governance – Proceedings of the Conference of ʿUlamāʾ Organised to Commemorate the 200 Years of the Establishment of the Sokoto Caliphate* (Sokoto, 2005).

Hakim, Besim S. and Zubair Ahmed, 'Rules for the Built Environment in 19th Century Northern Nigeria', *Journal of Architectural and Planning Research,* 23:1 (2006), 1–26.

Hall, Bruce S., *A History of Race in Muslim West Africa, 1600–1960* (New York, 2011).

Hall, Bruce S. and Charles C. Stewart, 'The Historic "Core Curriculum" and the Book Market in Islamic West Africa', in Krätli, Graziano and Ghislaine Lydon (eds), *The Trans-Saharan Book Trade* (Leiden, 2011), pp. 109–74.

Hamès, Constant, 'Problématiques de la magie-sorcellerie en islam et perspectives africaines', *Cahiers d'études africaines,* 189–90 (2008), 81–99.

Hamet, Ismail, 'Nour-el-Eulbab (Lumière des cœurs) de Cheïkh Otmane ben Mohammed ben Otmane dit Ibn-Foudiou', *Revue africaine,* 41:227 (1897), 297–320.

Hanretta, Sean, *Islam and Social Change in French West Africa: History of an Emancipatory Community* (Cambridge, 2009).

Hanson, John H., *Migration, Jihad, and Muslim Authority in West Africa: The Futanke Colonies in Karta* (Bloomington, 1996).

Herbst, Jeffrey, *State and Power in Africa: Comparative Lessons in Authority and Control* (Princeton, 2000).

Hiribarren, Vincent, *A History of Borno: Trans-Saharan African Empire to Failing Nigerian State* (London, 2017).

Hiskett, Mervyn, *The Development of Islam in West Africa* (New York, 1984).

—— 'An Islamic Tradition of Reform in the Western Sudan from the Sixteenth to the Eighteenth Century', *Bulletin of the School of Oriental and African Studies,* 25:1 (1962), 577–96.

—— '*Kitāb Al-Farq*: A Work on the Habe Kingdoms Attributed to ʿUthmān dan Fodio', *Bulletin of the School of Oriental and African Studies,* 23:03 (1960), 558–79.

—— 'Material Relating to the State of Learning among the Fulani before their Jihād', *Bulletin of the School of Oriental and African Studies,* 19:03 (1957), 550–78.

—— 'The Nineteenth-Century Jihads in West Africa', in Flint, J. E. (ed.), *The Cambridge History of Africa* (8 vols, Cambridge, 1977), vol. 5, pp. 131–51.

—— *The Sword of Truth: The Life and Times of the Shehu Usuman Dan Fodio* (Oxford, 1973).

—— *Tazyīn al-Waraqāt* (Ibadan, 1963).

Hogben, Sidney J., *An Introduction to the History of the Islamic States of Northern Nigeria* (Ibadan, 1967).

—— *The Muhammadan Emirates of Nigeria* (Oxford, 1930).

Hopen, C. Edward, *The Pastoral Fulbe Family in Gwandu* (Oxford, 1958).

Hunwick, John O., *Timbuktu and the Songhay Empire: Al-Sa'dī's Ta'rīkh al-Sūdān down to 1613, and Other Contemporary Documents* (Leiden, 1999).

Hunwick, John O. and Fatima Harrak, *Mi'rāj al-Su'ūd: Ahmad Baba's Replies on Slavery* (Rabat, 2000).

Hunwick, John O. and Rex S. O'Fahey, *Arabic Literature of Africa Volume 2: The Writings of Central Sudanic Africa* (Leiden, 1995).

Hunwick, John O., Ousmane Kane and Bernard Salvaing, *Arabic Literature of Africa Volume 4: The Writings of Western Sudanic Africa* (Boston, 2003).

Ismail, O. S. and A. Y. Aliyu, 'Bello and the Tradition of Manuals of Advice to Rulers', in *Nigerian Administration Research Project, Second Interim Report* (Zaria, 1975), pp. 54–73.

Jenkins, R. G., 'The Evolution of Religious Brotherhoods in North and Northwest Africa', in Willis, John Ralph (ed.), *Studies in West African Islamic History* (London, 1979), pp. 40–77.

Johnston, Hugh A. S., *The Fulani Empire of Sokoto* (London, 1967).

Kane, Moustapha and David Robinson, *The Islamic Regime of Fuuta Tooro: An Anthology of Oral Tradition* (East Lansing, 1984).

Kane, Ousmane, 'Arabic Sources and the Search for a New Historiography in Ibadan in the 1960s', *Africa,* 86:2 (2016), 344–6.

—— *Beyond Timbuktu: An Intellectual History of Muslim West Africa* (Cambridge, Mass., 2016).

—— *Muslim Modernity in Postcolonial Nigeria: A Study of the Society for the Removal of Innovation and Reinstatement of Tradition* (Boston, 2003).

Kani, Ahmad M., *Ḍiyā' al-siyāsāt wa-fatāwī-l-nawāzil mimmā huwa fī furū' al-dīn min al-masā'il* (Cairo, 1988).

—— 'Some Reflections on the Writings of Shaykh 'Uthman b. Fudi', *Kano Studies,* 2:1 (1980), 1–9.

Kani, Ahmad M. and Charles C. Stewart, 'Sokoto-Masina Diplomatic Correspondence', *Research Bulletin, Centre of Arabic Documentation, University of Ibadan,* 11 (1975), 1–12.

Kassim, Abdulbasit, 'Defining and Understanding the Religious Philosophy of Jihādī-Salafism and the Ideology of Boko Haram', *Politics, Religion & Ideology,* 16:2–3 (2015), 173–200.

Kennedy, Hugh, *The Prophet and the Age of the Caliphate* (New York & London, 1986).

Kriger, Colleen, 'Textile Production and Gender in the Sokoto Caliphate', *The Journal of African History,* 34:3 (1993), 361–401.

Lander, Richard, *Records of Captain Clapperton's Last Expedition to Africa with the Subsequent Adventures of the Author* (2 vols, Cambridge, 1830).

Landeroin, Moïse A., 'Notice historique', in Tilho, Jean (ed.), *Documents scientifiques de la mission Tilho, 1906–1909* (3 vols, Paris, 1909), vol. 2, pp. 309–552.

Last, Murray, 'Ancient Labels and Categories: Exploring the "Onomastics" of Kano', in Haour, Anne and Benedetta Rossi (eds), *Being and Becoming Hausa: Interdisciplinary Perspectives* (Leiden, 2010), pp. 59–84.

—— 'An Aspect of Caliph Muhammad Bello's Social Policy', *Kano Studies*, 2 (1966), 56–105.

—— 'The Book in the Sokoto Caliphate', in Jeppie, Shamil and Souleymane Bachir Diagne (eds), *The Meanings of Timbuktu* (Cape Town, 2008), pp. 135–63.

—— 'Contradictions in Creating a Jihadi Capital: Sokoto in the Nineteenth Century and Its Legacy', *African Studies Review*, 56:2 (2013), 1–20.

—— 'The Early Kingdoms of the Nigerian Savanna', in Ajayi, J. F. Ade and M. Crowder (eds), *History of West Africa*, 2nd edn (2 vols, New York, 1985), vol. 1, pp. 167–224.

—— 'From Dissent to Dissidence: The Genesis & Development of Reformist Islamic Groups in Northern Nigeria', in Mustapha, Abdul Raufu (ed.), *Sects & Social Disorder: Muslim Identities & Conflict in Northern Nigeria* (Woodbridge, 2014), pp. 18–53.

—— 'History as Religion: De-constructing the Magians "Maguzawa" of Nigerian Hausaland', in Chrétien, Jean-Pierre (ed.), *L'invention religieuse en Afrique: Histoire et religion en Afrique noire* (Paris, 1993), pp. 267–96.

—— '"Injustice" and Legitimacy in the Early Sokoto Caliphate', in Ajayi, J. F. Ade and J. D. Y. Peel (eds), *People and Empires in African History: Essays in Memory of Michael Crowder* (New York & London, 1992), pp. 45–57.

—— 'Innovation in the Sokoto Caliphate', in Bobboyi, H. and A. M. Yakubu (eds), *The Sokoto Caliphate: History and Legacies, 1804–2004* (2 vols, Kaduna, 2006), vol. 2, pp. 328–47.

—— 'The Pattern of Dissent: Boko Haram in Nigeria 2009', *Annual Review of Islam in Africa*, 10 (2009), 7–11.

—— *The Sokoto Caliphate* (New York, 1967).

Last, Murray and Muhammad A. Al-Hajj, 'Attempts at Defining a Muslim in 19th Century Hausaland and Bornu', *Journal of the Historical Society of Nigeria*, 3:2 (1965), 231–40.

Launey, Robert, *Beyond the Stream: Islam and Society in a West African Town* (Berkeley, 1992).
Lefebvre, Camille, *Frontières de sable, frontières de papier. Histoire de territoires et de frontières, du jihad de Sokoto à la colonisation française du Niger (XIXe–XXe siècles)* (Paris, 2015).
Levtzion, Nehemia, 'Early Nineteenth Century Arabic Manuscripts from Kumasi', *Transactions of the Historical Society of Ghana,* 8 (1965), 99–119.
Lockhart, Jamie Bruce and Paul E. Lovejoy, *Hugh Clapperton into the Interior of Africa: Records of the Second Expedition, 1825–1827* (Leiden, 2005).
Lofkrantz, Jennifer, 'Intellectual Discourse in the Sokoto Caliphate: The Triumvirate's Opinions on the Issue of Ransoming, ca. 1810', *The International Journal of African Historical Studies,* 45:3 (2012), 385–401.
—— 'Protecting Freeborn Muslims: The Sokoto Caliphate's Attempts to Prevent Illegal Enslavement and its Acceptance of the Strategy of Ransoming', *Slavery & Abolition,* 32:1 (2011), 109–27.
Loimeier, Roman, *Islamic Reform in Twentieth-Century Africa* (Edinburgh, 2016).
—— *Muslim Societies in Africa: A Historical Anthropology* (Bloomington, 2013).
Loimeier, Roman and Rüdiger Seesemann (eds), *The Global Worlds of the Swahili: Interfaces of Islam, Identity and Space in 19th- and 20th-Century East Africa* (Berlin, 2006).
Lovejoy, Paul E., 'The Ibadan School of Historiography and Its Critics', in Falola, Toyin and J.F. Ade Ajayi (eds), *African Historiography* (London, 1993), pp. 195–202.
—— *Jihād in West Africa During the Age of Revolutions* (Athens, Ohio, 2016).
—— 'Plantations in the Economy of the Sokoto Caliphate', *The Journal of African History,* 19:3 (1978), 341–68.
—— 'The Role of the Wangara in the Economic Transformation of the Central Sudan in the Fifteenth and Sixteenth Centuries', *The Journal of African History,* 19:2 (1978), 173–93.
—— *Slavery, Commerce and Production in the Sokoto Caliphate of West Africa* (Lawrenceville, 2005).
Mack, Beverly B. and Jean Boyd, *One Woman's Jihad: Nana Asma'u, Scholar and Scribe* (Indianapolis, 2000).

Madelung, Wilfred, 'Al-Mahdī', in Bearman, P., Th. Bianquis, C. Bosworth, E. van Donzel and W. Heinrichs (eds) *Encyclopaedia of Islam* (Leiden, 2012).

Mahibou, Sidi Mohamed, *Abdullahi dan Fodio et la théorie du gouvernement islamique* (Paris, 2010).

Mahibou, Sidi Mohamed and Jean-Louis Triaud, *Voilà ce qui est arrivé. Bayân mâ waqa'a d'al-Hâjj 'Umar al-Fûtî. Plaidoyer pour une guerre sainte, en Afrique de l'Ouest au XIXe siècle* (Paris, 1983).

Martin, Bradford G., 'Unbelief in the Western Sudan: 'Uthman Dan Fodio's "Ta'lim Al-Ikhwan"', *Middle Eastern Studies,* 4:1 (1967), 50–97.

McHugh, Neil, *Holymen of the Blue Nile: The Making of an Arab-Islamic Community in the Nilotic Sudan, 1500–1800* (Evanston, 1994).

Miers, Suzanne and Igor Kopytoff, *Slavery in Africa: Historical and Anthropological Perspectives* (Madison, 1977).

Moraes Farias, Paulo F. de, *Arabic Medieval Inscriptions from the Republic of Mali: Epigraphy, Chronicles and Songhay-Tuareg History* (Oxford, 2004).

—— 'Intellectual Innovation and Reinvention of the Sahel: The Seventeenth-Century Timbuktu Chronicles', in Jeppie, Shamil and Souleymane Bachir Diagne (eds), *The Meanings of Timbuktu* (Cape Town, 2008), pp. 95–107.

—— 'Local Landscapes and Constructions of World Space: Medieval Inscriptions, Cognitive Dissonance, and the Course of the Niger', *Afriques: Débats, méthodes et terrains d'histoire*, 2 (2010), 1–21.

Moumouni, Seyni, *Vie et œuvre du Cheikh Uthmân Dan Fodio (1754–1817): De l'islam au soufisme* (Paris, 2008).

Naylor, Paul, 'Abdullahi Dan Fodio and Muhammad Bello's Debate over the Torobbe-Fulani: Case Study for a New Methodology for Arabic Primary Source Material from West Africa', *Islamic Africa,* 9:1 (2018), 34–54.

Naylor, Paul and Marion Wallace, 'Author of His Own Fate? The Eighteenth-Century Writings of Ayuba Sulayman Diallo', *The Journal of African History,* 60:3 (2019), 343–77.

Nicolas, Guy, *Dynamique sociale et appréhension du monde au sein d'une société hausa* (Paris, 1975)

Nobili, Mauro, 'Back to Saharan Myths: Preliminary Notes on 'Uqba Al-Mustajab', *Annual Review of Islam in Africa*, 11 (2012), 79–84.

—— 'A Propaganda Document in Support of the 19th Century Caliphate of Ḥamdallāhi: Nūḥ b. al-Ṭāhir al-Fulānī's "Letter on the Appearance of the Twelfth Caliph" (*Risāla fī ẓuhūr al-khalīfa al-thānī 'ashar*)', *Afriques*, 7 (2016).

—— 'Reinterpreting the Role of Muslims in the West African Middle Ages', *The Journal of African History*, 61:3 (2020) 327–40.
—— *Sultan, Caliph, and the Renewer of the Faith: Ahmad Lobbo, the Tārīkh Al-Fattāsh and the Making of an Islamic State in West Africa* (Cambridge, 2020).
Nobili, Mauro and Mohamed Diagayeté, 'The Manuscripts That Never Were: In Search of the *Tārīkh Al-Fattāsh* in Côte d'Ivoire and Ghana', *History in Africa*, 44 (2017), 309–321.
Nobili, Mauro and Mohamed S. Mathee, 'Towards a New Study of the So-Called *Tārīkh Al-Fattāsh*', *History in Africa,* 42 (2015), 37–73.
Norris, Harry T., *The Arab Conquest of the Western Sahara: Studies of the Historical Events, Religious Beliefs and Social Customs which Made the Remotest Sahara a Part of the Arab World* (London, 1986).
—— *The Tuaregs: Their Islamic Legacy and its Diffusion in the Sahel* (Warminster, 1975).
Noth, Albrecht, *The Early Arabic Historical Tradition: A Source-Critical Study* (Princeton, 1994).
Ochonu, Moses, 'Colonialism within Colonialism: The Hausa-Caliphate Imaginary and the British Colonial Administration of the Nigerian Middle Belt', *African Studies Quarterly,* 10:2–3 (2008), 95–127.
Palmer, Herbert R., *The Carthaginian Voyage to West Africa in 500 B.C. Together with Sultan Mohammed Bello's Account of the Origin of the Fulbe* (Bathurst, 1931).
—— 'An Early Fulani Conception of Islam (Continued)', *Journal of the Royal African Society,* 14:53 (1914), 53–9.
Philips, John E., *Black Africa's Largest Islamic Kingdom before Colonialism: Royal Ribats of Kano and Sokoto* (Porter Ranch, 2016).
Piault, Marc H., *Histoire Mawri: introduction à l'étude des processus constitutifs d'un État* (Paris, 1970).
Piłaszewicz, Stanisław, *Hausa Prose Writings in Ajami by Alhaji Umaru from A. Mischlich/H. Sölken's Collection* (Berlin, 2000).
—— 'Legitimacy of the Holy War and of the Sokoto Caliphate in Some Fulani Writings, Oral Traditions and Court Practices', *Africana Bulletin,* 37 (1991), 35–47.
Rançon, André, *Le Bondou: Etude de geographie et d'histoire soudaniennes de 1681 a nos jours* (Bordeaux, 1894).
Renan, Ernest, *Œuvres complètes d'Ernest Renan* (8 vols, Paris, 1952), vol. 1.
Richardson, James, *Narrative of a Mission to Central Africa, Performed in the Years 1850–51* (London, 1853).

Robinson, David, 'D'empire en empire: l'empire toucouleur dans la stratégie et la mémoire de l'empire français', *Islam et sociétés au Sud du Sahara*, 16 (2002), 107–117.

—— *The Holy War of Umar Tal* (Oxford, 1985).

Rosenthal, Franz (ed.), *The Muqaddimah: An Introduction to History* (3 vols, New York, 1958).

Rossi, Benedetta, 'The Agadez Chronicles and Y Tarichi: A Reinterpretation', *History in Africa*, 43 (2016), 95–140.

—— *From Slavery to Aid: Politics, Labour, and Ecology in the Nigerien Sahel, 1800–2000* (New York, 2015).

Salau, Mohammed B., *Plantation Slavery in the Sokoto Caliphate: A Historical and Comparative Study* (Rochester, 2018).

—— 'Ribats and the Development of Plantations in the Sokoto Caliphate: A Case Study of Fanisau', *African Economic History*, 34 (2006), 23–43.

Sanneh, Lamin, 'The Origins of Clericalism in West African Islam', *The Journal of African History*, 17:1 (1976), 49–72.

Sartain, Elizabeth M., 'Jalal ad-Din as-Suyuti's Relations with the People of Takrur', *Journal of Semitic Studies*, 16:2 (1971), 193–8.

Savage, Elizabeth, 'Berbers and Blacks: Ibāḍī Slave Traffic in Eighth-Century North Africa', *The Journal of African History*, 33:3 (1992), 351–68.

Seesemann, Rüdiger, *The Divine Flood: Ibrahim Niasse and the Roots of a Twentieth-Century Sufi Revival* (Oxford, 2011).

—— 'Embodied Knowledge and the Walking Qur'an: Lessons for the Study of Islam and Africa', *Journal of Africana Religions*, 3:2 (2015), 201–9.

Shādhilī, Bahīja (ed.), *Infāq al-maysūr fī ta'rīkh bilād al-Takrūr* (Rabat, 1996).

Smaldone, Joseph P., *Warfare in the Sokoto Caliphate: Historical and Sociological Perspectives* (Cambridge, 1977).

Smith, H. F. C. (Abdullahi), 'A Neglected Theme of West African History: The Islamic Revolutions of the 19th Century', *Journal of the Historical Society of Nigeria*, 2:2 (1961), 169–85.

Smith, Michael G., *Government in Zazzau, 1800–1950* (London, 1964).

—— 'Hausa Inheritance and Succession', in Duncan, John and Martin Derrett (eds), *Studies in the Laws of Succession in Nigeria* (Oxford, 1965), pp. 230–83.

Sounaye, Abdoulaye, 'Izala au Niger: une alternative de communauté religieuse', in Fourchard, L., O. Goerg and M. Gomez-Perez (eds), *Lieux de sociabilité urbaine en Afrique* (Paris, 2009), pp. 481–500.

—— 'Salafi Aesthetics: Preaching among the Sunnance in Niamey, Niger', *Journal of Religion in Africa,* 47:1 (2017), 9–41.
Stewart, Charles C., 'Frontier Disputes and Problems of Legitimation: Sokoto–Masina Relations 1817–1837', *The Journal of African History,* 17:04 (1976), 497–514.
—— *Islam and Social Order in Mauritania: A Case Study from the Nineteenth Century* (Oxford, 1973).
—— 'Southern Saharan Scholarship and the Bilad Al-Sudan', *The Journal of African History,* 17:1 (1976), 73–93.
—— 'What's in the Manuscripts of Timbuktu? A Survey of the Contents of 31 Private Libraries' *History in Africa,* 48 (forthcoming).
Stilwell, Sean, *Paradoxes of Power: The Kano 'Mamluks' and Male Royal Slavery in the Sokoto Caliphate, 1804–1903* (London, 2004).
Stoler, Laura Ann, 'Colonial Archives and the Arts of Governance', *Archival Science,* 2 (2002), 87–109.
Sulaiman, Ibraheem, *The Islamic State and the Challenge of History: Ideals, Policies, and Operation of the Sokoto Caliphate* (London, 1987).
—— *A Revolution in History: The Jihad of Usman Dan Fodio* (London, 1986).
Triaud, Jean-Louis, 'Le renversement du souverain injuste: Un débat sur les fondements de la légitimité islamique en Afrique noire au XIXe siècle', *Annales. Histoire, Sciences Sociales,* 40:3 (1985), 509–19.
Turner, Bryan S., *Weber and Islam: A Critical Study* (London & Boston, 1974).
Umar, Muhammad Sani, 'Changing Islamic Identity in Nigeria from the 1960s to the 1980s: From Sufism to Anti-Sufism', in Brenner, Louis (ed.), *Muslim Identity and Social Change in Sub-Saharan Africa* (London, 1993), pp. 154–78.
Vikør, Knut S., 'Sufi Brotherhoods in Africa', in Levtzion, N. and R. L. Pouwels (eds), *The History of Islam in Africa* (Athens, Ohio, 2000), pp. 441–76.
Walz, Terence, 'The Paper Trade of Egypt and the Sudan in the Eighteenth and Nineteenth Centuries and its Re-export to the Bilād as-Sūdān', in Krätli, Graziano and Ghislaine Lydon (eds), *The Trans-Saharan Book Trade: Manuscript Culture, Arabic Literacy and Intellectual History in Muslim Africa* (Leiden & Boston, 2011), pp. 73–108.
Ware III, Rudolph T., *The Walking Qur'an: Islamic Education, Embodied Knowledge, and History in West Africa* (Chapel Hill, 2014).
Weber, Max, *The Theory of Social and Economic Organization,* trans. Talcott Parsons and Alexander Morell Henderson (New York, 1947).

—— 'The Three Types of Legitimate Rule', trans. Hans Gerth, *Berkeley Publications in Society and Institutions,* 4:1 (1958), 1–11.
Whitting, Charles E., *History of Sokoto* (Kano, n.d.).
Willis, John Ralph, 'Jihād fī Sabīl Allāh – Its Doctrinal Basis in Islam and Some Aspects of its Evolution in Nineteenth-Century West Africa', *The Journal of African History,* 8:3 (1967), 395–415.
—— 'The Torodbe Clerisy: A Social View', *The Journal of African History,* 19:2 (1978), 195–212.
Zehnle, Stephanie, *A Geography of Jihad: Sokoto Jihadism and the Islamic Frontier in West Africa* (Berlin, 2020). [Page references are for the 2015 PhD dissertation.]

Unpublished Theses and Papers

Al-Hajj, Muhammad A., 'The Mahdist Tradition in Northern Nigeria' (Unpublished PhD dissertation, Ahmadu Bello University 1973).
—— 'A Tentative Chronology for the Writings of Shehu ʿUthmān dan Fodio', delivered at Bayero University College Department of History Postgraduate Seminar, 18 January 1977, Kano, Nigeria.
Albasu, Sabo Abdullahi, 'A Glimpse at Muhammad Bello's Views on the Mahdi and Mahdist Expectation', delivered at Seminar on Amirul-Mumin Muhammad Bello organised by Centre for Islamic Studies, University of Sokoto, Sokoto, Nigeria, 15–18 April 1985.
Balogun, Ismail A., 'A Critical Edition of the Iḥyāʾ al-Sunna wa-Ikhmād al-Bidʿa of ʿUthmān b. Fūdī, popularly known as Usumanu Ḍan Fodio' (Unpublished PhD dissertation, University of London, 1967).
Bello, Omar, 'The Political Thought of Muhammad Bello (1781–1837) as Revealed in his Arabic Writings, more especially al-Ghayth al-Wabl fī Sīrat al-Imām al-ʿAdl' (Unpublished PhD dissertation, University of London, 1983).
Boyd, Jean, *'Asma'u Fodio's use of Power'* (Unpublished notes, 1990) in Jean Boyd Papers, SOAS special collections.
—— 'An Interim Report on the Yan-Taru Movement in the 20th Century, with an Account of its Origins', delivered at Popular Islam in the Twentieth Century, University of Illinois, 2–3 April 1984.
Brown, William A., 'The Caliphate of Hamdullahi, ca. 1818–1864: A Study in African History and Tradition' (Unpublished PhD dissertation, University of Wisconsin, 1969).
Collet, Hadrien, 'Le sultanat du Mali (XIVe-XVe siècle): Historiographies d'un État soudanien, de l'Islam médiéval à aujourd'hui' (Unpublished PhD dissertation, Université Paris 1, 2017).

Dantiye, Nasiru I., 'A Study of the Origins, Status and Defensive Role of Four Kano Frontier Strongholds (Ribats) in the Emirate Period (1809–1903)' (Unpublished PhD dissertation, Indiana University, 1985).

Diagayete, Mohamed, 'The Contributions of Fulani Scholars to the Development of Islamic Scholarship in Mali, 18th–19th Centuries', delivered at Wednesdays@PAS, Program of African Studies, Northwestern University, 28 September 2017.

Duffield, Mark R., 'Hausa and Fulani Settlement and the Development of Capitalism in Sudan: With Special Reference to Maiurno, Blue Nile Province' (Unpublished PhD dissertation, University of Birmingham, 1978).

Gwandu, Abubakar Aliyu, 'Abdullahi B. Fodio as a Muslim Jurist' (Unpublished PhD dissertation, Durham University, 1977).

Hunwick, John O., 'Al-Maghīlī's Replies to the Questions of Askia Al-Hajj Muhammad, Edited and Translated with an Introduction on the History of Islam in the Niger Bend to 1500' (Unpublished PhD dissertation, University of London, 1974).

Jumare, Ibrahim M., 'Land Tenure in the Sokoto Sultanate of Nigeria' (Unpublished PhD dissertation, York University, 1995).

Lovejoy, Paul E., 'The Kano Chronicle Revisited', delivered at Landscapes, Sources, and Intellectual Projects in African History: Symposium in Honour of Paulo Fernando de Moraes Farias, University of Birmingham, 12–14 November 2015.

Marcus-Sells, Ariela, 'Realm of the Unseen: Devotional Practice and Sufi Authority in the Kunta Community' (Unpublished PhD dissertation, Stanford, 2015).

Mathee, Mohamed S., 'A Seventeenth-Century Songhay Chronicler Learning (and Teaching) to be Muslim through Historiography: The Case of the Tarikh al-Sudan', delivered at Cadbury Conference 2016: Bodies of Text: Learning to Be Muslim in West Africa, Birmingham, UK, 30 June–1 July 2016.

Minna, Mahmud T. M., 'Sultan Muhammad Bello and His Intellectual Contribution to the Sokoto Caliphate' (Unpublished PhD dissertation, SOAS, University of London, 1982).

Ould Cheikh, Abdel Wedoud, 'Nomadisme, islam et pouvoir politique dans la société maure précoloniale (XIème siècle–XIXème siècle): essai sur quelques aspects du tribalisme' (Unpublished PhD dissertation, Université Paris V, René Descartes, 1985).

Philips, John E., 'Ribats in the Sokoto Caliphate: Selected Studies, 1804–1903' (Unpublished PhD dissertation, University of California, Los Angeles, 1992).

Starratt, Priscilla E., 'Oral History in Muslim Africa: Al-Maghili Legends in Kano' (Unpublished PhD dissertation, University of Michigan, 1993).
Stewart, Charles C., 'A Condensed Summary of Historians and History Writing in Nigeria: Sokoto's Past through 180 Years' (Unpublished draft, 1979).
Syed, Amir, 'Al-Ḥājj ʿUmar Tāl and the Realm of the Written: Mastery, Mobility and Islamic Authority in 19th Century West Africa' (Unpublished PhD dissertation, University of Michigan, 2017).
Zahradeen, Muhammad S., ''Abd Allāh ibn Fodio's Contributions to the Fulani Jihad in Nineteenth Century Hausaland' (Unpublished PhD dissertation, McGill, 1976).
Zebadia, Abdelkader, 'The Career and Correspondence of Ahmad Al-Bakkay of Timbuctu: An Historical Study of His Political and Religious Role from 1847 to 1866' (Unpublished PhD, SOAS, University of London, 1974).

Web-based Sources

Shareef, Muhammad, 'The Abundant Downpour' (2002) http://siiasi.org/wp-content/uploads/2014/12/Chapter-1-_Ghayth_.pdf [accessed 9 September 2020].
—— 'Advice to the Friend' (1990) http://siiasi.org/wp-content/uploads/2014/12/Tanbeeh-as-Saahib.pdf [accessed 9 September 2020].
—— 'Easy Expenditure' (2008) http://siiasi.org/digital-archive/sultan-muhammad-bello/infaql-maysuur [accessed 9 September 2020].
—— 'The Guiding Light of the Brethren' (2000) http://siiasi.org/wp-content/uploads/2014/12/Siraajl-Ikhwaan-2.pdf [accessed 9 September 2020].
—— 'A Letter of Healing' (1995) http://siiasi.org/wp-content/uploads/2014/12/Risaalat-LilAmraad.pdf [accessed 9 September 2020].
—— 'The Signs of the End of Time' (1998) http://siiasi.org/wp-content/uploads/2014/12/Tanbeeh.pdf [accessed 9 September 2020].

Index

Index compiled using TExtract.

Previously Published Titles in the Series:

Violent Conversion: Brazilian Pentecostalism and Urban Women in Mozambique, Linda Van de Kamp (2016)

Beyond Religious Tolerance: Muslim, Christian & Traditionalist Encounters in an African Town, edited by Insa Nolte, Olukoya Ogen and Rebecca Jones (2017)

Faith, Power and Family: Christianity and Social Change in French Cameroon, Charlotte Walker-Said (2018)

Contesting Catholics: Benedicto Kiwanuka and the Birth of Postcolonial Uganda, Jonathon L. Earle and J. J. Carney (2021)

Islamic Scholarship in Africa: New Directions and Global Contexts, edited by Ousmane Oumar Kane (2021)

Forthcoming:

Labour & Christianity in the Mission: African Workers in Tanganyika and Zanzibar, 1864–1926, Michelle Liebst (2021)

Sacred Queer Stories: Ugandan LGBTQ+ Refugee Lives & the Bible, Adriaan van Klinken, Johanna Stiebert, Sebyala Brian and Fredrick Hudson (2021)

The Rwandan Genocide & the Christian Churches: Between Grief & Denial, Philippe Denis (2022)

Competing Catholicisms: The Jesuits, the Vatican & the Making of Postcolonial French Africa, Jean Luc Enyegue, SJ (2022)